AN ARMY NEEDS AN AMBULANCE CORPS

A History of The Salvation Army's
Medical Services

AN ARMY NEEDS AN AMBULANCE CORPS

A History of The Salvation Army's Medical Services

by

Harry Williams

Salvation Books
The Salvation Army International Headquarters
London, United Kingdom

ISBN 978-0-85412-795-5

Cover design by Nathan Sigauke

Published by Salvation Books
The Salvation Army International Headquarters
101 Queen Victoria Street, London EC4V 4EH, United Kingdom

Printed by UK Territory Print & Design Unit

Contents

vi

Acknowledgements

I FIRST discussed the need for a new history of The Salvation Army's medical services with Commissioner (Dr) Paul du Plessis and Professor Norman Murdoch, and I am grateful to them for the material which they collated. I also appreciated having access to earlier material prepared by Lieut-Colonel (Dr) Herb Rader. Major Nanella Weir typed several drafts of the manuscript for this book and my daughters Fleur and Jennifer edited the final one. Many illustrations were supplied by the International Heritage Centre in London, and others came from sources around the world. Commissioner Paul du Plessis continued to help right up to the final draft, and my thanks go to all these people as well as to the editorial and literary personnel at International Headquarters who took the final manuscript through to publication.

It is now 37 years since the publication of *It Began with Andrews*, in which Lieut-Colonel Miriam Richards recorded the beginnings of The Salvation Army's medical work and traced its development through the first three quarters of the 20th century. Since then, both the concept of health and The Salvation Army's medical programme have diversified considerably.

The dramatic changes in the understanding of health became obvious towards the end of the 20th century. Writing in the foreword to *Health, Healing and Wholeness*, General Paul Rader said: 'This book puts us all in the picture. Every Salvationist, every corps … we are all, at some level or another, engaged in the redemptive work of health, healing and wholeness.'

Commissioner Paul du Plessis has defined health as 'a state of physical, mental, social and spiritual wellbeing … in harmony with our Creator, creation and with each other', and writing from a theological point of view, Commissioner Phil Needham says: 'Every Christian is called to experience personal healing, to participate in corporate healing and to represent Christ's healing power in the world.' This is a great stride forward from the concept of health represented in the institutional programme reported in *It Began with Andrews*.

An Army Needs an Ambulance Corps, while retelling the early history, is the story of this transition in perspective. As the then Commissioner (later General) Paul Rader, speaking at the 1990 Aids Conference in San Francisco as Territorial Commander, USA Western Territory, said: 'We're all in it now! If The Salvation Army doesn't care, who will?'

Harry Williams
Commissioner (Dr)
January 2009

Foreword

COMMISSIONER Harry Williams has taken the title for this book from an article published in *The Assurance Magazine* in 1898, which declared: 'No army engaged in actual warfare is complete without its ambulance and medical corps.' The article was commenting on the creation of the first Medical Department at International Headquarters. The title fits neatly with The Salvation Army's quasi-military metaphor. But an army's ambulance corps serves exclusively its own troops. The Salvation Army's medical services exist primarily for the sake of those outside its ranks – a huge difference. Salvation Army hospitals and clinics have never existed just for our own wounded soldiers, far from it. Perhaps more than any other avenue of Salvation Army service they have epitomised our philosophy of 'others' and of 'the whosoever'.

That has been both our glory and our burden. Carrying that burden has entailed a huge financial cost which has to be taken into account when the Army's leadership regularly, as a matter of wise stewardship, asks the same question that formed the title of the final chapter of *It Began With Andrews*: 'What of Tomorrow?'

The same question is asked and answered again in the final chapter of this book, but not before Commissioner Williams has enthralled, encouraged and inspired the reader with his account of the dedication and sacrifice of the thousands of Salvationist doctors, nurses and technicians who have, for a century and more, made the hundreds of Salvation Army clinics and hospitals and health centres on five continents into places of 24-hours-a-day, 365-days-a-year healing. Lives have been changed, lives have been extended, lives have been saved. What began in an amateur dispensary in a bathroom in Nagercoil, India, in 1893 has never stopped. *It Began With Andrews* tells the story until 1971. This book takes the story to 2009. There will be further books because there will be further stories.

But what of tomorrow? Harry Williams – despite having, at 95, the energy and passion for mission of a man half his age – has handed the final chapter of this book to Majors Dean and (Dr) Eirwen Pallant, International Health Services Coordinators at International Headquarters. Charged by the Army's leadership to prepare a blueprint for the future of the Army's international health services, their mindset is seen in the title they have given the chapter: 'Looking forward to a faithful future'.

They write: 'It is an honour for us to contribute this final chapter. The preceding chapters of this book remind us that we stand on the shoulders of giants. This is a privileged place but also a rather precarious position. It is precarious because Salvation Army medical ministry has scaled great heights over more than a century of service but, as this history reveals, hospitals, clinics and health programmes never stand still. They constantly change. The medical world does not stand still. The communities we serve do not stand still. Christian health ministry needs to be agile. We suspect that the God-faithful future for Salvation Army medical work will be very different to the past.'

However, say the Pallants, 'As Commissioner Williams repeatedly reveals, the history of Salvation Army medical service is one of faithful ministry in the midst of constant change. The future should not be any different – in the midst of chaos and change The Salvation Army must always be faithful to God.'

In this, there can be no better role model than the author of this book. Commissioner Harry Williams, OF, has devoted all his life, and every skill and talent he possesses – and they are many – to bring healing of body, mind and spirit to men and women, boys and girls, including the poorest and most deprived. He has been faithful in small things and large. We should read this book and marvel. And praise God.

Charles King
Major
Literary Secretary and Editor-in-Chief
International Headquarters
January 2009

Prologue

Doctors have been a peck of trouble to us

OF all the world religions, Christianity alone claims that God chose to reveal himself *uniquely* in the Incarnation of Jesus Christ. It is also distinctive for its emphasis on God as the foundation of health, so that the Gospels speak of Christ performing miracles in order that 'the works of God might be made manifest. It is small wonder that in the history of the Church, the periods of greatest spiritual clarity and effectiveness have been marked by progress in the art of healing.

In 325AD the Christian Church was able to declare publicly – thanks to Constantine – that it felt responsible for widows, strangers and the sick. It directed that every cathedral city should be provided with a hospital. In Britain, early provision, related to monasteries, was extensive and varied, including care for the blind, the mentally deranged and lepers. Lepers were numerous in Europe until the 14th century and treated by isolation. Lazar houses burgeoned outside towns – 2,000 in France alone.[1] Francis of Assisi had a profound effect on Christian thinking, when he embraced a leper instead of sidestepping him. He sent Agnellus and a party of friars in 1224 to visit lazar houses and provide care.

In Britain, by confiscating all the monasteries, Henry VIII effectively terminated the whole medical service. The only survivors were two in London: St Thomas's (which had been founded in 1123 by Rahere, the court jester) and St

Bartholomew's, reconstituted particularly as a gesture from the king. It wasn't until the 18th century that a spate of Christian philanthropy saw the opening of 'voluntary hospitals'. Starting with Guy's in London in 1724, it reached a total of 145 by the turn of the 18th century.

John Wesley, in launching the Methodist Church, provoked not only evangelical revival but also a renewed interest in health care. He opened the first free dispensary in Britain in 1745 and published a book of self-help advice, *Primitive Physic*, for those too poor to afford a doctor.

Springing from Methodist roots, The Salvation Army became well known as a branch of the Christian Church which successfully balanced evangelism with community service. In keeping with the outlook of William and Catherine Booth, the Army developed a medical expression of community care which was both rational and compassionate. It was therefore fitting that the first dispensary opened in South India was named 'The Catherine Booth Hospital'.

Catherine and William Booth, the founders of The Salvation Army, were manic in their approach to work; what Barbara Robinson calls 'chaotic activism'.[2] Catherine herself was exceptional. Despite an adolescent history of months on a day-bed, she bore eight children, travelled tirelessly on evangelistic exploits, whilst in between she maintained a disciplined home and took in lodgers. She, like William, had strong views on most things. As early as 1867, she protested against Jenner's cowpox vaccine as protection against smallpox. She developed her own diets, cookery, and treatments.

It is hardly surprising that William, with his disregard for his own wellbeing, became dyspeptic. For his treatment, he used remedies fortified with port or brandy. Catherine, with an alcoholic father, was strong in her abstinence, and soon converted William. When something more was needed Catherine produced a Spartan diet for her husband that was the despair of all who entertained him during his world travels as a fiery evangelist. He eventually became a vegetarian, and wrote to his officers, 'if you never see another mutton-chop in this world, I am quite sure that you will never see one in the next'.[3] He even wrote in the manual for officers, *Orders and Regulations*, much advice on health, 'but his personal theories on the subject remained. He was suffering when he first met Catherine; tentative, exploratory and open to revision'.[4]

Catherine, who grew up in Ashbourne, Derbyshire, a county with several spas, favoured hydrotherapy, and chose an establishment in Matlock. The family continued the emphasis with Florence Booth, their daughter-in-law, who embraced dietary reform in 1887 and pointed out its economical aspect: 'vegetables two pence against animal food one shilling'.[5] When, in 1929, Bramwell Booth opened the William Booth Memorial Training College in South London, the bias was still there. The main health provision was the hydro!

It is small wonder that when, at the age of 15, Bramwell declared his wish to become a doctor, he provoked a family upset which Barbara Robinson describes as an 'emotional debate ending with a devastated Bramwell'.[6] His mother continued the attack in letters telling of doctors who had lost their personal faith. In one of them she writes that the practice of medicine is a 'vortex which has swamped the religion of thousands of promising, piously trained young men', and praises God for the attack of rheumatic fever which finally ended his ambition to be a doctor.[7]

In her biography of her father, Bramwell Booth's daughter Catherine says that as a boy he loved 'dissecting rats and frogs and operating on his sisters' dolls'.[8] Bramwell's thwarted medical ambitions may explain his empathy and support for his protégé, Harry Andrews, when he opened his first dispensary.

As The Salvation Army grew, the founders not only worked out the theology, evangelistic techniques and training programmes, but also passed on their health regime which, as we have seen, called for little help from doctors. In this context it is of interest to quote the views of William on the subject of faith healing. A number of his officers had held such meetings in their corps, notably William Baugh at the Regent Hall, Oxford Street, in London's West End. The General had not interfered but wrote a memorandum approving a biblical approach. He warned against false notions. No officer was to teach that sickness was related to sin, or that failure to heal was a proof of lack of faith. All sickness, he maintained, was contrary to God's will, 'though by his death Christ did not procure for man healing of the body in the same way that he obtained salvation for the soul'.[9]

The Booths were Victorians and as such, great believers in self-help. They were 'do-it-yourself' enthusiasts in more than household decoration. Give Booth a small, ailing insurance company, and he did not just breathe a sigh of relief that cash was available for his latest extension, he turned the company round. He transformed the door-to-door collectors of pennies from the poor into an efficient, uniformed brigade of counsellors and friends to the policy holders.[10] In the same way, the development of a medical service on a global scale was due to a similar entrepreneurial spirit. The first Salvation Army missionary 'doctor', Harry Andrews, initially knew no medical college. The establishment of his first dispensary in 1893 called for little financial input from any headquarters and it would have shrivelled up swiftly had it done so. Income generated by the high quality of its services, which drew a stream of paying patients, subsidised those unable to pay. By 1950 there was a total of 1,000 hospital beds in India still supported in a largely similar way.

We remember the crowded years of Christ's ministry in The Holy Land as ones of teaching and healing – health in its fullest sense. His Church has always found the same priorities; his disciples have been in the vanguard in broadening the scope of its health service. This saga has been recorded in *Heralds of Health*,[11] and The Salvation Army is a part of it. But does its contribution differ from that of others, and if so, in what manner?

The tale now unfolding does not differ in fundamentals and underlying theology, but it does in emphasis. Most of the pioneering of the Church has been by men and women who were in the forefront in professional qualifications, but The Salvation Army has drawn largely on talented amateurs, enthusiasts who have learned by experience. Also, its contribution has been international throughout. From Victorian times, the service of the Western world has been given through missionary societies. The Salvation Army has never had such a branch: it has always been one throughout the world. It has been a self-generating and an expanding service, commonly springing up spontaneously without direct planning and minimal oversight from International Headquarters.

By 1900 there was a medical department at International Headquarters, which included the care of Salvation Army officers, although it wasn't until 1922 that Lieut-Colonel (Dr) Percy Turner was appointed Chief Medical Officer at International Headquarters – but he had limited executive clout. Some of his successors have had even less. So it is a racy story, rich in colourful personalities, with heroic episodes as varied as the characters.

The world-encircling service which, by the middle of the 20th century had annual totals of a quarter of a million inpatients, and in excess of two million outpatients, grew from twin impulses. The first was the pressing need for obstetric facilities for the unwed mother; a work which had started from the instinctive response of 'ordinary' Salvationists in Victorian times, when such women were regarded as social pariahs. Such services spread rapidly throughout the West. The second thrust came from countries where even the simplest medical care for the poor, or disaster relief, was lacking.

As the Army's medical programme expanded it called for a diverse array of expatriate professionals whenever the home-grown variety was inadequate. Such were not only expensive, but were also difficult for inexperienced commanders to handle. Employee doctors, usually from other denominations, were not accustomed to The Salvation Army's rigid discipline and were inclined to resent direction from non-medical leaders. It is not surprising, therefore, that when the young Harry Williams, an aspiring medical student, having had tea with Dr Turner was taken to see Commissioner Arthur Blowers, the International Secretary for Asia and Africa, the commissioner's opening gambit was 'doctors have been a peck of trouble to us!'[12] That same discipline, a distinctive feature of The Salvation Army over the years, has even proved difficult for some of its own doctors. A few have resigned and others have remained as soldiers, signing on for a limited period of service for a specific purpose.

Salvationist pioneers in India were quickly aware of the need for medical support from their own family tragedies. Their children, in hill-schools in the country, were fired to meet the need themselves. The first of these were Ted Barnett, Edgar Stevens and Dan Andersen. Their arrival resulted in the golden years of expansion in India, and a vision of the needs and possibilities in Africa.

In World War II a welfare state for Britain was blueprinted, its chief architect being Sir William Beveridge, who many years earlier had evaluated Booth's 'Darkest England' scheme.[13] Some of the components of the Army programme, such as employment exchanges, became part of the state set-up Britain knows today. In a similar exercise, with independence likely for India, the Raj commissioned a report from its Health Survey and planning committee, chaired by Sir Joseph Bhore – the Bhore Report published in 1946. This became the basis of India's present Health Service.

With the notable exception of the USA, much of the world has created welfare systems, differing mainly according to the finance available. Such variations have meant that some are still more dependent than others on the Church's contribution. In the United Kingdom in 1948, The Salvation Army's maternity service was absorbed into the National Health Service, but in India and elsewhere the take-over was partial and gradual.

Even though the treatment of leprosy and tuberculosis was pioneered by the Church, when governments commenced their own programmes, these proved inherently unpopular with doctors and in consequence leprosy and tuberculosis programmes remained largely voluntary. These are areas where vocational, rather than professional, medical qualities are called for.

The Salvation Army still maintains frontline troops in health services and is able to make thrusts in new forms of health promotion, as in alcoholism, now a worldwide service. Its inherent concern for the whole person gives it a role in formulating and demonstrating the social aspects of newer problems such as Aids. In The Salvation Army this was modelled at Chikankata in Zambia, when Aids was unknown to most people in the West. It is now recognised worldwide as an important model for clinical treatment and perhaps even more importantly, community involvement.

At the other end of the medical spectrum, early in the 20th century, there was a Salvation Army medical college in South India, and until recently there was one in Newfoundland, and other hospitals in which medical students received clinical training.

Enthusiastic amateurs have thrown up new challenges. In Papua New Guinea, a country with few roads and no railways, Dorothy Elphick, an officer-nurse in an isolated village, built a hospital from local materials and created a homespun health service. The Regional Commander needed a helicopter to reach her, but this did not deter Salvationist Rotarians from Australia from flying in a pre-fabricated hospital. This was at a time when a measles epidemic was killing children unchecked. The Highlands of that country now has a central hospital and for some years there were 'barefoot doctors', who were also envoys or pastors, supported by a village.

The greatest advances in recent years have been in community health services, varied, because tailored to local requirements.[14] Most of these programmes in various territories have a central hospital and a chain of dispensaries; some have mobile clinics.

In two world wars, not only have the troops had the 'Salvos' cup of tea, but on occasion a Salvation Army hospital has also become a military one. In World War I a complete ambulance brigade was fielded. At that time also, two Salvation Army doctors died in similar circumstances. Both were rescuing casualties under sniper fire. One doctor was from a middle class English family, the other a motherless waif from London's East End. That the motherless waif, Harry Andrews, received a posthumous VC and the 'gentleman' Charles Steibel was not even mentioned in dispatches, owes much to their differing personalities.[15]

The scientific base of medicine will continue to expand, both in knowledge of pathology and in the discovery of newer and newer remedies. But there is a human, even a spiritual aspect of health, which is highly individual, demanding empathy and compassion. These are the elements which were so rich in Christ's ministry. The many cadres required in the provision of health care will always benefit from those who find in it a spiritual vocation. There will be new possibilities for pioneers. A recent one has been the hospice for the terminally ill; an area in which the state has been slow to realise a need. The Army has opened several hospices and some of its doctors and nurses have served in others. It operates rehabilitation services, notably in Canada, with state support.

It has always been claimed that when the Church has been most vital, its missionary outreach has been an index. The conventional form of missionary zeal in the 18th and 19th centuries was west to east. It is now two-way, although some countries have discouraged the use of expatriate church staff.

The challenge to The Salvation Army is to continue to alleviate suffering and to promote health by every means it can find, especially encouraging self-help and local forms of development as it builds on a spiritual dynamic, a holistic salvation of body, mind and spirit. General Arnold Brown wrote, 'Salvationists sense the needs of mankind and reach out to meet them. Without this dynamic the Army's social enterprise would be mechanical … if it existed at all.'[16]

In 1977 Earl Mountbatten presented the World Humanity Award to The Salvation Army and the then Prime Minister of Great Britain – James Callaghan – said of Salvationists, 'They proclaim with selfless conviction and sincerity, that people matter, and that there is no greater calling than the service of others.'[17]

So the tale which follows is being told in the belief that a purposeful communication with a race of illustrious forebears can inspire the present age.

---

[1] Reported by Roy Porter in *The Greatest Benefit to Mankind* Collins, London 1997 p. 122
[2] Robinson, B. *Bodily Compassion* PhD Thesis, Ottawa University
[3] Ibid
[4] Ibid
[5] Ibid
[6] Ibid
[7] Booth-Tucker, F. *The Life of Catherine Booth Vol II* SP&S, London 1893 p. 419
[8] Bramwell-Booth, C. *Bramwell Booth* Rich & Cowan, London 1933
[9] Wiggins, Arch R. *The History of The Salvation Army Vol IV* Nelson, London 1964, Appendix A p. 382
[10] Williams, H. Personal observation
[11] Browne, S. G. *Heralds of Health – The Saga of Christian Medical Initiatives* Christian Medical Fellowship, London 1985
[12] Personal Diary, unpublished
[13] *In Darkest England and The Way Out* was published in London in 1890 and raised a considerable sum, which became the basis of all The Salvation Army's social services in the UK.
[14] see chapter 5
[15] see chapter 2
[16] Gariepy, H. *Mobilized for God, The History of The Salvation Army Vol VIII (1977-1994)* The Salvation Army, Atlanta GA 2000 p. 15
[17] Ibid p. 14

Chapter one

The early years

THE Salvation Army was virtually launched when William Booth led revival meetings in a second-hand tent on a Quaker burial ground in the East End of London. It was not a solo effort. In fact, he was taken on as the preacher at the last minute. The organisers, The East London Revival Association, were a miscellaneous group, including some men of Huguenot descent. They were typical evangelicals of the period.

Jan Morris, writing of the British Empire, calls the Victorian era 'an evangelical age'.[18] It is a description of the way that Victorians approached everything, including their religion. As a doctor of more recent times wrote, on taking up his post at a Salvation Army hospital in Africa, 'New Testament Christianity has a radical effect on one's life once it gets hold of you. There is only one thing … to know God's will and to do it.'[19] The experience the empire builders had at first hand, or in the writings of others, led them to believe that what they possessed was superior to what those whom they served possessed, or believed. They had something to sell and felt virtuous in sharing it freely with others.

They saw things in black and white. They were Christian whilst all the rest were heathen. 'In those days to show hesitation was to court disaster; the grander you were, the safer,' wrote Jan Morris, adding that this included 'evangelical Christianity with its strange mixture of arrogance and humility'.[20] So they sailed adventurously round the globe, sharing beliefs, inventions both scientific and medical, as well as their culture of home and community. The *Pax Britannica*, as well as the fact that a British passport provided an entrance anywhere, helped them. As a young private secretary to Commissioner Blowers, Erik Wickberg (a Swede) had to resist the pressure of his single-minded boss,[21] who assured him that British nationality would facilitate his service.

The early history of The Salvation Army is scarred by violent opposition to its methods. It went too far, too quickly for its religious contemporaries. But in its ebullience and energy, its uncompromising acceptance of hard work, and a willingness to suffer in pursuit of an ideal, it was a true child of its age.

Initially William Booth was only the General Superintendent of the Christian Mission, subject to the decisions of an Annual General Meeting. With Booth at its head, it evolved as a child of Methodism in its theology, its use of the laity, and in many practical matters, such as the class-meeting structure at local level, ensuring a disciplined training of recruits. But in one direction, on social issues, it exceeded the emphasis of John Wesley. It was impecunious, so its charity would need to find its own support. William Booth's compassion for the hungry was rooted in his Nottingham boyhood, but soup kitchens for the half-starved still had a price, if only a farthing.

As already mentioned, John Wesley had also strong views on health.[22] He published booklets to guide his people, and opened dispensaries. His brother Samuel was involved with the launching of the first voluntary hospitals in London in 1720.[23] In this concern the disciple was slow to follow; the founders of The Salvation Army had little place for doctors. When Dr Morrison was converted at the Whitechapel corps and joined the ranks, he was not appointed as a medical adviser, neither was he asked to open a dispensary at the People's Market. Instead he shared the billing at that venue for The Great Salvation Fair, with the pocket-size evangelist, Elijah Cadman, with 'come and see our giant and dwarf' – Morrison weighed 35 stone (490 pounds)![24] Even 15 years later, when Dr Percy Turner became a Salvationist and then an officer, he accepted without cavil, an appointment as a corps officer. It is tempting to attribute this blind spot to Catherine's influence on her husband. She would certainly be happy in these days of 'alternative' medicine.

The first 20 years of the organisation were marked by continual experimentation. Starts and stops were frequent, caused sometimes by paucity of suitable staff, but more often by lack of cash. In one direction, namely the rehabilitation of prostitutes, the social programme was continuous. They formed a sad, steady stream to the penitent-forms all over Britain. It was hard to find suitable accommodation and to pay the rent. In the records, rescue homes appear and disappear.[25] If Booth hated poverty from his own experience as a boy, his years as a pawnbroker gave him a horror of debt. However, the work continued, largely due to the readiness of Salvationists to open their homes to needy girls. But for this, the demands of the needy would have reduced the mission to bankruptcy.

For long enough the problem was more fundamental. Booth had doubts about the wisdom of mixing social work with evangelism. Until his dying day he emphasised the priority of spiritual regeneration over social amelioration. Catherine's illness brought the watershed in his thinking. It was in these harrowing months that the 'Darkest England scheme' was born.[26] The programme outlined in this scheme would require a far greater expenditure than had been possible in the past. In the event, the instant appeal of his book *In Darkest England and The Way Out* provided the necessary funding.

Recent critics[27] have suggested that the originators of this programme were Commissioner Frank Smith and Brigadier Susie Swift, whilst the book was the work of the editor of *The Pall Mall Gazette*, W. T. Stead. It is fortunate that Stead, hearing like criticism in 1890, wrote and published a letter.[28] In it he revealed that William had been hesitant a year earlier, whilst Smith in America had been enthusiastic even three years before. During these years Bramwell Booth was making all 'the tentative efforts towards social work' and only with this success was his father convinced. William Booth started to write the book at his wife's bedside and 'it was then that the General asked William Stead to find him a literary hack to lick the huge and growing mass of material into shape. 'I volunteered to hack' Stead concludes.[29]

Robert Sandall, writing in the third volume of the official history of The Salvation Army, devotes a whole chapter to 'The General's change of mind'. In 1887 Booth had written an article on his 44 years of Christian experience, in which he explained something of the way in which his mind worked; leading periodically to a change in policy or organisation. The social experiment outlined in his book was the most important one. He had reached the conclusion that 'Salvationists were to be servants of all'.[30] Christ, speaking to Paul on the Damascus Road, had called him to be both a servant and a witness.[31] Health Services were to move nearer to an understanding of this dual compulsion in later years. General John Larsson expressed this vital link between evangelism and service as 'an Army that flies on two wings' even though force of circumstance may sometimes make one of those wings invisible.[32]

Overcrowding and insanitary conditions prevailed in many of Britain's cities. In each of the decades from 1830 there were major cholera epidemics. The one which broke out in 1865 took a national death toll of 14,378, of which 5,596 were in London, mainly in the East End. Twenty years later, Railton – who himself contracted cholera and was nursed in the Booth household – wrote: 'The extremity of that East End misery had a great deal to do with many of the early arrangements in connection with the General's work'.[33] That usually meant provision of food and clothing for families left destitute by the epidemic. In 1869 the *East London Evangelist* reported that: 'The Sick Poor Visitation Society still pursues its quiet way'. Thinking in the Booth family was proceeding along similar lines.

Two young women, attracted by Catherine Booth's preaching in Margate in the summer of 1867 became the

Booth's paying guests, thus enabling the Booths to move to a quieter and more commodious house near Victoria Park in east London. The first was Miss Mary C. Billups, whose parents in Cardiff supported the mission financially for some years. The second was Miss Jane Short, a Congregationalist moving against the advice of her minister.[34] Jane described William Booth's launch into feeding the poor at Christmas 1869. The previous year he had determined to have 'a thoroughly happy old-fashioned Christmas' with his family. In the event he burst out: 'I'll never have another Christmas Day like this again!' and told of the experience he had earlier that day in Whitechapel where 'The poor have nothing but the public house'.[35] The *Christian Mission Magazine* reports an increasing effort for the destitute poor as Jane Short records 'in no more useful way can money be spent in relieving the poor than in visiting them when sick and dying'. She, herself, became one of the first district visitors.[36]

The General had many in the ranks who were true evangelists and who also saw in the experience of childbirth a unique opportunity to speak of Christ, 'for the tenderest and most holy feelings of a woman's heart are called forth in these early hours of motherhood'.[37] The same spiritual argument surfaces in proposals to train nurses and to use them to care for poor Salvationists and others. There were 'hundreds who would welcome, more than gladly, a really saved nurse, who would not only tend their body, but with a heart full of love and joy, also care for their soul at the same time'.[38] It was also argued that, in addition to training nurses, it would attract better-educated women to Salvation Army programmes. Dr Hart, Medical Adviser in 1893, wrote 'there would be an opening here for well-educated young women … a Salvation Sisterhood of capable, intelligent people – (the) more brainpower the better'.[39] There was a response. A corps officer in East London, Ensign Will Gilks estimated that 20 or 30 individuals were attending religious services as a direct result of nursing intervention; five became soldiers and several more, recruits. Gilks asserted that the nurses had radically altered neighbourhood opinions about The Salvation Army. He observed that 'there are streets and squares around London Fields, the Broadway and Cambridge Heath, in which Salvationists always got molested, insulted or pelted, until the last six months, and now we can stop in any square and have a good meeting, and if anyone interferes, out will come a woman, or her stronger half, to say to the offending one, "hold yer tongue; yer don't know what yer talking about; yer don't know or yer'd listen, or taker yerself hoof." What made the change? It has not been the corps work, but the steady continual work of the nurses amongst the poorest of the poor.'[40]

The year 1884 also saw the start of the Cellar, Garret and Gutter Brigades. These were under the direction of Emma Booth, who was in charge of the Training Home for Women Officers. In the Christmas edition of *The War Cry* in 1883, the Founder wrote of 'the temporal miseries of the extreme poor of the great City of London'. Work started with distribution of spring flowers and cards, with bold wording in everyday language 'Give the Devil the slip; Sin is horrid, chuck it up'. However, the concept of a base in the slums, dressing as the people did, and then visiting them, came after an all-night of prayer for guidance. Blanche Cox gave oversight; women cadets staffed the brigades for a month at a time. They visited homes, washed the children, scrubbed the floors, nursed the sick and listened to heart-rending tales of woe. Evening activities included tract distribution and personal dealing with people about their souls.[41]

In 1895 the first Salvation Army hospital was opened in Amsterdam, Holland, by Miss Brinkman, described as one of a nursing elite, experienced in general nursing, obstetrics and psychiatry. She was influenced by reading *In Darkest England and The Way Out* whilst matron of Holland's largest psychiatric hospital. She knelt at the penitent form after six month's 'careful study of his humble servants in a Dutch slum hall'.[42] Anna Knuttell, who became an officer from Arnhem, joined her in the first year. Anna came from a wealthy background and was also running a hospital when she met the Army. Again, seeing true spirituality in a medical setting attracted her. For many years there was also a hospital in Germany.[43]

It is time to return to the specialisation in obstetric practice, which was the result of the predominant requirement in the earliest years of the Christian Mission. Catherine Booth had been especially concerned about young women, 'fallen outcasts of society, often more sinned against than sinning'.[44] It started with Mrs Elisabeth Cottrill inviting girls from the street into her own home. This eventually became too much for her, and more especially for her husband, so by 1868 the Booths had opened a temporary refuge for 'poor, friendless, penniless girls' in Bishopsgate, London. Another one was operating in Hastings by 1871. A network of Rescue Homes was being established across the country. Bramwell Booth took responsibility for the work in 1884, with his wife Florence, whose father was a physician, providing active oversight.[45] 'Flo had better go down and see what she can do in her spare time. Let her superintend,' was the Founder's suggestion.

As early as 1887 Florence Booth had seriously considered purchasing a small hospital in London.[46] Three years later, at the fifth anniversary celebrations of the rescue work, held at the Exeter Hall, she made the announcement. 'In this hospital,' read the War Cry report, 'they will be able to train Salvationist nurses, for, of course, salvation would be first in this branch of the work as with every other.' Captain (Dr) Hart was medical officer to the City Colony. Dr Edith Huntley, already acting as medical officer to the rescue staff and training home, would undertake the medical work. However, a multitude of difficulties led to delays, and Dr Huntley left for missionary service.

A Dr Wilson, and then Mrs Frazer Nash, supported the rescue work professionally. Florence Booth still pursued her dream of a hospital. A statement in The Deliverer in 1891 announced the expansion of the training of midwives at Ivy

House, to strengthen not only the rescue work, but also for soldiers and friends in the wider community. If these trainees were to be sent to paying patients, the fees would help support the home. It seems that even those admitted to Ivy House were charged a shilling a week for 10 weeks, so that the 1892 Report of the Commission of Inquiry upon the Darkest England Scheme concluded that the object was rather to train nurses than to afford charitable relief.[47] So Ivy House in Clapton, near the Congress Hall, became the hub of obstetrics in 1890. Ivy House had four wards, accommodating 25 patients, and was described as 'a charmingly fresh and bright institution'.

As many of the women seeking shelter in the refuges were unmarried and pregnant, so in 1888 The Salvation Army decided to dedicate Ivy House to the confinement of unmarried mothers. Although maternity hospitals had existed in Britain since the 18th century, these were almost entirely reserved for married mothers. This was the first time that maternity hospital facilities had been combined with a 'Home of Refuge'.[48] In 1885 Bramwell Booth had collaborated with W. T. Stead in the abduction of a girl in order to expose how easily under-age girls could be sold into prostitution.[49] Some of those involved were convicted for their efforts to expose the issue but their efforts led to a change in the law. Dr Heywood-Smith, the gynaecologist who had collaborated with verification that the abducted girl remained a virgin, lost his post at the Lying-In Hospital.[50] Ivy House was, by 1896, described as a 'maternity receiving house', as distinct from a 'rescue receiving house'. A definite change had taken place – babies needed to be accommodated with their mothers. 'A properly qualified medical man' gave oversight. The scope of care was widening.[51]

Adoption was often suggested to mothers in the refuges, but when the health of one of the first clients broke down at the thought of separation from her child, staff found themselves supporting both mother and baby – the so-called 'double difficulty'.[52] A string of Mother and Baby Homes sprang up, the first in Chelsea, London, in 1886. Further 'rescue officers' were appointed, early among them Caroline Frost, an experienced midwife from Guernsey – her husband's military experience being no doubt applied to midnight patrols.[53] By May 1894 *The Deliverer* reported 'the transformation of our maternity home into a hospital'. Major Sapsworth was to be appointed superintendent, Caroline Frost was to be matron. The rescue home moved elsewhere, thus allowing for a doubling of maternity cases at Ivy House.

The arrival of an experienced midwife, Annie Sowden, at Ivy House meant that Caroline Frost was free to pursue fresh paths in the cause of the East End's ever-expanding population. Though based at Ivy House, she inaugurated what was first named 'Slum Maternity Work' and later, and more appropriately, 'District Nursing'. When similar work was being consolidated in the USA, it was Caroline Frost who was appointed in 1897 to help guide it.[54]

In 1891 Florence Booth reported that the Army had a competent band of trained nurses ready to go to any part of the country. She advertised for more recruits. The response was excellent.[55] The *Social Report* published in 1894 listed three additional maternity centres, in South Hackney, Clapton Park and Limehouse Causeway. A complete delivery and nine days' after-care were given for a fee of seven shillings and sixpence, the fee being waived for the very poor. The nudge towards a more general medical component came from Emma Booth's Cellar, Gutter and Garret Brigade, as part of the first training course for women cadets, which grew into the Slum Department. This development also occurred in the USA, Finland, Sweden and Holland. It covered the nursing of the most destitute in their own homes, by officers with suitable training, who lived in simple quarters in the same area.

This growing obstetric service was notable for the quality of the women who were being attracted to it.

Elizabeth Sapsworth, 'a Clapton lady of middle age and independent means', had been attracted to the Army. So, on the steps of the Clapton Congress Hall in 1884, Bramwell Booth thrust a five pound note into her hands, urging her to go and finance the work and keep the books. Florence described her as having 'a brain like a statesman's for strength and comprehensiveness, a cultured methodical scholar in Greek, Hebrew and mathematics'.[56] But working with Mrs Cottrill was not easy and, although Florence Booth regarded Elizabeth Sapsworth as her most able helper, she had, on more than one occasion, to intervene in disputes.[57]

Miriam Castle was another who was to play a prominent part. In 1893 she answered an advertisement in *The Deliverer* inviting 'any young woman not having platform ability' to offer 'for nursing amongst the poor'. She was not a Salvationist, but had heard her father say that 'they were the people who most faithfully carried out the Master's teachings'. She was already a trained nurse, but was advised to join a local corps. She soon trained to be an officer and was appointed to Ivy House, thus commencing 53 years in obstetric practice.[58] Yet another trained nurse was Hannah Carr. While still a cadet she was drafted into Emma Booth's 'Cellar, Gutter and Garret Brigade'. Hannah nursed Catherine Booth in her final illness and, on her death, accompanied Emma and Frederick Booth Tucker[59] to India, and continued with them when they moved to the USA.

Annie Sowden was yet another in this pioneer group. A midwife, already middle-aged and with four sons who were 'now off her hands', she approached Ivy House for help with one of her own maternity cases. She was impressed by the way in which the assistant assigned to her 'lived salvation'.[60] This impression was strengthened by observing Elizabeth Sapsworth and her family, and Mrs Sowden soon reckoned that if they could commit themselves to the poor, instead of living comfortably, so should she. Afternoon tea with the Sapsworths turned into a dedication service. She abandoned her hard-won position among a wealthy and influential clientele, accepting the meagre allowance of a Salvation Army officer. For 16 years, Sapsworth, the hospital superintendent, and Sowden, the matron, fast friends by now, worked to make Florence Booth's dream of a hospital come true.[61] Amongst their greatest challenges were finance and the requirements of the London Obstetrical Society.[62] Elizabeth sensed the need for midwifery qualifications and passed all the theory examinations

Because The Salvation Army had become an international organisation, developments in one country rapidly followed elsewhere. The USA quickly explored health needs in the community although its main thrust remained evangelical. Zeal and enthusiasm for evangelism blended with a ministry of compassion that marked the early day Army. A variety of small-scale relief operations – more like little acts of kindness – started in many corps. The Commander in the USA was William Booth's second son, Ballington. His wife, Maude (daughter of an Anglican rector) was responsible for the development of community services in New York. She was committed to providing opportunities for women to minister to women. A background experience to such work in her early days with the Army in London provided the focus on 'the new woman'. The transformation of others was the goal of all they attempted; their own transformation was what fuelled their activity.[63]

Street evangelism had brought Salvationists into close contact with prostitutes. In 1886 a rescue home was inaugurated in Brooklyn, New York, the 'Rescue Home for Fallen Women and Homeless Girls'. 'Salvation Army to the Rescue', was the *War Cry* headline announcing the venture. Mrs Booth put the programme on a firmer footing when she opened a home for women in New York's Upper Manhattan, in the summer of 1892. An experienced English officer, Captain Denison, arrived to oversee the work, which was expanding nationwide. It was from this that a network of Booth maternity hospitals was to evolve across the nation. A special training programme for rescue work was started alongside the Manhattan home.[64] Four years later the Rescue Home for Women was relocated to East 15th Street. Here the Army's first venture into hospital ministry in the USA was launched with an operating room, doctor's office, small laboratory, ward and two private rooms. The public's demand for access to the unit was so great that a major expansion was needed four years later.

A broader-based, health-related ministry had begun when Emma J. Bown first sent her 'Slum Sisters' into the streets of New York in 1890. These women simply did whatever came to hand. Their sole ministry was to be helpful and speak of Christ when asked their motive. They bathed and fed helpless stroke victims; in crowded flats, they washed and cuddled the extra baby or two, cooked meals, made beds, patched clothing, scrubbed floors, bundled returning drunks into bed, washed and dressed the dead for undertakers (who simply delivered a coffin, took payment and left). The Slum Sisters wore no Army uniform, but dressed unobtrusively in nondescript clothes. They encountered the worst poverty imaginable. 'No food, no fire, no comfort – filth, vermin, cold and despair were all we found that day,' wrote one in 1895. The Slum Sister programme had spread by then to Brooklyn, Boston, Buffalo, Philadelphia, Chicago and St Louis. Even the Army's worst critics fell silent before this ministry, which the many more sympathetic observers regarded as being close to angelic.[65]

The drive was evangelical. To 'rescue fallen women' was one of the ways in which this young and growing mission expressed its strong commitment to practical holiness. Samuel Brengle, one-time Methodist theologian, had become a Salvation Army officer in 1887. In his writings he articulated the Salvationists' holiness experience as 'nothing more than a pure heart, filled with perfect love, and a clear conscience toward God and man, which comes from a faithful discharge of duty and simple faith without hypocrisy'.[66] Holiness teaching reinforced the Salvationists' motivation to serve others in the spirit of Christ.

Commissioners Frederick and Emma Booth-Tucker succeeded Ballington Booth in leadership. It was they who had guided the development of medical work in India. Their protégé, the amateur Harry Andrews had opened the inauspicious dispensary in Nagercoil. From this burgeoned general hospitals countrywide. The Booth-Tuckers brought to the appointment in the USA the experience of India, but here reinforced the predominantly obstetric approach to health programmes.

In the early 1900s the Rescue Homes, many of them now supplemented by maternity services, conducted their expanding programmes in an atmosphere which, at the Army's insistence, was kept small, comfortable and homely. Even the sharpest critics of the Army's social programme called these Rescue Homes the most effective of their kind in the country. Such good reports encouraged public support for an innovation – in 1914 the Army opened a small general hospital in Covington, Kentucky, a suburb of Cincinnati. Not only did it provide the local population with a service, it also provided a training base for the 31 Rescue Homes around the country. The credit for the success of the rescue work went to the indefatigable matrons.[67]

On the other side of the globe in New Zealand, where the Army began in 1883, evangelism was again the primary thrust. But the Army's close contact with the more needy elements in the population made it aware of the need for more emphasis on social rehabilitation, despite the generally better economic climate of the 1890s. In 1892 the Army was running four rescue homes for women in the main cities and one maternity hospital for unmarried mothers in Christchurch. The report for 1900 indicated that, in the previous year, 466 women and girls had passed through the four rescue homes, fewer than 30 of whom had been declared unsatisfactory, and 187 men had passed through the prison-gate homes, with only 14 being declared unsatisfactory. Also, 111 unmarried mothers had passed through the maternity home in Christchurch. The comments of the *Taranaki Herald* on the 1897 Social Report entitled *Hope* ran as follows: '... the Army has a network of social agencies which are undoubtedly saving the colony many hundreds of pounds annually, by the rescue of poor, unfortunate girls, and reclamation of criminals who are, in many cases, permanently reformed. In addition, there is the noble work performed by the Army nursing sisters in the Maternity Homes, besides the efficient aid rendered to the out-of-works at the Industrial Homes at Auckland and Wellington …'[68]

As an example of the work being done, the case of Lizzie Roach may be cited. She was a Dunedin 'character' who had over 400 convictions for drunkenness. Sister Agnes Scott of the Dunedin *War Cry* Brigade met Lizzie in a hotel one evening and gave her a white rose which she had been carrying with her bundle of *War Cry*s. This kindly gesture led to Lizzie attending the Army meeting the next day, which was a Sunday, in order to seek out Agnes who, in true Salvation Army style, took her home for a meal, counselled her and led her to a point of spiritual decision. Accommodation was found for her in the Dunedin rescue home and suitable employment. Lizzie eventually became an understanding and efficient sergeant in a Salvation Army institution in Australia.

In Australia a similar story unfolds – nine maternity hospitals and one general hospital in Australia in 1953, although by 1977 there were only three.[69] The cost of medical services had always proved an anxiety, even as far back as the 19th century during the command of both countries by William and Catherine's third son, Herbert. 'Social Annuals' were introduced, where audited reports were published, and fresh appeals were launched by the governors or other leading citizens, such as Sir Robert Stout and Sir William Fox.[70]

If the worldwide medical work of the Army sprang from small beginnings, so did the Army's hospital work in Canada. Two of the five young officers, who journeyed from Toronto to Winnipeg in 1886 to pioneer the work, were faithfully serving six years later when, one bitter winter night, there was a knock on the door of the women officers' quarters. A pregnant girl, with nowhere to go, made a tearful plea for help. Accommodated and cared for, she was the first of a long queue of deserted wives, homeless women and unmarried mothers that came for aid.[71] When The Salvation Army initiated its rescue work in 1886 its purpose was the reclamation of 'fallen women'. Havens for unmarried mothers were endowed with titles such as Fort Hope, The Homestead, The Anchorage and Redemption Home. Staffed by trained nurses, and aided by volunteer medical doctors, the transition from post-natal care, in which the rescue homes had specialised, to complete maternity care seemed inevitable. In 1890 the St John Rescue Home was being used as a maternity facility. City doctors offered their services free of charge. Only official accreditation and recognition were wanting.[72]

The Army's Rescue Home in Winnipeg, established in 1890, became so quickly overcrowded that, by 1894, a larger property was needed. When, by 1902, even this failed to meet the demand for maternity care, a larger building was contemplated. At this point, several favourable circumstances combined. First, public approval of its work in Winnipeg had exceeded expectations; among supporters were a large number of church and civic officials. Second, both the municipal and provincial governments were prepared to support the Army's work financially in an unprecedented manner. And third, and perhaps most important, was the fact that several influential doctors recognised and encouraged the work of the Rescue Home (now called Fort Rescue).[73] Redevelopment led to increase in capacity beyond initial thinking. Between 1906 and 1910 almost 2,000 admissions of married and unmarried mothers were recorded in Winnipeg. Those who had no home to return to were offered a chance to recuperate in the adjoining Rescue Home. Children with no home care were also admitted while their mothers were patients at the hospital. In due course the Grace gained both the expertise and right to train its own nurses.

On the world scene, The Salvation Army has provided nursing education in many countries. The first officer to foresee the value of training was Ensign Hart. By 1895, Dr Hart, Chief Medical Officer at the Hackney Rescue Home, had full plans for nursing education. In the first year of training the nurse would be both a cadet and a probationer; in the second year she would be a nurse, holding the rank of lieutenant; by the third year she would be a sister with promotion to captain. As the service expanded Hart expected some to become assistant matrons with staff rank.

In 1895 there had been a great leap forward in terms of an official medical programme. Word appears here and there of doctors who had become Salvationists and commenced charitable work whilst continuing private practice, even wearing uniform. Edward Evatt (LRCS Edin) had a practice near Cambridge[74] and mention has already been made of Ensign Hart (MD Edin), who became Corps Cadet Guardian[75] at the Congress Hall in London. He was an assistant in the Aural Department of The London Hospital, and had already helped the Army in India.[76] In 1895 he became the Medical Officer to the Hackney Rescue Headquarters. He must have had a very busy schedule, dividing his time between visits to all rescue facilities and daily clinics for Salvation Army officers. Every second day he lectured to trainee midwives at Ivy House.

In *All the World* in August 1916, Major Bell of the International Headquarters Medical Department wrote: 'In our ranks today in different parts of the world, are officers who entered the service of the organisation from the Regent Hall which surely holds the blue ribbon for the number of its members who have volunteered.' No doubt he would be thinking first of his boss, Dr Henry W. Williams, who opened the Medical Department at International Headquarters in May 1898. The programme was on public display at the Army's exhibition at the Agricultural Hall, Islington, the next year.[77] Dr Hart was designated as Williams's assistant. It is noteworthy that Hart's practice was recorded as giving priority to evangelism.

The same emphasis was true for Williams. His testimony was published in *The War Cry*. He writes that he first entered the Regent Hall in 1895. He was an Anglican, commissioned by some of his friends to give his opinion on the new organisation and its startling methods. He found that the emphasis on the penitent form was off-putting but he stayed to learn more of the holiness teaching. It moved him, and he eventually claimed the experience for himself. As he wrote, 'It was the most fortunate thing that ever happened to me.' He became an Auxiliary[78] and was gazetted as Staff Auxiliary, with the rank and privileges of Staff-Captain attached to the Subscribers' Department.[79] He started to help with screening of candidates for training, and soon gave up his lucrative practice to serve as an officer, although he retained his honorary posts of Consulting Physician to the Hospital for Consumptives, Margate, and Senior Physician to The Western Skin Hospital, Great Portland Street, London.[80]

Regarding the new Medical Department, Major Thonger said: 'No army engaged in actual warfare is complete without its ambulance and medical corps.' He went on to describe how the department was moving into overseas commitments. The newly created Salvation Army Assurance Society was concerned about the heavy claims following the deaths of children, and ran a series of articles in its magazine *Assurance* on the treatment of coughs, colds and diet, written by its Chief Medical Officer. According to Thonger it was similar disquiet at the cost of ill health which prompted the Chief of the Staff to launch the new department. There had been negative publicity on the care of officers. 'The bodily health of our people suffers through the hardness of the fight.'

So the parameters of the Medical Department's programme were set as:

1. to advise the Chief of the Staff on purely medical matters;
2. to supervise the various medical institutions of The Salvation Army, both at home and abroad;
3. to give advice on surgical treatment to officers and employees, including wives and children;
4. to constitute a central medical bureau for information on the most suitable hospitals for professional advice and treatment;

5. to examine cadets, even outlining a countrywide service with corps, divisional and provincial surgeons, who might also train doctors and nurses for missionary work.

In 1901 a leaflet was discovered amongst scrap paper, which listed charges for treatment. It bore the signature of Commissioner Carleton, of the Assurance Society:

1. consultation including medicine: one shilling;
2. home visits and treatment: two shillings and sixpence plus travelling expenses;
3. extraction or scaling of teeth: one shilling;
4. candidate's certificates: two shillings and sixpence;
5. operations: from two shillings and sixpence.

Dr Williams died in 1917 after 27 years' service. He was always proud of his uniform and, said his colleagues, 'he was one of nature's gentlemen'.[81]

At the close of the 19th century, the development of obstetric hospitals had become widespread. Early developments in the USA have already been described. In 1892 the first hospital for the USA opened in Oakland, California. Grand Rapids was next, then Chicago. The next year it was Milwaukee, with St Louis not far behind. The latter attracted the support of James and Martha Stewart, local residents who donated a property in 1897. The work continued to spread throughout the USA. In 1896 it was Omaha and by 1898, St Paul, 'the Army's most luxurious institution'. By the last year of the century it included Des Moines and Detroit. The facilities in these hospitals varied, some including gynaecology and even psychiatry and dentistry. All had the valuable help of honorary doctors, many of local eminence. Typical of these was Charles Sumner Bacon of Chicago, who was consultant to three other hospitals in the city. All of these hospitals continued to grow in the new century.

New Zealand has a similar story, where a series of Bethany hospitals developed from the initial rescue homes for women in Auckland, Gisborne, Wellington, Christchurch, Dunedin and Napier, already noted.

The last quarter of the 19th century saw a change in the place of medical services by evangelicals in Western countries. Previously, doctors, and medical students in particular, had been morally suspect, but by 1893 their work was described as 'that sober, absolute, positive science … the relief of human suffering'.[82]

The care of overworked officers was not neglected. Even as early as 1886 there is record of 'homes for the sick and wounded' in the UK. These must have included nursing, with visiting doctors. The first was a large mansion in the Rhondda Valley, donated by the Cory brothers, ardent supporters of William and Catherine Booth.[83] With the stimulus of the medical services at International Headquarters in 1898, such provision presumably increased. Convalescent homes for officers who broke down under strain of their demanding work or demanding leaders[84] were opened in Sausalito California in 1890 and in North Long Beach, New Jersey in 1891. Another early expression of health care services was for neglected women and children, in Grand Rapids Michigan, and Oakland, California, in 1887. There were new twists and emphases, marking local needs, in the spread of slum and obstetric services in Europe, Japan, Australia and South Africa. In those formative years the tale unfolding is that of the enterprise of zealous individuals many of whom were women. Service development was usually a response to perceived local need. As a Chinese nurse in the Ting Hsien hospital was often heard to say, 'If you don't do it, no one else will!'

[18] Morris, J. *The Spectacle of Empire* Faber and Faber, London 1982
[19] Richards, M. *It Began with Andrews*, SP&S London 1971
[20] Morris, J. Ibid
[21] Commissioner Arthur Blowers, a pioneer of The Salvation Army in India, was then International Secretary for Africa and Asia at International Headquarters.
[22] Bready, J. W. *England Before and After Wesley* Hodder & Stoughton, London 1939
[23] Andersen, D. Introduction to *It Began with Andrews*
[24] Sandall, R. *The History of The Salvation Army Vol I* Nelson, London 1947 pp. 203-4
[25] Fairbank, J. *Booth's Boots – Social Service Beginnings in The Salvation Army* The Salvation Army British Territory, London 1983 Chapter 2

[26] With the publication of *In Darkest England and The Way Out* in 1890, The Salvation Army's social programme in the UK was launched. Money poured in from the public and a committee of prominent citizens was set up to oversee its use. The plan outlined was in three sections. Stage one provided shelters and employment in selected towns; stage two, a land colony with training in agricultural skills, whilst the third stage envisaged overseas colonies where trainees could be settled. The last never truly emerged although more than a quarter of a million people were assisted to emigrate under supervision. Later developments can be traced in *Hadleigh Salvation Army Farm: A Vision Reborn* by Gordon Parkhill and Graham Cook, The Salvation Army UK Territory, London 2008

[27] Murdoch, N. Paper to USA Social Services Commission

[28] Stead, W. T. *The Star*, 2 January 1891

[29] Ibid

[30] Sandall, R. *The History of The Salvation Army Vol III* Nelson, London 1955 Chapter 9

[31] Acts 26:16 *Weymouth*

[32] Larsson, J. *Saying Yes to Life – An Autobiography* International Headquarters, London 2007 p. 242

[33] Moyles, R. *The Blood and Fire in Canada* AGM Publications, Edmonton, Canada 2004

[34] Sandall, R. *The History of The Salvation Army Vol I* p. 83

[35] Ibid p. 135

[36] *The Deliverer*, SP&S, London August 1909

[37] Ibid Christmas 1891

[38] Ibid September 1893

[39] Ibid June 1928

[40] Gilks, W. 'Our District Nurses from a Field Officer's Point of View', *The Deliverer* January 1896

[41] Sandall, R. *The History of The Salvation Army Vol II* Nelson, London 1950 Chapter 16

[42] *The Deliverer* 1938

[43] Rader, H. in *Historical Dictionary of The Salvation Army* John G. Merritt (Ed), Scarecrow Press, Lanham, Maryland 2006 p. 210

[44] Fairbank, J. *Booth's Boots – Social Service Beginnings in The Salvation Army* UKT, London 1983 p. 10

[45] Ibid Chapters 9, 10

[46] Ibid p. 33

[47] Ibid p. 36

[48] Archives of St Bartholomew's Hospital, London

[49] Fairbank, J. *For Such a Time – The Story of the Young Florence Booth* IHQ, London 2007 Chapter 12

[50] Ibid p. 115

[51] Fairbank, J. *Booth's Boots – Social Service Beginnings in the Salvation Army* UKT, London 1983 p. 33

[52] Fairbank, J. *For Such a Time – The Story of the Young Florence Booth,* IHQ London 2007 p. 123

[53] Fairbank, J. *Booth's Boots – Social Service Beginnings in the Salvation Army* UKT, London 1983 p. 28

[54] Ibid p. 39

[55] Fairbank, J. *For Such a Time – The Story of the Young Florence Booth* IHQ, London 2007 pp. 123-124

[56] Ibid p. 66

[57] Ibid p. 71

[58] *The Deliverer* 1928

59 Frederick Tucker was an assistant commissioner in the Indian Civil Service, his grandfather having been the chairman of the East India Company. He established The Salvation Army in India in 1882. On his marriage to Emma, the second daughter of William and Catherine Booth, he changed his name to Booth-Tucker by deed poll.

60 Ibid 1917

61 Fairbank, J. *Booth's Boots – Social Service Beginnings in the Salvation Army* UKT, London 1983 p. 37

62 Inaugurated in 1858 and with membership open to practitioners throughout the country, the society was devoted to advancing the knowledge of obstetrics and of the diseases of women and children.

63 Winston, D. *Red Hot and Righteous – The Urban Religion of The Salvation Army* Harvard University Press, Cambridge, Massachusetts 1999 Chapter 2

64 McKinley, E H. *Marching to Glory* (Second Edition) – *The History of The Salvation Army in the United States, 1880-1992* William B. Eerdemans Publishing Company, Grand Rapids, Michigan 1995 pp. 68-69

65 Ibid p. 70

66 Brengle, S. L. *Helps to Holiness*, The Salvation Army, London 1896, facsimile edition by Salvation Army Supplies Department, Atlanta 1992, Chapter 3, p. 16

67 McKinley, E H. *Marching to Glory* (Second Edition) – *The History of The Salvation Army in the United States, 1880-1992* William B. Eerdemans Publishing Company, Grand Rapids, Michigan 1995 p. 125

68 Bradwell, C. *Fight the Good Fight – The Story of The Salvation Army in New Zealand* A. H. & A. W. Reed, Wellington 1982 p. 55

69 Rader, H. in *Historical Dictionary of The Salvation Army* John G. Merritt (Ed), Scarecrow Press, Lanham, Maryland 2006 p. 207 ff

70 Bolton, B. *Booth's Drum – The Salvation Army in Australia 1880 – 1980* Hodder & Stoughton, Sydney 1980 and Bradwell, C. *Fight the Good Fight – The Story of The Salvation Army in New Zealand* A. H. & A. W. Reed, Wellington 1982 p. 55

71 Brown, A. *The Gate and the Light* Bookwright Publications, Toronto 1984 p. 176

72 Moyles, R G. *The Blood and Fire in Canada* AGM Publications 2004 p. 121

73 Ibid

74 *All the World* 1917

75 A section in each corps for the training of young people.

76 *All the World* 1899

77 Ibid 1916

78 Well-wishers of The Salvation Army who became regular supporters financially and in other practical ways.

79 *The Officer* 1897

80 *All the World* 1899

81 *The War Cry* London, 1917

82 Cathcart, G. *The Medical Charities in the English Metropolis* Garland Publishing, New York 1984

83 Sandall, R. *The History of The Salvation Army Vol II* Nelson. London (1950) p. 342

84 Rader, H. in *Historical Dictionary of The Salvation Army* John G. Merritt (Ed), Scarecrow Press, Lanham, Maryland 2006 p. 207 ff

Chapter two

Pioneers in the developing world

THE Catherine Booth Hospital at Nagercoil, 12 miles from Cape Cormorin, India's southern tip, is The Salvation Army's oldest general hospital in the developing world. Its opening in 1901 was due to collusion between the amateur, Harry Andrews, and the professional, Dr Percy Turner. Both Bramwell Booth and his father, William, had a hand in it.

In this saga, Harry Andrews is the most colourful character, the first of many who, without formal training and with scant apprenticeship, sparked medical centres in various parts of the world. There was little link between them until Turner was appointed Chief Medical Officer at International Headquarters in London in 1922.[85] The establishment of a medical department at IHQ in 1898 has already been described, but its warrant to control and inform overseas programmes never became a reality.

In the early years of the Christian Mission, Bramwell Booth, when visiting people living in workmen's cottages near Victoria Park in the East End of London, accepted the care of a baby from its dying Salvationist mother.[86] The baby boy posed a problem for Catherine Booth, who eventually decided he could stay in her home if her daughter Emma assumed responsibility for his care. So Emma looked after little Harry until she launched the first Training Home for Women in Clapton. Here she was able to transfer her charge to the nursery. Bramwell retained his interest in the boy, and it was he who detected the boy's empathy with the sick and a talent for healing.

At the age of 15, Harry arrived in India with Emma, by now Commissioner Rahman, wife to Frederick Tucker, who had changed his name to Booth-Tucker at his marriage.[87] Two years later Harry was trained as an officer in Bombay and appointed to assist Major William Stevens at the divisional headquarters in Nagercoil, Tamil Nadu. Stevens was a charismatic pioneer, a jeweller from Worthing, who had sold up and joined the ranks as an officer on hearing Catherine Booth preach. Harry's appointment was as educational inspector and later as cashier. He was reported to be a quick worker 'driving his pony like Jehu'.[88] Mrs Stevens noted his concern for the sick that he met, and handed over a bathroom at the end of the verandah for his use. It became the first recorded missionary dispensary of The Salvation Army. As such, the teak doors were preserved as the entrance to the physiotherapy department of the Catherine Booth Hospital, a reminder of the tiny acorn from which grew the oak, India's largest Salvation Army mission hospital.

In 1897 a separate building was erected with a local donation. Thus, even before the Catherine Booth Hospital was formally opened by the Diwan[89] of Travancore State in 1901, two wards of bamboo and thatch were ready for use. Bramwell kept in touch with his protégé, sending a parcel of simple surgical instruments, including dental forceps. He subsequently arranged for Andrews to be enrolled for a six-month dresser's course at The London Hospital. It was at this point that Andrews heard that a Dr Turner was working as a corps officer in Lewisham, and sought him out. After gaining Percy Turner's permission, he approached Bramwell to secure his services for India. Turner pursued his studies for two years, obtaining the practical experience he felt essential to tackle the medical challenge of India. By 1901 he was installed at Nagercoil with Andrews as his assistant.[90]

After a year or so Andrews was transferred to Anand in Gujarat, where The Salvation Army had seen rapid progress. He was reminded that his role was as an evangelist, but by 1903 he was building a hospital funded by a donation from Miss Emery, a Canadian lady living in the USA, in memory of her sister. Even before the hospital was up and running, Andrews had amputated the leg of a patient who had been mauled by a crocodile.[91] So the Emery Hospital was built, revealing Andrews' talent as an architect, in the form of a quadrangle, the paved courtyard at its heart being ideal for meetings. Four years elapsed before it was arranged for Andrews to receive full medical training in Chicago. He made his mark there. Dr Blake, one of his tutors, would always remember the student who was already an experienced 'surgical operator'.[92] Returning to India in 1912, he was given a new Salvation Army assignment in North India, at the walled Mogul city of Moradabad, 100 miles from Delhi, where The Salvation Army had a Criminal Tribes' Settlement.[93] Miss Emery again weighed in with a donation, this time in memory of her father. Even before the Thomas Emery Hospital was opened, the doctor had been busy operating in his quarters, so that the donations of a string of grateful patients enabled the addition of long wings of private wards to the impressive frontage. There was wide publicity when the Governor of the United Provinces of Agra and Oudh, Lord Meston, opened the hospital. It was hailed in government circles as a model for district hospitals.[94] The brass plates of those grateful patients were still in place in 1940, when Dr Harry Williams was stationed there. Having cause to modify rooms at the front entrance, he found that all the original bricks were stamped SA!

With the outbreak of World War I the government of India, faced with a shortage of beds for casualties, requested the loan of the Thomas Emery Hospital and its Chief Medical Officer.

This was agreed, Andrews remaining in charge as a captain in the Indian Medical Service (IMS). Andrews still had not ended his pioneering days for, at the behest of Commissioner Booth-Tucker, he prospected for a new hospital in the Punjab. Land was purchased at Batala, 24 miles north of Amritsar. It was some years before funds were available, by which time the

New Egerton Woollen Mills, 12 miles to the north in Dhariwal, asked for the hospital to be built on land near the mills and to assume responsibility for the health of the company's covenanted staff. So The Salvation Army's MacRobert Hospital was opened in 1926 in Dhariwal. Andrews was not around to design it, but its long colonnaded frontage, reminiscent of Moradabad, is an unconscious tribute to him. The land he had bought in Batala became the site of a boarding school.

The tale of the London waif turned military surgeon, and his posthumous Victoria Cross is often told. The Thomas Emery Hospital was returned to The Salvation Army at the end of the war, but Andrews had been posted to the North West Frontier where he was killed on 22 October 1919 whilst removing casualties from 'no man's land'. His bravery is memorialised by a painting, which hung in the headquarters of the Royal Army Medical Corps at Woolwich[95] until it was presented to The Salvation Army – it is now in the International Heritage Centre. He had set a challenge to other Salvation Army medical enthusiasts who, seeing a need, opened dispensaries and hospitals around the world.

Many early hospitals became training centres, firstly for compounders – pharmacists, who often acted as doctors. They were even registered by some government departments as Licensed Medical Practitioners. It was from this source that many of the branch hospitals of the Catherine Booth Hospital in Nagercoil were staffed. By the end of World War I, the Catherine Booth Hospital was reported as having 'more than 60 beds … staffed entirely by Salvation Army officers, of whom all those belonging to the country have received their entire training in the Salvation Army medical department … all obtaining the diploma recognised by the state'.[96] One outstanding convert, a man named Sundaram, of the Church Missionary Society at Dohnavur, 30 miles from the Catherine Booth Hospital, was attracted to the Army by Stevens. He took full medical training and was appointed to Kulathummel Hospital (now in Kerala), and served finally at Nagercoil.

Quite early in this phase of medicine in the developing world, a degree of specialisation occurred, notably in leprosy and tuberculosis. The first leprosy hospital was opened at the request of the Dutch colonial government at Pelantogoen, Sumatra in 1896, thus antedating the Catherine Booth Hospital.[97] These leprosy centres were usually called settlements, emphasising the predominant place of tender loving care, curative treatment being undiscovered at that time. It was only in the 1950s that new drugs changed the picture and prognosis in both leprosy and tuberculosis. (It is interesting to note that the two bacilli, which cause these diseases, are almost identical under a microscope.) It was fortunate that such selfless, devoted care was available in abundance in those gifted amateurs, the pioneer missionary officers. Commissioner Booth-Tucker wrote: 'It is in times of suffering and sickness that we appreciate, as at no other moment, the kindly touch of sympathy and prayer.'[98]

As has already been noted, there were doctors who became Salvationists whilst still continuing private practice. In addition to their own charitable work, some of these became, or encouraged others to become, pioneers in Salvation Army hospitals. They sometimes responded to specific appeals made by William or Bramwell Booth. The first was a Dane, Vilhelm Wille, who responded to Bramwell's appeal for help for the sick in the poorest countries, when he visited Copenhagen in 1906.[99] Born in 1862 to a famous sculptor, by 1882 Wille was a medical student. These were the days when Lister's carbolic spray was in use in the operating rooms. First working as an obstetrician, Wille moved to ophthalmology, which became his life's work.

Whilst serving as Corps Sergeant-Major[100] in Koge, his patients knew of his strong disapproval of alcohol, as well as his evangelism and care for the poor. After his interview with Bramwell Booth, Wille sold up his Koge practice, and set out, with his wife and four children, for Java in the Dutch East Indies (Indonesia). Following floods in 1901, the colonial government had opened a settlement for beggars at Bugangan.

They asked the Army to take it over. It was a low, barrack building of plaited bamboo, a most unlikely place for eye surgery when the Willes arrived there in 1908.

However, miracles of restored sight soon attracted patients. The first was a blind Chinese man. The restoration of his sight silenced the local priests who had warned against treatment by a foreigner. It was an uphill fight, success depending largely on the fact that the family worked as a team. But gradually Wille's reputation spread throughout the region. Government hospitals in Semarang began transferring patients with venereal or skin infections. Despite such unhelpful additions to his workload, he continued to develop his own speciality.

Mrs Wille wrote: 'I think it is the most glorious work in the world to be a Salvation Army officer.'[101] Doctor Wille set the pattern for all pioneers by putting Christian witness above professional skill. Writing to his friends back in Koge, he said, 'I am grateful about my position, for I can use all my strength in work for Jesus, in a manner that reminds me so much of his own.'[102]

Soon though, in awe of this bearded enthusiast, Dutch and other expatriates were consulting him. Their fees helped him to create what became a hospital within a colony intended only for beggars. The figures speak for themselves: 1908 – 2,000 consultations; 1909 – 24,000, and by 1913 a staggering 41,000. In these five years there were 5,000 inpatients and 3,000 major operations. Initially his wife was his only assistant, though she was quickly able to relieve him of minor cases whilst he trained new assistants. Soon his daughter, Elisabeth, joined the team. Wille was remarkably patient, but by 1915 his ambition was realised and a custom-built hospital, devoted entirely to ophthalmology, was opened in Semarang. It still exists today.

The family paid a price for this dedication. Even before their first furlough in 1913, malaria, typhus and dysentery took their toll in the settlement. Their second daughter, Andrea Wilhelmina, died of typhus.

Many of the pioneers suffered professionally from the parochial outlook of the professional bodies in their adopted countries. Wille's Danish qualifications were not recognised, so he had to sit Dutch qualifying exams. His examiners were embarrassed when they realised that they had an eminent consultant on their hands. Such problems for expatriates have continued. Even as late as the 1970s Captain Janette Davies had to sit Bolivian exams because her UK nursing qualifications were not recognised. Even more remarkable is the experience of Major Gwyneth Evans of the United Kingdom. A highly qualified nurse with great experience when appointed to Suginami, Japan, she not only re-qualified, but did so using the Japanese language.[103]

The Semarang hospital, which Wille opened in 1915 with donations from grateful patients and a generous government grant, was well designed. In addition to laboratory, operating room, darkroom and wards, there were adequate staff quarters. The new milieu was suited to professional reflection: papers by Wille commenced to appear in the medical press. One was on xerophthalmia, a vitamin A deficiency which can cause blindness. He found it widespread in Java. His cure, by means of a diet that included milk, eggs, liver and cod-liver oil, added to his fame. The incessant work for weeks and months on end is hard for us to envisage. It was from 8 am to 8 pm with a three-hour siesta. Evangelical ardour was unabated. Mrs Wille took her guitar and went visiting in the poorest areas of the city, with a blind girl as her translator. Meanwhile, the doctor entered prisons with his message.[104]

It is small wonder that when General Bramwell Booth instituted the Order of the Founder, for those deemed to have given outstanding service of a kind that would have delighted William Booth's heart, Major (Dr) Vilhelm Wille was one of the first group of recipients in 1920. It should have been awarded to his wife as well! King Christian X of Denmark had already appointed Wille, Knight of the Order of the Dannebrog, and in 1921, Queen Wilhelmina of his adopted country made him an Officer of the Order of Oranje-Nassau.

Mrs Wille died in 1925 and Vilhelm retired in 1931. He remarried and settled into private practice, first in Semarang and later in Bandung. Even as late as 1938 he had an article published in the *British Journal of Ophthalmology*. His uniformed figure was familiar on the streets of Bandung until his serene death in 1944. Indonesian doctors, notably Dr Oey Khoen Lian, took his place in the hospital. During the Second World War the Japanese overran the Dutch East Indies, commandeering the hospital. When the war was over and Indonesia became independent, the hospital was completely refurbished. Dr Oey Khoen Lian had continued to work in the ravaged hospital during the war. It is recorded that he performed the most difficult operations by the light of a bicycle lamp. When the wife of the Minister of Health reopened the hospital in 1950, Dr Wille's widow again stressed the spiritual foundation by presenting a new flag on behalf of the family.

With the passage of time the Wille reputation faded and, even with the support of consultants from Semarang university's department of ophthalmology, it became clear that diversification into a general hospital was essential for its survival in a competitive environment. When the former Chief of the Staff, John J. Allan, visited as the General's special representative in 1955, he submitted a well-reasoned report, highlighting several causes for low occupancy. Principal among these, he felt, were strained relations between doctors and administrators. He concluded by putting in a strong appeal for appointment of a missionary doctor of repute to save the hospital. But the proposal did not materialise.[105] However, Finnish, American, Dutch, Canadian and Swedish officers administered the hospital in various capacities until the 1980s when Captain Ann Powell, a British officer who had graduated from radiographer to hospital administrator, guided developments.

Early in the century, the government in Surabaya had invited the Army to undertake medical work there, and the small general clinic, which opened in 1915, developed into the William Booth Hospital, which stands on the Djalan Peninsula

(Diponegoro). Nurse and midwife training were significant from early days. The hospital suffered, as did many other Salvation Army centres, during the Japanese occupation. Officers from countries perceived as 'friendly' were permitted to carry on in some places. Scandinavians were among those permitted to 'hold on' at the hospitals.[106]

Conflict did not cease with the Japanese surrender in 1945 because Indonesian nationalists fought for both independence and political control. After the recognition of Indonesian independence in 1949 the William Booth Hospital in Surabaya regained its Norwegian matron, Malene Berge, replacing the Swiss Elizabeth Rufener, Swedish Tora Ryden and Finnish Elli Walo. The hospital has been notable for the variety of nationalities on its staff and for its adaptability. In its early history there were four polyclinics attached to the hospital. The main hospital had evolved over the years, until a Norwegian officer, Major Oscar Enstad, developed a master plan as its administrator. Also Captain Britt Alhbin, a Swedish officer-nurse, spent many years at the hospital, both as Head of Nursing, and later as Administration Officer. Captain Basuki Kartodarsono, hospital administrator in the 1980s, took over the project, and gradually it came to fruition. The captain became Commissioner Kartodarsono, territorial commander for the Indonesia Territory.

In the rural beauty of Turen, East Java, a simple medical service which had commenced in 1918, had by 1936 developed into the Bokor General Hospital. At this stage, it was handed over to The Salvation Army. Many patients came from the plantations in the southern ranges. Surgery had become a major priority, accounting for 50 per cent of the patients. Dr Jim Smith, an Australian, worked at Turen for many years. Careful financial management enabled the hospital to apply small profits to redevelopment and upgrading. A new outpatient department was the result in 1988.

In Bandung a 25-bed maternity clinic was opened in 1930.[107] It transferred to a rented house in 1938 and was named 'Beatrix

Clinic' after the recently born Dutch princess. Esther Petterson, in spite of having lost an arm in a traffic accident, delivered babies and trained Indonesian helpers. Bungsu, Indonesian for 'last born', and the local name affectionately given to the hospital in Bandung, was appropriated by the occupying Japanese during World War II.[108] It reopened as a general hospital. Salvationist doctor Charlie Kristianto, did much to upgrade the hospital during the 1980s, but he died of lung cancer at an early age, leaving his wife, Pratiwi Kristianto, to consolidate the upgrading process. She later became territorial medical secretary.

In Japan it was William Booth himself who set the country ablaze in 1906, appealing eloquently for help for the sick poor, to whom his officers had introduced him. Amongst the vast crowds who heard him was Dr Sanya Matsuda, already attracted to the treatment of tuberculosis, which so afflicted the poor.[109] Reared as a Buddhist, Matsuda first heard the Christian gospel at the age of 16, when a student at Doshida college in Kyoto. He was immediately attracted. In these years he met Gunpei Yamamuro who had witnessed the launch of The Salvation Army in 1895. Matsuda was baptised whilst a medical student at Dai I Koto Gakko college and continued his studies at the Imperial University. He felt led to apply for his first post at the tuberculosis sanatorium, where the superintendent was a known Christian. Like many converts, he wanted to go the whole way as a disciple of Christ. He met Dr Wakiya, who was treasurer of Hongo Corps, who invited him to hear William Booth preach. In the previous year he had been in charge of a Red Cross team during the Russo-Japanese war, and felt that a military approach might be suitable to the needs of the sick poor.

William Booth made a profound impression in Japan. A newspaper reported 'if this man remains long in Japan he will change its religion, for he speaks not as professors, but as a man with a soul in possession of secrets'.[110] So it is not surprising that, when Booth died in 1912, there was a national move to create a memorial. The consensus was that a hospital would be most appropriate. Donations poured in and the emperor added his gift of a suitable building, which became the nucleus around which the hospital quickly developed. The Salvation Army pioneer Gunpei Yamamuro appealed for a doctor to become the superintendent, and Matsuda responded. By this time he had attained some eminence as a professor at Tokyo Medical College. He became a Salvationist and followed the example of Frederick Tucker in fixing an Army ribbon around his hat.[111] He was appointed superintendent of The Salvation Army Sanatorium in Tokyo.

To his peers, Matsuda was known primarily for his Christ-likeness. Even as a superintendent and professor he still made domiciliary visits to patients in the Tokyo slums. Many were consumptive. He was a tall man, and a visitor's description of seeing him 'bending low' to pass under the lintel of a tiny house had more than the physical connotation. It is small wonder that he eventually contracted the infection himself and died in 1930. He, like Yamamuro, was admitted to the Order of the Founder. By this time he had attracted others. Professors from the medical colleges brought their students to study his methods. A team developed around him, headed by a young woman, striking in appearance and manner, Dr Rin Iwasa.

In 1891, only four years after the establishment of The Salvation Army in Japan, Rin Iwasa was born to an aristocratic family of Nagoya. Her high-principled, peace-loving father gave her a good education. She was a brilliant student, but as she excelled in Japanese folk-dancing and sports, she remained a popular figure, with an 'infectious gaiety'.[112] Her portrait as a Salvation Army officer shows a tall, slim and beautiful woman. Reared in the Buddhist-Shintoist religion at home, she had read widely and was an idealist, with Florence Nightingale as role model. Admitted to Tokyo Medical College, she met Matsuda and immediately responded to his insistence that character was of prime importance to a doctor. He was the only Christian among her teachers, but he had a profound influence on the whole student body. Led by Rin, about a third of them would find opportunity to seek his counsel at his home. That was scarcely likely to endear her to the rest of the staff.

Once she became a doctor her father expected her to return to Nagoya and set up practice among his Buddhist friends. When she announced that she had applied for a post on Matsuda's staff, her father was bitterly opposed. He forbade her to become a Christian. Despite this, her forays into the slums of Tokyo to treat very ill patients only drew her nearer to her chief. Influenced by him, she attended The Salvation Army International Congress in London in 1914. When she returned to Japan as a captain in 1915, to her great joy her parents, seeing her good works, gave her their whole-hearted support. Soon her name was linked with that of Matsuda in public estimation, so that when he died in 1930 there was no hesitation in appointing her as his successor. Awarded the Order of the Founder, this was followed by Japan's Order of the Blue Ribbon in 1944. Two years later she received an invitation to lecture on tuberculosis to an audience in the palace. There were no limits to her commitment. In 1948, only a year before her death, she was in the thick of medical relief, following floods that swept the plain on the outskirts of Tokyo. At the time of her death she was superintendent of both Suginami and Kiyose hospitals.[113]

Another medical missionary pioneer, Charles Steibel, was again well qualified but self-effacing. His background was distinctive, for he came from an upper middle class Jewish home in the West End of London. His sister had become a Christian. Whether or not this raised questions in his mind, it was on impulse that one evening in 1910 he entered the well-lit foyer of the Regent Hall. A meeting was in progress and he sat it out. Intrigued, he went again and eventually convinced that Christ was alive and calling him to discipleship. The corps officer, Major Frank Barrett, had a vivid memory of this Jew labouring with the problem of the divinity of Christ.[114] Charles's education in his wealthy home had commenced with French and German governesses, followed by public school at

Clifton College, near Bristol. Intent on becoming a doctor, he took the Natural Sciences Tripos at Trinity College, Cambridge before going on to clinical studies at St Thomas' hospital. This hospital, on the south bank of the Thames opposite Parliament, was of ancient foundation. In its long, open wards Florence Nightingale had commenced the formal training of nurses. Years later, Steibel sought surgical experience and was directed to Marylebone hospital 'for its maximum air and quiet'.[115] It was here that Florence Nightingale opened her second school for nurses. And it was here that Steibel met one of its probationers, Agatha Cook, whom he later married. He had already served a long apprenticeship in general practice, both in the UK and South Africa. But his conversion in 1910 meant a radical change in direction. As with others, for him to be a disciple meant serving the sick poor. He commenced the training he considered to be necessary for a medical missionary, studying eye surgery at Moorfields Eye Hospital in London, then general surgery in Newcastle, before appearing for the Fellowship of the Royal College of Surgeons, Edinburgh.

He took himself in hand by embarking on a life of self-denial. His spartan diet and cold room horrified his sister, huddled in her furs. Before any state health service, Christian missions had established clinics in various parts of London. Steibel chose to work in Islington. By this time he and Agatha were of one mind. They were interviewed at International Headquarters by Commissioners Fakir Singh and Dutini (to give the Booth-Tuckers their Indian names). Married on 12 February 1912, Charles and Agatha set sail for India the next day.

At the Catherine Booth Hospital they proved to be a godsend to the Turners. Charles taught surgery to medical students, leaving Percy Turner to concentrate on medicine. Both the wives could train nurses. Mrs Turner has the distinction of being the first formal nursing educator in The Salvation Army.

At the end of 1912 Drs Steibel and Turner were faced with the dilemma brought about by a raging cholera epidemic. 'Is it right to bring virulent infection within the hospital walls?' They solved the matter by making a hole in the hospital compound wall, well away from the other wards. They built temporary structures of plaited leaves over a bamboo frame – built in just 12 hours and which could later be burnt – to accommodate the cholera patients. But their vital contribution was a tireless campaign to organise safe water and control of practices which spread infection. For weeks they had little more than three or four hours sleep per night.

By 1913 the Steibels were on the move again, this time to take charge of the Emery Hospital at Anand, Gujarat. Next year the clouds of war swept in, and Charles, conventionally patriotic, volunteered for the Indian Medical Service. He was sent to the Middle East. His standing as a surgeon would have ensured his employment in a base hospital or on a hospital ship. He did indeed reach a hospital ship in the Mediterranean by 1916 but, true to his sense that he should be in the front line tending casualties, he agitated for a change. Thus by 1917 he was in the trenches outside Kut in Mesopotamia. He was caught by a sniper's bullet as he was applying a field dressing. There was no mention in dispatches, though Agatha received a sympathetic letter from his commanding officer.[116]

The Maharajah of Travancore had approved and funded a medical school at Catherine Booth Hospital. Although the school only lasted for a few years (1908-1914) some officers graduated. They were Brigadier T. Chacko Joseph and Senior Majors S. Ghanaiah and J. Manuel, who had long careers in the medical service. These were in charge of branch hospitals, whilst Dr Sundaram was attached to the main hospital.

As already reported, a measure of specialisation, especially in the field of leprosy, had already occurred in the formative period of medical programmes. The first 'Army' leprosarium in India was opened at Bapatla in Andhra Pradesh; two followed in Kerala.

In Japan, the treatment of tuberculosis was a special emphasis. At a later date much was done in this field in India by special units attached to a number of existing hospitals. The Emery Hospital, Anand, and the Evangeline Booth Hospital, Ahmednagar, both had separate blocks, ensuring isolation.

From the early years, the training of hospital staff was important, and husband and wife teams were the basis of most of the training programmes. In 1899 Harry Andrews had married Gena Smith, a childhood sweetheart, at the nursery in Emma Booth's Training Home in Clapton. She and her sister gained a reputation for fearlessness from their service in evacuating victims of cholera and plague from their homes in Poona, when others had refused.

William Noble, who had emigrated with his parents from Fraserburgh in Scotland to the USA, graduated from the new Emery University, Atlanta in time to serve in France with American troops. He married Etna Dodds in 1919 and they became officers. They sailed for India immediately to take charge of the Thomas Emery Hospital in Moradabad, recently released from its wartime use by the Indian Government. The next year they were transferred to Nagercoil where they worked with the Turners until 1922, when the Turners were posted to International Headquarters. For the next 38 years Noble developed the hospital until it was the largest mission hospital in India. Though fully qualified, Noble fits the pattern of the pioneers in his complete dedication to work for the poor. He was unorthodox, keeping irregular hours, commonly operating and doing rounds in the middle of the night. The Nobles were the first in a stream of doctors and nurses from the USA. As with most of the pioneers, the Nobles were an excellent team. Etna was her husband's public relations officer, facilitating his demanding schedule and making it work. Her heroic efforts to maintain adequate supplies of rice and coconuts to feed hundreds of patients in days of rationing will always be remembered. The coconut shells were used for fuel to obtain the high temperatures required for 'Ma's' 100 loaves of bread each day![117] Dr Noble was admitted to the Order of the Founder in 1957.

Whilst Dr Noble maintained the branch hospitals, which Dr Turner had created, and built two leprosaria, his main concern was the ever-growing base hospital. The pattern of an attractive village was maintained with local granite employed in the buildings. Many of the new blocks were two or three storeys high. Private accommodation, from simple rooms to the four-suite nursing home, earned an income that enabled hundreds to be treated free. He kept outpatients' medicines as cheap as possible, but his huge desk was piled with sample drugs from his friends in the USA. The patients coveted one of these sophisticated cartons to supplement the pills or bottle from the pharmacy. Under Turner the pharmacy, with an English pharmacist, was large and turned out vast supplies of medicines for the branch hospitals. In addition it trained 'compounders', the first of the barefoot doctors. These apprentice graduates were capable of running branch hospitals. It was always part of Andrews's plan and Noble continued it in each of his hospitals

Some form of *ad hoc* training was in operation in every situation. Those instructed in circumscribed tasks proved to be excellent, particularly in sterilisation and theatre techniques. The most notable of such was Brigadier Lautala, a Finnish officer posted to Nagercoil, whom Dr Noble trained to run the routine of his operations and post-operative care. She was on the go from five o'clock each morning throughout her service, personally washing all the theatre linen. Another was Mabel Poole, from Somerset in the UK, who was seconded to nurse the infant Maharajah in the Trivandrum Palace, Travancore State.[118]

Formal training of nurses made rapid advances in the US and Canada. By the 1930s many officers with the diploma of one of the Canadian Salvation Army hospitals were at work in India. State registered courses had to come eventually. The first were in India at Moradabad, Anand and Nagercoil. At the Catherine Booth Hospital, William Noble had a trained nurse from Virginia qualified to commence such a course. Brigadier Katherine Lord saw 67 nurses through to graduation and a state-registered diploma. This registration was in the lower grade. The upper grade course wasn't possible until a later Maharajah of Travancore opened a School of Nursing building in 1947. The then Captain Vera Williamson was appointed as Matron.

Lieut-Colonel Vera Williamson of New Zealand was one of the first to devote the whole of her career to nursing education. She had nursing diplomas in general nursing and in administration. She describes the battles she had with 'Doc', who said, 'Vera, I guess you and I live in two different worlds.' He couldn't be persuaded that state registration demanded buildings used only for education and nursing administration. 'In his view all a nurse needed was a pair of willing hands, an ear for the doctor's orders, and what he termed "a missionary spirit"'.[119]

One of Andrews's trainees at Moradabad was Samuel Burfoot, son of the most famous of the Army's missionary linguists, Major Burfoot, editor of all the vernacular papers published in Bombay. Samuel was sent to run a dispensary. His Swedish wife was a nurse, and by working as a sister in Bombay's main teaching hospital she was able to pay her husband's fees as he studied for the Licentiate of the College of Physicians and Surgeons. He qualified in time to take charge of The Salvation Army MacRobert Hospital (opened by the Governor of the Punjab) in 1926.

Alfred Barnett was another compounder trained at the Catherine Booth Hospital, Nagercoil. He was sent the length of India to open a dispensary at Chini, within sight of Tibet, on the Hindustan-Tibet Road, which Kipling's Kim had walked with his Buddhist Lama. Barnett subsequently left the medical wing, and during World War I raised an Indian Labour Battalion of which he became commander as a lieut-colonel. Later, as lieut-commissioner, he succeeded Arthur Blowers as International Secretary for Missionary Countries. He had a son, Ted, who figures in the next chapter. The opening of the dispensary had been hazardous. Adjutant Jang Singh (Walker) was one of Andrews's compounders at Nagercoil. He was sent to Chini in 1911 whilst on his honeymoon. It was envisaged as being a 12-mile trek from Simla, and muleteers were sent with food supplies for their arrival. But the muleteers had an agenda of their own and it was a month before they turned up in Chini. Meanwhile the Walkers had to eke out an existence on a bag of potatoes, for the people they had come to serve were hungry themselves. But there was no shortage of officers prepared to follow them. One was Hannah Carr (the nurse who had cared for Catherine Booth in her last illness) who had gone to the USA with her daughter, Emma. She arrived at the dispensary, opened at Ani in the Sutlej valley with a Norwegian, Major Hansine Weie.[120]

There were two officers trained at Indian medical schools. Lieut-Colonel Sara Daniel trained at Christian Medical College, Vellore in South India and served at CBH for 26 years. Lieut-Colonel K. C. Joseph graduated from Miraj, Maharashtra, near Ahmednagar and served with distinction at CBH branch hospitals and at Puthencruz Leprosy Hospital, where he became a specialist.

Alongside all this development in India and other developing countries, pioneer efforts continued throughout the rest of the world. Australia was in the picture by 1904 with the opening of a community hospital in Melbourne. It was re-built in 1938 with accommodation for 110, well equipped and with a nurses' training school in three adjoining houses. Four general hospitals were operating in Canada and Newfoundland in the first half of the 20th century. They had each started with obstetric facilities, becoming general by community demand.[121] They were staffed by honorary doctors but administered by officer-matrons, who had usually graduated from one of them.

In the USA in 1914, a large mansion in Covington, Kentucky, was donated and became a general hospital, the Booth Memorial, together with another in Cincinnati, Ohio.[122] Probably the most lasting benefit of these hospitals was the training of nurses. In Covington in 1924 Colonel Clara van der Schouw reported that, in the state examinations, Booth memorial graduates had thrice secured the highest marks, and stressed the value of these graduates to The Salvation Army. In 1918 the influenza epidemic led to a corps building in Charleston, West Virginia, being pressed into the service. The epidemic over, it continued to operate as a general hospital by popular request. It even took over a whole floor of the new corps building for obstetrics. Another general hospital was opened in Boston, Massachusetts.[123]

With the passing years, the solo efforts of a doctor, or a duet with a nurse, gave way to teamwork, the number and variety of paramedicals ever increasing. The Salvation Army trained some of these cadres itself. Stanley Beer had served in the Royal Army Medical Corps before becoming an officer, so before departing for India he was sent to Livingstone College in the East End of London for a short course in medicine. He was appointed as business manager at Anand, a title which covered a great variety of tasks in addition to finance. He was the first to operate an x-ray plant and opened and worked the first clinical laboratory. In the 1930s he felt the need to take full medical training and he qualified with the Bombay Licenciate of the College of Physicians and Surgeons. He returned to Anand to become a valuable assistant to Dr Bramwell Cook. His story takes another twist in the next chapter, but already fits the pattern of the enterprising entrepreneur.[124]

There was a dearth of Salvationist doctors in the 1920s and the employees who were contracted belonged to a variety of denominations. Dr Arthur Swain was a member of the Plymouth Brethren and a marked evangelist from the beginning of his valuable service in The Salvation Army. His first appointment was to China. He arrived there to find that the hospital under construction at Ting Hsein, Hopei, was not viable, so in 1917 he was transferred to India and to the Emery Hospital. He found that a staff of non-smokers looked askance at the pipe always at the corner of his mouth. He gave it up, but he replaced the pipe with his fountain pen, to the amusement of his colleagues. With financial assistance from Rabindranath Tagore, Staff Captain (Dr) Thomas Draper extended the hospital with an Ophthalmic Department.

However, the hospital in China was revived and Swain returned to find it complete, and a model for the country. It was rural in setting and catered for 800 villages. Built in a hollow square it included, in addition to the usual wards and departments, a separate block for tuberculosis. A tower topped the mass of one-storey buildings, which was to prove valuable in the troubled years which followed. Mary Layton, an officer-nurse, joined him. She not only assisted him in establishing a workable routine, but also set up a School of Nursing for a state diploma; the training included general nursing, midwifery and tuberculosis.[125] Swain, like so many of the pioneers, overworked, and after three years he had a breakdown in health. He had a rest in the hills, but relapsed on his return. With his wife to nurse him, he set out on the long journey to the UK. His staff loved him, and many travelled to the Peking railway station to sing and pray with him. Within four days of the docking at Tilbury of the SS *Rawalpindi*, Arthur Swain was promoted to Glory.

Other employee doctors were Maxwell, Sessions, Windsor and Jones, who served in Anand for limited periods. Two Salvationist doctors had longer periods there. The first was a Norwegian, Dr Johannson, whom the visiting General Bramwell Booth made a major on the spot. As already mentioned, Dr Thomas Draper was transferred there from Nagercoil, where in 1911 he trained pharmacists for a hospital diploma. He was well liked and older staff members were delighted to see him when he returned for the golden jubilee celebrations in 1954.

The African story opens with the Western pattern of maternity work in South Africa. Medical work grew out of three hospitals opened between 1901 and 1933: Booth Memorial in Cape Town, William Eadie in Northern Transvaal,

ABOVE: Major (Dr) Henry Williams in his consulting room at IHQ in 1899.
Picture: International Heritage Centre

ABOVE: A painting by Lindsay Cox of a meeting between a Salvation Army welfare officer (Lieutenant William Hooper) and an Australian soldier during the Boer War in South Africa in 1900 based on a line drawing published in the Melbourne *War Cry*.
Picture: Australia Southern Territory Archives

LEFT: Lieut-Colonel (Dr) Harry Andrews, whose amateur dentistry as a teenager led to the founding of the Catherine Booth Hospital at Nagercoil, pictured below in 1899 and as it is today.
Pictures: International Heritage Centre

ABOVE: Major (Dr) and Mrs Percy Turner, circa 1908.

RIGHT: Dr Turner teaching a class of medical students at Nagercoil, in the early 1900s.

Pictures: International Heritage Centre

LEFT: Staff Captain Emma Bown with Captain Ida Kenison and Ensign Beatrice Gilbert to her left and right.

RIGHT: Staff Captain Emma Bown with Cadet Martha Johnson in slum sister uniform.

BELOW: The White Shield Home, Portland, Oregon, USA, 1920.

Pictures: Salvation Army US National Archive

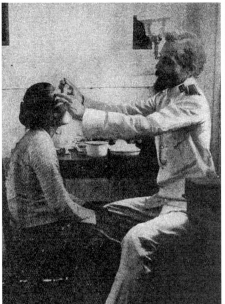

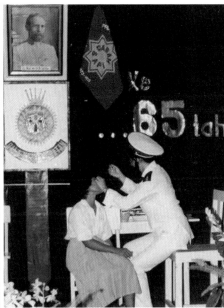

Picture: International Heritage Centre

Picture: Major Ann Powell

ABOVE LEFT: Adjutant (later Lieut-Colonel) Villhelm Wille treating an eye patient in Bugangan. RIGHT: The same scene depicted 65 years later in a play about his life at the eye hospital close by at Semarang.

ABOVE: William Booth Memorial Eye Hospital in Semarang as it was in 1915.

BELOW: As it was in the 1980s, with scaffolding for a new block in the background.

Top picture: International Heritage Centre. Lower picture: Major Ann Powell

ABOVE: An Australian Salvation Army nurse, circa 1915. BELOW: A grittier First World War image, used in a series of postcards.

Pictures: Australia Southern Territory Archives

ABOVE: A British Salvationist transporting a wounded soldier in France during the First World War.

Picture: Australia Southern Territory Archives

BELOW: The Salvation Army Ambulance Band under Adjutant Taylor from the Editorial Department pictured at Boulogne, France during the First World War.

Picture: International Heritage Centre

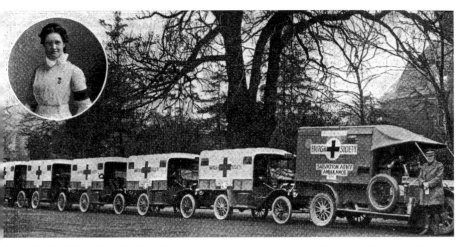

During the First World War, The Salvation Army sent ambulances to the front from countries around the world. ABOVE: Ambulances from the United Kingdom. BELOW: One of four ambulances sent from Australia, driven by volunteer Salvation Army bandsmen. This ambulance later saw service in either Egypt or France.

Picture above: International Heritage Centre. Picture below: Australia Southern Territorial Archives

During the First World War the Indian Government requested the loan of the Thomas Emery Hospital. Its Chief Medical Officer, Brigadier (Dr) Andrews remained in charge as a captain in the Indian Medical Service. Seen here is a military ambulance at the hospital.

Picture: Harry Williams

LEFT: A 1950s ambulance at Nagercoil, Southern India.

BELOW RIGHT: A 1960s ambulance donated to The Salvation Army by Oxfam is seen in the background as health instruction is given at Ahmednagar, Northern India.

Pictures left and below: International Heritage Centre

ABOVE LEFT: Dr William Noble meets a patient arriving on a stretcher at Nagercoil in 1954.

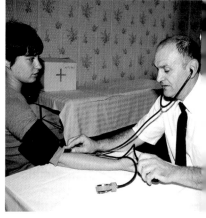

ABOVE LEFT: A Salvation Army clinic and ambulance in Moldova, pictured in 2001.

LEFT: Rural mobile clinic in action in Moldova in 2001.

ABOVE RIGHT: Salvationist Dr Nicolai Caraman treating a teenage patient in the clinic pictured here.

Even a wheelbarrow can serve as an ambulance. ABOVE LEFT: An Afghan refugee is greeted by Dutch Salvationist Wim Kanis as he brings his son to the Haripur Basic Health Unit in Northern Pakistan in 1988 (pictured ABOVE RIGHT).

Pictures by Afghan Refugee Project personnel

Picture above: Australia Southern Territorial Archives. Pictures below: Malawi Command

ABOVE: Nurses based at the Bethesda Hospital in Australia in the early 1900s used bicycles to visit sick people in the surrounding district. Even today, bicycle ambulances are particularly useful in Malawi (see BELOW RIGHT) while an oxcart ambulance is also valuable in rural Africa (BELOW LEFT).

ABOVE LEFT: The commissioning of Cadet (Dr) and Mrs Seamans by Commissioner Alexander Damon. Called to service in Africa, and accepted for India, the Seamanses eventually served in both China and Japan before returning to USA at Covington (pictured LEFT).

ABOVE RIGHT: Major (Dr) Clesson Richardson, who also served at Covington, after service in India with his wife Mary, also a doctor.

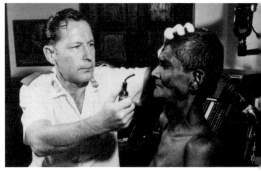

Picture above courtesy International Heritage Centre, all other pictures on this page courtesy US National Archive

ABOVE LEFT: Colonel (Dr) and Mrs William Noble who served for 38 years at Nagercoil. ABOVE RIGHT: Major (Dr) Lyle Alloway treating a patient at Catherine Booth Hospital, Nagercoil in 1969. LEFT: Candidate Hilda Mary Plummer in 1924, who was appointed to India in 1926. As a brigadier (RIGHT) with the Indian name Jiva Ratnam, Hilda Plummer stayed in Bapatla after retirement, still using her nursing skills until in old age she herself was cared for lovingly by her adopted Indian family until her promotion to Glory in 1980.

and Mountain View in Natal. Because of the spiritual ministry among the farm workers by the corps officer, Mountain View Hospital was developed on a 4,000-acre farm purchased by The Salvation Army in 1910 for a school for children of the tenants. Basic medical care led to the establishment of a six-bed hospital by 1933. There were obstetric clinics elsewhere, including The Mothers' Hospital in Durban, which was famous for its midwifery school. The rest of the continent where the Army was at work was less sophisticated. The William Eadie Maternity Hospital opened in Vendaland, and there were clinics in Rhodesia. But it was in Northern Rhodesia, later to become Zambia, that new ground was broken in 1946.[126]

Medical initiatives in Africa were to set a new pattern in community health and have changed as rapidly and radically as the nations in which they exist. The work was often started by untrained Salvationists responding to urgent need, and later taken over and developed by highly-trained physicians and nurses. The work was affected by local politics and economics, world wars, and by a series of internal liberation struggles.

Catherine Booth Hospital in Zululand began as a nine-bed clinic in the mid 1930s, to support Salvation Army ministry to the people of South Zululand. Expanded into a large hospital, it was taken over by the KwaZulu homeland government in 1979 to become a district hospital. Expatriate mission staff worked there until the end of 1980. Major Hilda Sigley of Australia started the Msunduza Clinic in the shanty town on the outskirts of the capital, Mbabane, in Swaziland in 1988. In 1993 Captain Betty Moone of The Netherlands was appointed matron, developing a programme of Aids care.

In 1923 Mrs Major Kirby, from Canada, informally started health services in Glendale in Southern Rhodesia.[127] But it was at Howard on land granted by the local chief that Brigadier Agatha Battersby from South Africa opened a clinic in which the training of nurses was commenced in 1939. By 1956 the clinic had become a general hospital. With independence,

Zimbabwe and Zambia rapidly developed community health policies. Of the new schemes which burgeoned, Chikankata was the most impressive, becoming a major health provider for the Southern Province of the country. Mobile clinics became a feature as the programme developed.[128]

But there had been an earlier 'community' emphasis with mobility the key during World War I. Bramwell Booth, as General of an international Christian fellowship, was a true pacifist. He was grieved by the outbreak of hostilities that would pit Salvationist against Salvationist. 'War is a confession of failure', he wrote, 'but I am appealing for men and money to run an ambulance service.' He added 'some good things emerge and stand up and challenge'.[129] In that war the British government was prepared to use a non-governmental agency and agreed to the formation of the Salvation Army Ambulance Brigade, operating nominally under the wing of the British Red Cross. It employed its own personnel under the command of an officer carrying the rank of captain.

Commencing with five ambulances in 1914, a further 20 were added the next year. The last six were inspected by Queen Alexandra and bore her name. Staff-Captain Aspinall was the first Commandant. He had a small musical group, which consisted of a cornet and five ocarinas. His successor, Adjutant Taylor from the Editorial Department, was a staff bandsman, and quickly formed a full brass band, which became famous under his baton. Taylor was heard to say, with a wry smile, 'Twenty-six of my bandsmen were corps bandmasters.' The bandsmen were all ambulance personnel and, when in base at Boulogne, the band was available for programmes on Sundays in base camps over a wide area. On the last Christmas of its existence it played to audiences with a total of 30,000 men. It was highly popular with both men and top brass. In addition to the fleet of ambulances in France, there were seven more in Italy and Russia.[130]

85 Baird, C. *Little Doctor VC* SP&S, London 1944
86 Williams, H. *Booth-Tucker, William Booth's First Gentleman* Hodder & Stoughton, London 1980
87 Ibid
88 Baird, C. *William Stevens (Yesu Ratnam): Jeweller and Missionary* SP&S, London 1944. See 2 Kings 9:20
89 Prime minister
90 Richards, M. *It Began with Andrews* SP&S, London 1971
91 Baird, C. *Little Doctor VC* SP&S, London 1944
92 *The Officer* January 1916
93 Nomadic tribes in various parts of India, with a reputation for robbery. The Salvation Army assumed responsibility for many of them, settling them on land provided by the Raj.
94 *The Officer* 1967
95 Richards, M. *It Began with Andrews* SP&S, London 1971
96 Turner, P. *The CBH for One and Twenty Years* Printed locally
97 Bridson, T. *Lightening the Lepers' Load.* SP&S 1946
98 Correspondence
99 Richards M. *It Began with Andrews.* SP&S London 1971
100 The senior 'lay' elder in every Salvation Army corps
101 Wille, J. *Lys og Mørke* Copenhagen 1950.
102 Ibid
103 Williams, H. Personal recollection
104 Richards, M. *It Began with Andrews* SP&S, London 1971
105 Allen, J. *Report of the General's Special Delegate to Indonesia 1955*, Salvation Army Heritage Centre, London
106 Coutts, F. *The Better Fight – The History of The Salvation Army Vol VI (1914-1946)* Hodder & Stoughton, London 1973 Chapter 8
107 Ibid
108 Brouwer, M. *History of The Salvation Army in Indonesia* The Salvation Army, Australia 1996
109 Unsworth, M. *Great was the Company* SP&S, London 1963 Chapter 1
110 Wiggins, Arch R. *The History of The Salvation Army Vol V (1904-1914)* Nelson, London 1968 p. 155
111 *All the World* 1913
112 Unsworth, M. *Great was the Company* SP&S, London 1963 Chapter 1
113 Ibid
114 Williams, H. 'Under Two Flags' *The War Cry* New Zealand 1973
115 Ibid
116 Ibid
117 Hansen. L. *The Double Yoke* Citadel Press, New York 1968
118 Neeve, E. *Nurse by Royal Command* SP&S, London 1958
119 Williamson, V. *The Inside Story.* New Zealand
120 Smith, S. *By Love Compelled* SP&S, London 1981 pp. 97-100
121 Coutts, F. *The Better Fight – The History of The Salvation Army Vol VI (1914-1946)* Hodder & Stoughton, London 1973 p. 271
122 Murdoch, N. A Protestant Hospital for Covington: Booth Memorial Hospital 1915 – 1985' *The Journal of Kentucky Studies*, 3 October 1986.
123 Coutts, F. *The Better Fight – The History of The Salvation Army Vol VI (1914-1946)* Hodder & Stoughton, London 1973
124 Atkinson, J. E. *Dr Beer Returns* SP&S, London 1957
125 Ah Kow, A. *Mary Layton* SP&S, London 1957, Chapter 27

[126] Richards, M. *It Began with Andrews* SP&S, London 1971
[127] Kirby, L. *Led and Protected by the Omnipotent God* – Autobiography of Isabel and Leonard Kirby
[128] McInnes, B. *Flag Across the Zambesi* The Salvation Army, Zambia 1997
[129] Copping, A. *Serving the King's Men* Hodder & Stoughton, London 1918
[130] *The Deliverer* 1915

Chapter three

Enter the professionals

The archives of the Royal College of Midwives contain the history of the battle to recognise the worth of midwives by central registration. The Salvation Army entered the battlefield. In 1902 the Midwives Act was passed in England, followed in 1915 by a similar one for Scotland. Until then there had been a dingdong battle of words between those who thought that midwifery should be under the control of doctors, and those who argued for their registration. Florence Nightingale, heroine of Scutari, and a power in the land, led one group, while the other, campaigning for nursing registration, was led by an equally formidable figure, Ethel Bradford Fenwick, daughter of a Member of Parliament and wife of a doctor. She was an articulate, trained nurse who, at the age of 24, was Matron of St Bartholomew's Hospital in London. In the contest, The Salvation Army, with years of experience in the business of training midwives at Ivy House and later at The Mother's Hospital, well after Florence Nightingale's death, continued to contend for full professional certification and accreditation. That's what finally happened. It's a surprising fact, especially given the history of Salvation Army medicine as the triumph of gifted amateurs. A great protagonist in the battle for professional standards had been Florence Booth, the daughter of a family doctor, then married to Bramwell Booth, and committed to development of medical work from the rescue work for which she was responsible.[131]

In truth, we have already met the professionals, that is, doctors and nurses with appropriate degrees and diplomas.

However, the first 30 years of the 20th century were still the days of the amateur with native skills. Even the doctors who joined forces or took over, were themselves insistent that theirs was an evangelical calling; serving Christ as disciples, their Lord's compassion their chief endowment.

Percy Turner had learned from Socrates that to separate body from soul was a great mistake. Minnie Mayger, the sister on the paediatric ward of the Maidstone Eye Hospital, where Turner was gaining experience in ophthalmic surgery, wrote, 'before many days had passed … he had enquired of most patients as to the state of their souls'. It was during his time at Maidstone that he was introduced to The Salvation Army and to Minnie, whom he later married. He gave the hospital staff a pressing invitation to attend the Salvation Army meetings. Surely he was an extraordinary medico? They thought so. However, as Miriam Richards writes, 'he set the standards', which were to be the accepted norms for the rest of the century.[132] Dr Turner was known to a whole generation of Salvation Army officers in the UK as a dignified consultant, thorough in examination, but undemonstrative. To some, his detailed probing in interview was off-putting. He was a psychiatrist before the specialty was well known.

At his retirement from IHQ Adjutant (Dr) Hart, of the original medical department, spoke of Turner's misleading exterior: 'He had mastered Greek and Latin and had first-class medical qualifications, yet was unobtrusive in a group.'[133]

Percy Edward Hedgman Turner was born on 10 March 1870, the eldest of 11 children. His father had been apprenticed at The Apothecaries' Hall in London at the age of 16. In this heyday of Victorian learning by doing and assisting, the diploma Percy's father obtained at the final examination was registrable with the new General Medical Council, for general practice in the UK.

He attended a school in Islington, but when the family moved to Kensington, Percy was sent to a boarding school, and confirmed in the Anglican Church. A holiday in Folkestone saw him apprenticed to an enterprising pharmacist. In days when every doctor made up his own pills and potions, this was quite valuable experience. But it was also the town in which he met The Salvation Army in the form of five lively sisters, who carried him off to the meetings. He found his new company 'religious all day long … and jolly and happy to boot'.[134]

When he reached St Bartholomew's Hospital he took the opportunity of listening to Catherine Booth, who was preaching in the Exeter Hall on the Strand every Thursday afternoon. He and another student became Salvationists and attended their lectures in Salvation Army guernseys. He took his final examinations in 1893 and promptly entered officer training. He was appointed as a captain to Dartford in Kent. Appointments were of short duration in those days but with many meetings a week his sermons still ran out! He was moved first to Forest Hill and then to Lewisham, when into this evangelical routine burst Harry Andrews, as outlined previously.

Turner had thought through the opportunity given him at Nagercoil. It was within the native state of Travancore, half the size of Holland with a population of three million. It was fertile country and almost entirely rural. He aimed at a medical service covering as large a population as possible. To the central hospital which Andrews had prepared was added a chain of branch hospitals that provided a training programme for staff to cover epidemics. Turner kept in touch with the Durbar physician[135] and with the Maharajah of Travancore's own personal doctor. He quickly became a Durbar physician himself, with access which enabled him to influence the medical thinking of the state. He obtained permission to start a medical course to provide a diploma for 'sub-assistant surgeons' to be recognised by the state. These new graduates would take charge of his branch hospitals as well as any others in Travancore. His first students were Salvation Army officers, who served well until retirement. One of the first class of government registered nurses at Catherine Booth Hospital was Grace Sugantham, the daughter of one of these, who remained permanently at the main hospital. This bright, attractive girl grew up with the missionary children on the compound and shared their aspirations. She was admitted to the Order of the Founder in 1988 by General Eva Burrows.

The development of the Catherine Booth Hospital was itself unusual. A visitor said, 'I never expected to see a garden city.' It was an attractively landscaped village of wards, operating theatre, laboratory and a variety of staff quarters. At the top of the hill was the two-storey bungalow, with a Malabar tiled roof, which housed both the Turners and the Andrews. It is still there today, overtopped by a multi-storeyed, concrete block, the nurses' home, on the other side of William Booth Road.

Travancore was a matriarchal state, each Maharajah being the son of his predecessor's sister. It meant that the ruler had no interest in a personal family, and usually had consorts in various areas. One of these consorts had her palace in Nagercoil and was Turner's patient. She provided a new block of wards.

The advent of Charles Steibel, a well qualified surgeon, greatly increased Turner's effectiveness at Nagercoil. He complemented Turner in teaching students, and the two years that they were together were the high point of the training programme. Their wives shared in the nurses' training.

In later years it was possible to discern two streams of thought. There were those with an open mind about the type of appointment that would be acceptable within a medical calling, whilst others were more rigid in their commitment to traditional expressions of medical ministry. Turner retained the confidence of his General, carrying in his pocket a goodbye letter, in which the old man's huge quill-pen handwriting assured him 'of the great interest I feel in your undertaking and my earnest prayers for its success'. Those who followed Turner became increasingly recognisable consultants, with good equipment and an equally professional staff. Some, like Dan Andersen, even made time for research, publishing articles in the medical press.

As already told, the professional standard of The Salvation Army's tuberculosis service in Japan, under Matsuda and Rin Iwasa, was unquestioned, but both retained compassion for the sick poor that made them continue domiciliary visits in the Tokyo slums. Vilhelm Wille was astonishing in the way that he produced a professional eye service in the beggars' camp in Indonesia, to which he was appointed, and he provided simple care for them as well.

But there was another factor in the ethos of Salvation Army officership, which regards all officers as interchangeable according to 'the exigencies of the war'. It did not change with Turner's arrival at Nagercoil or at International Headquarters. Later medical candidates entering training at the International Training College were reminded that officers could not be guaranteed a medical career.

In 1948, General Orsborn, perhaps the last of the authoritarian generals of the stamp of William Booth, was visiting India and stayed for a week with Dr Harry Williams, the CMO at Dhariwal. Over dinner one night he surprised the doctor with, 'What would you say if I gave you a non-medical appointment?' Nonplussed, the doctor responded, 'But you couldn't do that, General; you haven't enough doctors.' 'Doctors,' snorted the General, 'we can find doctors, what we need is leaders.' The doctor was to remember this when, 20 years later, he received a cable in the middle of the night: 'The General is appointing you territorial commander. Cable acceptance.'

Over the years Bramwell Cook, Harry Williams, Pratipathi Devararam and Paul du Plessis have all been Territorial Commanders; Bill McAllister was Governor of the Men's Social Work in the UK and Sidney Gauntlett was Chief Secretary of the same service. It is profitable to reflect that this style of administration has cross-pollinated the various components of top level administration, with profit both to the organisation and the individuals involved. Numerous other officers with experience in the Army's health service have been appointed senior leaders. Commissioner Robin Dunster, a long-time nurse-administrator, was appointed Chief of the Staff in 2006.

However, the passing years showed a decreasing number of lifetime commitments to officership, and either by resignation or specific terms of employment, a greater number has given service of limited duration.

There was a more obvious professionalism in the wave of Salvationist doctors who began to appear in the 1930s. They were the children of Indian missionaries, educated in India, who made their own judgment that medical work was a priority for the organisation. The first of these, who arrived at a near-moribund Thomas Emery Hospital in Moradabad, in 1932, was Ted Barnett. He was a son of the erstwhile compounder at Chini on the Tibetan border. He believed that high professional standards would bring the best results, and started from scratch with a nurses' training school of state-recognised standard. A grant for it was obtained, but he felt that IHQ help was tardy and inadequate. He battled on until 1936, when impatience overcame him and he departed for London to appeal to the General in person. But General Eva (Booth), in the stamp of her father, would not see an officer who was 'awol' (absent without leave).

Fortunately a second officer was in the wings, a well-trained surgeon, Captain Edgar Stevens. Again he was the son of pioneers, no less than the divisional commander in whose nest Harry Andrews had laid the cuckoo's egg that became the Catherine Booth Hospital of Nagercoil. Compassionate and quietly spoken, Stevens was pre-eminently a dignified surgeon. Before long it was noised abroad throughout the United Provinces that Moradabad was back to its 1913 glory. The tally of influential patients grew, and by 1938, at the time of the hospital's Silver Jubilee celebrations, the Governor of the United Provinces was presiding. Two years later, and a new block was built behind, but parallel to, the original colonnaded front. By the end of 1939 Stevens had a junior officer-doctor to train. Captain and Mrs Harry Williams had newly arrived. But the clouds of war were drifting over and Stevens reacted as Steibel before him. Fortunately for the hospital and his successor, it was 1941 before he was called up to become a lieut-colonel in the Indian Medical Service. He was not to return to Moradabad at the end of hostilities, though as a consultant in the National Health Service, he became the medical adviser to the Salvation Army Assurance Society.

It must have delighted Turner's heart that in his last years in office he could lead a Sunday's meetings at the Regent Hall in Oxford Street, with the support of half a dozen doctors and medical students preparing to follow him. One of these, as has been mentioned, in many ways the prototype of all the professionals was Dan Andersen, who arrived at IHQ holding a British Council grant for the study of the bowel deformity volvulus.[136] This interest commenced in his active years at Ahmednagar as a surgeon, where the condition was very common.

General Evangeline Booth, despite her cavalier treatment of Ted Barnett, did have an interest in missionary medicine. In fact, her interest in medicine generally continued. As Territorial Commander for Canada and as National Commander in the USA she actively encouraged the growth of medical services, even when her brother, Bramwell, did not completely agree with such an emphasis.[137] A number of hospitals in India bear her name. The first, under Captains (Drs) Mary and Clesson Richardson, was already a successful rural hospital at Nidubrolu in Andhra Pradesh, South India, when the General visited in 1936 and gave her name, and a grant for a radiological department. The second hospital (at Ahmednagar) she bought from the American Marathi Mission, also in 1936. It was a three-storey block in granite and already beloved throughout the Deccan plain of central India. The mission was unable to keep it going and it was to remain empty until the Andersens arrived in 1939. Dan knew it from boyhood, when his father was in charge of the boys' boarding school in the town.

Captain Ludwig Andersen, Dan Andersen's father, was the first Norwegian officer to arrive in India and the seven years prior to his marriage were typical of the sadhus who survived by their begging bowls and the villagers' generosity. Dr Ruth Hume, of the American Marathi Mission, who was there to welcome Ludwig's son at the reopening of the Evangeline Booth Hospital, remembered him affectionately. Ludwig had an absence of 26 years, largely in the USA, where there was a very large Scandinavian contingent. He was married with three children when he returned to India, and three-year-old Dan had his first sight of the Dagadhai Daukhana,[138] the hospital's local name. The boy was fascinated by the way his father could put a violin to his shoulder and quickly attract a crowd. He was equally interested in his mother's black bag, which was being unpacked at the periphery, full of simple remedies for a clinic.

Dan tells his own story of the long odyssey before he found his ultimate calling, but once found, it was held with tenacity. His parents left him as a junior clerk in The Salvation Army Fire Insurance Department, where he showed his ability in obtaining the requisite diploma to practise as an underwriter. His vision to be a doctor was crystallising, and to fulfil his dream he sought medical scholarships. The qualifications which he obtained showed his professional skill. He acquired surgical skills in a number of appointments in the smaller voluntary hospitals which then dotted the London scene, principally at the Connaught Hospital in Walthamstow. Appointed CMO of the Ahmednagar hospital, he served for an unbroken 21 years. More than for any other, it was his professional fulfilment.[139]

Solveig Hammer, who was to become Dan's wife, was a Norwegian doctor, daughter of the Corps Sergeant Major, first at Oslo 1, then at Ålesund. She spoke of her teenage rebellion during those years, but she won through to become a founder member of the university's Christian Union. They were married and off! Solveig was to show tenacity in maintaining her own professional calling in India, despite four children and a husband sometimes slow to appreciate the emancipation of women. She continued to supervise the obstetric wards.

In a rural setting, the Society for the Propagation of the Gospel (the oldest Anglican missionary society) had many clinics in the area. Dan Andersen held a monthly meeting with them and geared his programme to support their needs. During the war years, Ahmednagar was full of troops and there was a demand for the care of families. Both Dan and Solveig saw the need for modern nursing education, but in typical manner Dan looked not primarily to donations but sought a government grant from 'the Raj'. He made a start with lectures in a basement room, where a British Surgeon-General, stumbling in the gloom, was heard to exclaim 'This is a rum hole!' The wife of the Governor of Bombay was the next visitor. Lady Colville was an enthusiast for the scheme and promised 50 per cent of the cost of an impressive building. It was opened in an independent India, with the reassurance that probationers could be of any faith or caste. The new government gave its support.

Throughout the years it needed persistent teaching of illiterate villagers, usually arriving in bullock carts, to reach modern levels of hygiene and order. In early days Solveig found a man in bed in one of the women's wards, his wife, the patient, was curled up under it! Solveig's indignation startled him and he appealed to Dan, who must surely appreciate a man's point of view. But the concept got through to one returned villager who told his neighbour, 'You must do what the doctor says, for God has sent him to help us.'

One of the first building schemes was a dharmsala, a large open building in which the patient's relatives could camp out and cook for their patient. The final extension was to treat tuberculosis. This too was a striking block, and was opened by the Christian Princess, Raj Kumari Amrit Kaur (who was Minister of Health in the first Congress administration and Gandhi's personal physician).

As the tale unfolds of new medical developments appearing spontaneously all over the world and the appointment of

Turner to direct it all, it might have been expected to usher in a new era of central planning, as foreseen in the establishment of that first medical department, under Dr Henry W. Williams in 1898. But it did not happen. It is easy to see the absence of a substantial war chest as the cause. It undoubtedly crippled Turner's efforts to build up schemes of which he approved, but even when, half a century later, ever-increasing development funds became available from a variety of sources, state and private, the ever increasing number of projects monitored by IHQ were still locally developed.

The new Planning and Development Department, set up in 1978, secured large SAWSO (Salvation Army World Services Organisation) grants from the American Government, but these were for the holding of a global series of seminars to teach nationals how to perceive their own needs, design suitable schemes and then to secure the necessary international funds. This fundamental design of a successful Salvation Army empire gave a major degree of independence to territorial commanders. Commissioner Harry W. Williams was appointed as the first International Secretary for Planning and Development in 1978. Although considerable expertise in social work lay at the centre, and periodic International Social Work Conferences were held, only one International Secretary for Social Work had ever been appointed before, namely Commissioner David Lamb, who was responsible for the last regular International Conference in 1921. As organiser for the International Congress of 1978, Commissioner Williams was able to include an International Social Conference at the same time. There have always been medical components in such social schemes, especially in disaster relief. In the 1970s IHQ could put together immediate relief work in earthquakes such as those in Peru and Guatemala. In Peru, the hostel at Callao was rebuilt and in Guatemala, the rebuilding of the town of Tecpan resulted in the establishment of The Salvation Army in that country. There is now a permanent section created to amass the personnel and funds immediately required for disaster relief, as in the December 2004 Indian Ocean tsunami.

Dan Andersen felt strongly that there should be a Chief Medical Officer at IHQ. There was no enthusiasm for such an idea but he was determined and eventually, in the early 1960s, was given the new appointment of Medical Secretary for Missionary Hospitals, with a modest budget that permitted occasional visits of inspection. He had no executive authority, however, and when he died, at his post, no successor was appointed.

Although Lieut-Colonel Miriam Richards of the Literary Department authored *It Began with Andrews* it was virtually Andersen's work. He wrote the excellent introduction and supplied much of the information, with the help of Major (Dr) Sidney Gauntlett. He felt a handbook of information should be available, and the trends noted in that volume are still being worked out now, almost four decades later.

By this time doctors had seen the light, and took a more tactful approach to authority. When Commissioner (Dr) Williams appeared at IHQ as International Secretary for the Americas and Australasia, he was asked to carry the separate office of Medical Adviser. He had no *aide memoire* but was expected to be available to give a medical opinion when needed, to give individual medical assistance to staff at IHQ or in overseas appointments, to interview cadets with medical qualifications and to advise on their commissioning appointments. He retired six years later and Major (Dr) Paul du Plessis (from Chikankata) succeeded him in a similar role. With du Plessis's appointment as a Territorial Commander in India, Captain (Dr) Ian Campbell, also from Chikankata, became the new Medical Advisor. When working in Africa he had developed a first class programme of care, prevention and treatment of HIV and Aids which he saw as an overwhelming priority in his new role. His single-minded approach, supported by an Australian Government grant for the treatment of Aids, caused some of the old problems of authority to re-emerge.

Other aspects of the service were catered for separately with a succession of medical officers taking responsibility for the health of personnel. These included Drs Eileen Thompson, John Lowther and John Tomlinson. The latest move, in 2007, was the creation of an International Health Services Coordinator in the Programme Resources Department at IHQ, the first appointees being Majors Dean and (Dr) Eirwen Pallant.

Back at the front line, the arrival of Indian doctors, educated at the new missionary medical schools, was a landmark. The first was Captain (Dr) Sarah Daniel, who qualified from the Women's College, run by Dr Ida Scudder at Vellore. Subsequently this became a co-educational college and was the joint responsibility of many missions, including The Salvation Army. Doctor Sarah, as she was always affectionately known, served her whole career at Catherine Booth Hospital in charge of obstetrics. She was to be seen in the outpatients' department every day, her consulting room wide open on two sides, and she was on call for deliveries day and night. She seemed to have no private life. Her nephew, Dr Varughese, qualified at Vellore and served for a while at Nagercoil.

The American Presbyterian Church had opened a medical school at Miraj, in central India. Dr Joseph from Travancore was educated there, and served not only with Dr Noble at Nagercoil, but also became the medical superintendent of the leprosarium at Puthencruz, in the northern part of Kerala. He became an authority on leprosy. A third doctor, who qualified with the Bombay LCPS, and served with Dr Cook and Dr Williams at Anand, taking charge in 1959, was Major (Dr) Isudas Christian.

Mention has already been made of Lieut-Commissioner (Dr) Bramwell Cook, a New Zealand officer who was a brilliant academic, mopping up degrees and diplomas, yet remaining a compassionate physician. At Anand in Western India, the Emery Hospital was universally known as Cook's Hospital and he himself as a Gujarati. In his later appointments in Australasia he had a powerful influence in directing The

Salvation Army's programmes for dealing with alcoholism and addiction.

A later arrival from New Zealand was Kingsley Mortimer, who prior to his medical qualification, had arrived in Rhodesia in 1931, and pioneered the Army's work north of the Zambesi.

Two other professionals served in Anand, Envoy (Dr) John Lowther from UK and Captain (Dr) Melvin Brieseman from New Zealand. From the USA came not only Colonel (Dr) Noble and Major (Dr) Lyle Alloway but also the Majors Richardson (both of whom were doctors), and who opened the Evangeline Booth Hospital at Nidubrolu, Andhra Pradesh. They were followed by Major George Scott and his wife Major (Dr) Hazel Scott, as Administrator and Medical Officer respectively.

In Dhariwal in the Punjab, Captain (Dr) Walter Lucas from Australia died whilst serving as CMO. Doctor J. B. Alexander then gave up his practice in the UK to take charge at Dhariwal for three years.

In 1961 Major (Dr) Ernest B. Pedersen from Australia, followed Colonel (Dr) Dan Andersen as CMO at Ahmednagar.

Indian nurses, mostly graduates of Salvation Army schools, began taking diplomas in teaching and administration. This led to the appointment of Brigadier Sughanantham as Nursing Superintendent at CBH and to Major Grace Punjalal taking over at Anand.

Reference has been made to the degree of specialisation that had taken place in leprosy and tuberculosis. Another specialism was the development of dentistry in South America. An efficient dental department also developed at Nagercoil, with the arrival of Captain and Mrs James Kennedy from the UK in the 1930s. His ability in prosthetics brought a stream of patients to the Nursing Home. Mrs Kennedy had been a Sister at the Glasgow Royal Infirmary and took over the European Nursing Home. When the Kennedys were transferred to district evangelism, a local Indian dental surgeon took over.

Gradually, Salvation Army hospitals gave a lead in the training of paramedicals in a variety of disciplines. These were linked by the Christian Medical Association of India (CMAI) which ran the courses, held the examinations, and issued the diplomas which were registered by the government. Even before unified training was started, Major Ruth Woolcott from Canada was training laboratory technicians at Dhariwal. Radiography at Anand, under Captain Ken Tutton, and at Nagercoil, under Captain Keith Wylie, was also under the CMAI banner. The physiotherapy training school, started by Dr Beer, was the first of its kind in India. Its first graduate was Lieutenant Jethulal.[140] Many more followed and found employment in new departments which sprang up in the medical college hospitals throughout India.

The discipline developed further at Nagercoil, where Mrs Rosemary Collins, MCSP, ran a school, from which Captain Ruby Samuel was one of the first graduates. Ruby went on to qualify as a doctor at Vellore and ran obstetrics at Nagercoil in succession to Major (Dr) Hazel Scott, who in turn had followed Lieut-Colonel (Dr) Sara Daniel. Mrs Collins had a constant stream of young orthopaedic patients, who then progressed through occupational therapy to provision of prostheses, from calipers to artificial limbs. At this point, enter Major George Scott, BSc who had studied vocational training at the Royal Orthopaedic Hospital at Stanmore, UK. Eventually there were three vocational training centres, two of them for women, concentrating on office skills from accounts to computers, as well as running a printing works. For men, the old branch hospital at Aramboly was converted into metal workshops and a factory producing all types of hospital furniture, from beds to operating tables and wheelchairs. In this, George had the cooperation of Sundar Egbert, disabled by polio, who had been the quality control officer at the Swedish Red Cross Centre at Vellore.[141]

In this field, the final stage of Salvation Army expertise in leprosy emerged. Dr Williams developed operations, invented by Paul Brand, to reanimate paralysed hands and feet, and added plastic surgical treatment for facial deformity and rapid healing of ulcers.

Certainly, The Salvation Army's first specialisation was in eye surgery. Dr Wille's work at Semarang, in what is now Indonesia, has already been described. But even earlier was the department at Nagercoil, opened by Dr Turner and built up by Dr Noble, then taken over by Dr Lyle Alloway. A new ophthalmic block was opened in 1965. Dr Bill McAllister, who had also worked under Dr Noble, took his skill to Chikankata and then to Dhariwal, where the eye department still flourishes under an employee consultant, currently performing 3,500 cataract operations each year.

The greatest advances professionally were made in Canada and the USA. Eventually Covington, Kentucky, and Cincinnati, Ohio both closed but the Booth Memorial Hospital on Long Island, New York, continued to grow until Major (Dr) Herb Rader, following a successful 13-year term in surgery at Nagercoil, returned to the USA and became the medical director in 1984. Eventually, it became so big an undertaking, involving financial liabilities too great for The Salvation Army, that it was sold. Herein lies a recurring challenge in health care which needs more debate.

Though the emphasis in this chapter has been on medical professional complexity, one important development in this period was not. In 1943, Minnie Carpenter, wife of the fifth General of The Salvation Army, inaugurated the Nurses' Fellowship. It was taken up enthusiastically with branches in most territories. It was recognised that nursing duties often made routine corps responsibilities difficult, and it provided a forum for discussion and fellowship. It was subsequently renamed the Salvation Army Medical Fellowship with a wider membership.

---

[131] Fairbank, J. *For Such a Time – The Story of the Young Florence Booth* IHQ, London 2007 Chapters 9-10

[132] Richards, M. *It Began with Andrews* SP&S, London 1971 p. 9

[133] Hart, A. *The War Cry*, India January 1901

[134] Turner, P. *The War Cry* London 8 December 1900

[135] Physician to the court of an Indian prince

[136] An axial twist of the intestines, fatal if not corrected surgically

[137] Murdoch, N. 'A Protestant Hospital for Covington: Booth Memorial Hospital 1915 – 1985' *The Journal of Kentucky Studies,* 3 October 1986

[138] The stone hospital

[139] Richards, M. *It Began with Andrews* SP&S, London 1971 Part Two, Chapter 6

[140] Lowther, J. *The Story of a Hospital: The Salvation Army Emery Hospital, Anand, Western India. Centennial Celebrations 1903 – 2003* Published privately

[141] Williamson, V. *The Inside Story* New Zealand

Chapter four

The mid century – a golden age of hospitals

THERE is no doubt that the formal and informal training of health professionals, which was a vital part of Turner's vision of a comprehensive health programme, aroused widespread interest amongst the children of those apprenticed in this way. It was to produce a rich harvest in India from the 1930s onward. As has already been noted, before World War II, Turner could call on half a dozen doctors or medical students to assist him in a Sunday's meetings in London. This wave of recruits was to usher in an era of expansion and innovation, which became the golden age in India and the springboard for an African chapter too.

It started with Alfred Barnett who, after training as a compounder at the Catherine Booth Hospital, Nagercoil, was considered fit to open a dispensary as far away as it was possible to be, yet still in India. Commissioner Frederick Booth-Tucker had returned to India with his third wife. Her background was not unlike his own. Her father had retired from the ICS (Indian Civil Service) as acting Governor of Ceylon. By the rules of this typical Victorian service, unmarried daughters were entitled to an allowance of £250 per annum, and Colonel Minnie Reid enjoyed this income until she married Fakir Singh and became known as Commissioner Dutini.[142]

Tucker made his headquarters for the whole country in Simla, the summer capital of the Raj, in the Himalayan foothills. Minnie bought them a house with extensive grounds and outbuildings, which gave scope for his latest interest in mulberry leaves and silkworms. He proceeded with the opening of weaveries for both cotton and silk, together with training schools which earned the enthusiastic support both of his Indian Civil Service contemporary, Sir Louis Dane, and also the Parsee tycoon, Tata. This northern eyrie encouraged him to develop outlets in the Punjab. It was on the Hindustan-Tibet Road, popularised by Kipling's Kim (who walked it with his lama) that Barnett was appointed to open a dispensary at Chini.

He was followed by others with similar training. The first was Samuel Burfoot, whose father was, at that time, The Salvation Army's most notable linguist, being editor of the vernacular papers published in Bombay, and translator for the Tamil speaking Territorial Commander. In the style of some of the pioneers he married an Indian convert. Samuel was sent to Andrews in Moradabad for training and also had a term at Chini. After this he was posted to a branch hospital at the land colony at Muktipur, Gujarat and from there to Dohad among the Bhil tribes. He finally returned to the Punjab to open the dispensary at Dhariwal, which became the MacRobert Hospital.[143]

By the 1920s the children of missionary officers were being educated at hill schools and Ted Barnett (Alfred's son) was already taking his BSc when he felt his calling to become a doctor. He was the first in a line of Salvationists to live in the Highbury hostel of the Medical Missionary Association (MMA) of London, whilst studying at The London Hospital. This 18th century voluntary hospital, with attached medical college, had a long humanitarian tradition. Among its most famous sons were Hudson Taylor of China repute, Grenfell of Labrador and Barnardo of Dr Barnardos fame. It welcomed students recommended by the MMA. According to what Harry Williams heard, when he was a student resident in the Highbury hostel, Ted Barnett was remembered by his student friends as both brilliant and independent, and certainly unconventional in his study pattern.

The next arrival came from New Zealand in 1933, though his father had become an officer from London's Regent Hall. Bramwell Cook had an outstanding academic record from the day he entered Otago Medical College with the support of a donor who had spotted his talent. He completed his higher qualifications in the UK before entering Salvation Army officer training. Appointed to the Emery Hospital, Anand, he quickly became known as 'the white Gujarati'.[144] He was one of a number who had the gift of losing themselves amongst an alien people and devoting long hours to their care.

An incident occurred at Adas in Gujarat, in which some Congress Party demonstrators were fired upon by troops. Cook brought the wounded to Anand for treatment and was awarded the Kaiser-I-Hind silver medal soon after. His bride, Captain Dorothy Money, arrived from New Zealand in 1936 and over the next 20 years the hospital grew in both fame and size, reaching a capacity of 250 beds with a modern nurses' home. Cook was an impressive clinician, quick in diagnosis. He would have one patient on the stool beside his desk and a couple of benches of fascinated onlookers. He would have already looked them over and spotted a hookworm anaemia or an incipient palsy. These interminable outpatient sessions must have been exhausting.[145]

Cook was joined by Captain (Dr) Reg Neeve from the UK, who had been a pharmacist before embarking on medicine. With his wife (née Marjorie Boot) he reached Anand in 1939, in time to cover the first homeland furlough for the Cooks. By 1941 war clouds had gathered and the doctor joined the Indian Medical Service. He commanded a mobile surgical unit in North Africa and Italy. After the war he returned to Salvation Army service and served a very successful term at the Thomas Emery Hospital, Moradabad.[146]

At the end of 1939 Captain (Dr) Harry Williams, with his wife Eileen (née Neeve), was posted to Moradabad as assistant to Edgar Stevens. Again the Regent Hall enters the story, for Harry was the grandson of two of the first soldiers. He carried on at Moradabad when Stevens went off to the war, but by 1943 the government remembered the profitable assistance given by the hospital in World War I and took over again. This time it was by the addition of many blocks to the main hospital and the production of a 2,000-bed base hospital. Captain Lilian Abel, the matron, remained as the Deputy Nursing Superintendent; Captain Geoff Parker was the RASC (Royal Army Service Corps) officer in administration. But Dr Williams was posted to the British Base Hospital at Poona for grading as a surgeon. His final posting was postponed following the tragic death of his eldest daughter in the hospital. In October 1944, Burfoot having left Dhariwal, Williams was released for 'a post of civil importance', to Dhariwal, liable to recall if the war went badly. At the close of hostilities the hospital at Moradabad, with added buildings and equipment, was returned to The Salvation Army and Major Reg Neeve became the Chief Medical Officer.

Dhariwal grew to 100 beds with a nurses' training school. Captain (Dr) Sidney Gauntlett was posted to Dhariwal from 1949 until 1951 when he exchanged appointments with Major (Dr) Bill McAllister at Chikankata in Zambia.

In 1934 a new 30-bed rural hospital was opened in Andhra Pradesh, at Nidubrolu, by a mature American officer-couple from New York, Drs Cleeson and Mary Richardson who had spent their first two years with the Nobles at Nagercoil. The land for the hospital, five acres of banana-growing quality, was given by the farmer, Pamulapati Parandaya.[147] The Richardsons were the only expatriates in a population of 30,000 illiterate villagers and had a lot of learning as well as educating to do. The first fee for a confinement was a pair of used sandals. It took a long while for Captain Albert Senaputra, the business manager, to establish a cash basis for payments. The pressure of patients meant overcrowded wards and verandahs. The patients wanted to touch the doctors, feeling that virtue would flow from them. With a small car, they started village clinics. Mrs Senaputra, being a nurse, made this possible. General Evangeline Booth visited in 1936 and gave her name to the hospital, plus a donation to cover the erection and equipment of an X-ray Department. By 1938 the acreage was doubled and more wards added. The training of nurse-aides was commenced and this led, eventually, to a state-registered nursing school.[148]

Meanwhile, the Richardsons had moved on to the Far East. They reached Yong Dong in the Chung Chong province of Southern Korea in 1940. The first hospital had been burnt down but the second was ready for them. Once again the political situation deteriorated and they had to leave. The Japanese used it as a military hospital. When peace came the Richardsons returned to an extended 75-bed institution serving a rural population of about 15,000. Mary handled the obstetrics and Cleeson the surgery. Experienced nurses joined them. First from Switzerland came Brigadier Anna Hackler, already fluent in the language and then two from the UK, Captains Agnes Cage and Mildred Stone. Three Korean doctors rounded off the professional team. But again the Richardsons had to leave as bullets began to fly. They retired as brigadiers in 1961, the latter part of their service being as chaplains at the William Booth Hospital, Covington, Kentucky. They were foreshadowing the much later development of hospices, where the scientific and the spiritual blend in terminal care.[149]

Lieut-Colonel Clifford Seamans MD was a physician in a Presbyterian hospital in North Carolina when he and his wife felt called to service with The Salvation Army in Africa. Their story is not unusual. They were accepted for India but reached China! When they arrived as officers in 1939, the Army was running numerous refugee camps with clinics, and to this service they were directed. Reference has already been made to Dr Swain's hospital at Ting Hsien. It had been hoped to use it again, but eventually a clinic was opened in the Nan K'ai district of T'ient'sin, and they had to operate with military permits. When these were eventually withdrawn, Seamans had already seen more than 60,000 patients.

The Seamanses were interned by the Japanese, but on release in 1944 they served at Covington, in the same capacity as the

Richardsons would later serve. By this time there was little chance of any more medical work in China so, as Lieut-Colonel (Dr) Rin Iwasa's health was failing, the Seamanses were appointed to the tuberculosis hospitals in Tokyo, with a combined bed capacity of 435. By 1949 Lieutenant (Dr) Nagasaki had joined them and more Japanese doctors were on their way. Following five years in the Salvation Army Home and Hospital in St Louis, Missouri, Lieut-Colonel (Dr) Seamans had his last appointment in New York, with responsibility for the medical care of homeless and alcoholic men in eight of the Men's Social Centres.

Not all the doctors who worked with Dr Noble in Catherine Booth Hospital were Americans. Doctor Margaret Round arrived from the UK in 1927. She worked for four years in the women's wards and then broke new ground, as the first Superintendent of the State Leprosarium at Koratti in Cochin (Kerala). She was posted to Nidubrolu in 1938 with good nurse support in Major Ellen Evanson and Captain Dorothy Narraway. When she returned from furlough in 1950 she had Dr Samson as her assistant and Captain Gwen Rust from Australia as Matron. She made extensions, including a row of private wards. A word of caution is needed here, for the constant reference to these private wards may suggest a wrong slant in a Christian practice. Many of these private wards were very small and cheap, but they provided that degree of privacy, and proximity of a relative, which was so important to village patients. It was 'home from home' as far as possible, but deadly to normal hospital discipline.[150]

Two more couples from the USA were to serve at Nagercoil. Captain (Dr) and Mrs Lyle Alloway, from the Western Territory, arrived just before the Nobles left. Lyle was to take over the extensive eye practice (including obtaining his specialist qualifications). He also worked with Dr Williams and relieved him of much of the general surgery. Ruth Alloway was a nurse who taught in the School of Nursing. Their later service included a posting to Booth Hospital in New York and then a spell at Howard Hospital in Zimbabwe.

Major (Dr) Herb Rader and his wife followed the Alloways. They served there from 1970 until 1983, raising the hospital's reputation for surgery yet again. As previously mentioned, Herb was to round his career as Medical Director of Booth Memorial Hospital in Flushing, New York, until it was deemed too vast a financial undertaking for the Army to maintain, and it was sold.[151]

A maternity clinic was maintained in Buenos Aires, Argentina, from 1929 until 1958. Bethesda was run by a well-known consultant, Dr Guismondi. It was noted for its tolerant atmosphere, its daily devotions being shared by Jews, Catholics and evangelicals. The evangelist, Luis Palau, was born there.

Severe floods which caused havoc in the poorest districts of Porto Alegre, capital of State Rio Grande do Sol, were the Army's introduction to medical work in Brazil.[152] All these autonomous medical programmes add up to a large global service. The annual statistics published in 1941 by International Headquarters give a total of 62 hospitals and 32 dispensaries, of which 17 were in the USA, four in Canada, 12 in India, four in Australia, six in New Zealand and eight in the then Dutch East Indies. Throughout that year there were nearly 200,000 inpatients.[153]

There was a steady stream of talent to maintain the growing tally of hospitals in both India and Africa. Captain Eileen Stanford was the sister at the clinic opened at the Howard settlement in Rhodesia. She subsequently took medical training, married, and as Mrs Brigadier (Dr) Mackintosh, was the Medical Officer at Kolanya Hospital in Kenya from 1956 to 1958. Three years at Nidubrolu hospital in India followed and then she returned to Howard Hospital as its medical officer. In retirement, she brought her expertise as University Lecturer in Community Health to the task of Medical Adviser for Zimbabwe. Dr Stanley Pearson, also from the UK, served for a term in India, first at Nidubrolu and finally at Anand.

Captain (Dr) Jock Cook came from his native Scotland and served for two years at Chikankata, Zambia, before transfer to

India for 1959/60. Back again in Africa, he spent a full term at Chikankata, serving finally at Howard until 1969.

The next doctor and his wife were from Germany. Guntur and Ursula Gramsch were drawn to The Salvation Army by its relief operations at the close of World War II. Ursula became a secretary with one of the teams and it was there that an Afrika Korps veteran, a doctor, was glad to accept her help. They fell in love and following training they were off together to India in 1953. Guntur was CMO at Thomas Emery Hospital, Moradabad, until 1958 and then served for a second term at Dhariwal. He was a dedicated physician and when they returned to Germany he joined the staff of the famous Missiones Hospitallet at Tubingen. They are still an inspiration in the small corps at which they soldier.[154]

Many non-officer professionals dot these years. We have already noted that in 1963 Dr J. Bennett Alexander, an Anglican, gave up his practice in the English Lake District to serve for a term in Dhariwal. He later became a Salvationist and, in retirement, was a choice spirit at Wymondham, Norfolk. Doctor Stafford Bourke was a New Zealander who served as CMO at Chikankata for two years, while Dr Gordon Carter spent two terms there between 1955 and 1970. One of the longest-serving was Dr Rupert Clarke from the UK, who was CMO at Turen hospital in Java from 1958 to 1966. Doctor Terence Daymond from the UK was in Dhariwal from 1968/70 and Dr Stig Pettersen from Sweden, held the fort at Howard during the same years.

This part of the story closes with a happy memory of the wedding of Dr and Mrs Robert Hart in the chapel at Catherine Booth Hospital, Nagercoil. A Baptist, Robert came to Nagercoil as a registrar, the hospital being recognised by the Royal College of Surgeons of Edinburgh for its Fellowship examination. They subsequently moved on with their family to a Baptist hospital in Assam.

One remarkable story is that of Colonel (Dr) Bill McAllister. Bill's father was an ardent socialist, a friend of Keir Hardie, and he had first seen his calling as being to politics. However, he became a Salvation Army cadet in 1896. He must have had a strong interest in medicine, for his three sons became doctors and all his daughters became nurses. Bill was the only one to become a Salvation Army officer. He set out for India in 1940 and spent his first term with Dr Noble in South India. Whilst on furlough he shared a seminar with Adjutant Eunice Guillot of the Editorial Office in Paris. They fell in love and married before being appointed to succeed Adjutant and Mrs Mortimer at Chikankata where Adjutant McAllister's experience in both ophthalmology and leprosy proved to be of great value. Dapsone, the drug developed from sulphanilamide, had just become available, and was known to arrest leprosy, thus changing the prognosis for the disease. A school of nursing was opened with government approval, and the first girls graduated before Dr McAllister was off back to India. Leprosy work at Chikankata then developed even more strongly under the guidance of Captain (Dr) Sidney Gauntlett, as described below.

Reference has already been made to the development of a variety of specialised clinics by The Salvation Army in South America where the gulf between the rich and the poor was so apparent. Lieut-Colonel Richard Christiansen, a Danish pioneer, was sent to Porto Alegre in Brazil. A doctor and his wife were among his first converts. Together they visited the slum huts and determined that something must be done. The doctor decided to give up his practice for a time and opened a clinic in Navegantes. To support it 'helping brigades' were established, members making a monthly or quarterly subscription. Dr Leopoldo Rossler continued the practice for 30 years, being awarded the order of Distinguished Auxiliary Service in 1967.[155] There was a further development in Brazil, when in 1953 a clinic was opened at Campinas, 59 miles from São Paulo, with the services of Dr Antonio Milone Sobrinho and Sergeant (Nurse) Izabel Godio. Two American doctors later gave their services, Donald Gordon and Maphalia Price. A third, an erstwhile Peace Corps worker, Dr Henry McKnight, opened a dental clinic.

Dental Clinics were to become popular in South America. The first was opened in Argentina at Territorial Headquarters (THQ) in Buenos Aires. A major supply company provided equipment and paid salaries. Dr Jorge Martinez opened a branch in The Salvation Army's Eventide Home in the city and again it was financed by the company. It continued to burgeon, Dr Edit Schnoerr joining the staff and running school clinics. Dr Martinez became the second doctor to be awarded the Order of Distinguished Service.

Zambia and Zimbabwe

The greatest advance, however, was made in Africa, with the coming of independence to Zambia and Zimbabwe. Back in 1967 the hospital in what was then Rhodesia was administratively separated from the educational setting of Howard Institute, with officer-physicians, Major and Mrs James Watt, taking charge in the early 1970s. Although 1972 to 1980 were war years, the hospital never closed. 1980 to 1984 were years of rebuilding. The hospital has since been designated a government district hospital and is a major provider of inexpensive health services. It has become even more innovative as the concept of a hospital-based, integrated community development model has taken shape. This includes an evangelical focus, vocational training, agriculture, water development, traditional crafts, income-generating projects and recreation to reduce out-migration. The community health programme concentrates on food supplementation at the 80 pre-schools, which are visited regularly by a mobile team.[156]

Zambia is on the edge of the great escarpment of the Zambezi. If Zambia can be visualised as a butterfly, with the capital Lusaka at the head, then Chikankata is in the middle of the left wing. When Adjutant and Mrs Kingsley Mortimer (both doctors) arrived, a hospital, modern in concept and equipment, was already taking shape. But let Dr Mortimer tell the story.

It was designed to serve the peoples of the Zambezi valley, that vast expanse where time has stood still for a thousand years, where smoke rising from the villages is the ageless sign of the unchanging centuries; where dirt, squalor and ignorance are a reigning triad, with only one greater god – the great god PAIN! The BaTonga people are inured to suffering … with a philosophy that to be stoical is the supreme virtue.[157]

The hospital was to be a joint venture with major government support. The Mortimers were from Australasia, he from New Zealand and she from Australia. Kingsley had already served as an officer in Rhodesia, from where he proceeded to study first in South Africa and then in the UK. He gained an arts degree through part-time study, and then was given the opportunity to qualify in medicine at St Bartholomew's Hospital in London. After working in a war-time London hospital during the blitz, Mortimer married Dr Mavis McKenzie, daughter of Commissioner McKenzie, the Australian chaplain of Gallipoli and China fame. The Mortimers commenced to win the trust of their rural clientele. They later moved on to Asia to take charge of the hospital in Surabaya, Indonesia. After resignation from officership, Kingsley worked in the Anatomy Department of Auckland Medical College, eventually becoming Professor of Anatomy. Kingsley and his successor, Dr McAllister, were followed by a line of doctors who became lovers of Africa and under whose care the hospital grew in size and scope.

From 1951 Captain (Dr) Sidney Gauntlett built up the Chikankata Hospital over a period of 16 years. With the aid of government capital grants for building work, and much help from the Beit Trust, Chikankata developed to a 200-bed facility, with a further 400 leprosy patients and Dr Gauntlett, who enjoyed a long and distinguished career in Africa, not only ran the hospital but became responsible for the leprosy control programme for the Southern Province of Northern Rhodesia (later Zambia).[158]

During Zambia's freedom struggle, though little or no violence occurred at Chikankata, talk of a possible uprising led local farmers to express disquiet when the hospital authorities made it plain that they would treat casualties on both sides equally. Kenneth Kaunda himself was an in-patient not long before independence, and became a personal friend of Dr Gauntlett, able to share with him some of the burdens of his office as well as his deep Christian faith. When General Eva Burrows visited Zambia, the president let her know that the fortnight's stay in Chikankata saved his life.

By way of interest, Dr Gauntlett adds: 'The policemen who came to the hospital asking if they could 'plant' a patient in the ward to check on the *anti-government activist* Kaunda and try to ensure that he did not abscond, were the very same ones who, some months later, came early to the hospital to check on the security afforded to *President* Kaunda and saluted him when he arrived.'

He also notes, on reflection, that even in the 1960s he treated patients whose rapid development of Kaposi's sarcoma and flare-ups of pulmonary tuberculosis, now lead him to think they were suffering from Aids, long before it was described. Much later, with the spread of the Aids pandemic, Chikankata was in the thick of it, becoming the focal point for the development of an understanding of the social, spiritual and community aspects of the disease. Treatment and counselling evolved and in 1987 the former leprosy settlement became a hospice for Aids sufferers. By 1993 a total of 68 community counsellors had been trained. Since that time, Dr Ian Campbell and his wife Alison have carried the lessons of the Chikankata experience round the world. They have continued to give oversight to this expanding programme, particularly by conducting seminars.

The Chikankata Hospital programme has been singularly successful. It has trained hundreds of people to deliver health services to a rural community of more than 100,000. Mobile units make monthly visits to a network of 30 community-based village health centres, supported by 60 trained community health workers and 30 birth attendants, who are drawn from the League of Mercy programme.[159] The Chikankata progamme has also been visited by teams of Salvationists and others from Sudan, Niger, Ghana, Nigeria and South Africa. This has meant that since 1985 Aids care has been a special focus and area of expertise for The Salvation Army throughout Africa and beyond. Training has been focused on community and extended-family-based programmes rather than institutional facilities. Aids has been accepted as a community phenomenon and responsibility, and in some countries legislation against negative cultural practices has been attempted in order to try and reduce the spread of the virus.

One final story must be told. It concerns Tshelanyemba in Zimbabwe, already referred to earlier. It starts a few miles away at Mbembeswana, then the Divisional Headquarters (DHQ) of the Semokwe District. A Swiss officer, Brigadier Gertrud Wackernagel described the water situation: 'In the rains all the tanks would be overflowing, but come the dry months the dispensary and the quarters each had padlocked tanks. If these gave out, it was cartage by donkeys from four miles away'. When Major Leonard Kirby was appointed as Divisional Commander (DC), he made the vital decision that DHQ must follow the water, and the move to Tshelanyemba was on. Mrs Kirby was a nurse and was joined by Major Ruth Hacking from the UK. The nearest medical facilities were 30 miles away. The building of simple quarters was scarcely complete before patients commenced arriving. The villagers agreed to make bricks and a first ward went up. Within weeks it was inadequate, so a second ward was run up 'around the beds on which the patients were already lying!' Plans were drawn up for a 35-bed hospital and a government grant was promised, but THQ had no funds and the scheme lapsed.

In the end the Kirbys did it themselves and the present 100-bed hospital is the result. The story should be told in the Major's own words. He read in a newspaper 'that a fertilizer factory was offering £3 per ton for bones. Due to the severe drought in the area, which had resulted in the death of many animals, large amounts of bones were lying around. These were collected by the school children and a few weeks later we had a heap of five tons … and a neighbour loaned a lorry for the 100 mile journey to Bulawayo'. To Kirby's surprise the price had risen and he came away with £45. They commenced to make bricks and dig foundations, and all the while money came from all directions, including major grants from the Beit Trust. The £45 soon became £5,000.[160] In this remote spot in Zimbabwe major emergencies are common but Major Evelyn Munn from the UK and Major Doris Wright from Canada, with a Zimbabwean staff, managed to cope, with increasing help from international agencies.[161] It is a thriving hospital and one of its former nursing staff, Commissioner Robin Dunster is currently Chief of the Staff of The Salvation Army at International Headquarters.

Papua New Guinea

It was thanks to officer nurses that an extensive medical service at grass-roots level developed in Papua New Guinea. In a country with very limited infrastructure, young women lived alone in isolated villages, a new portent in the region. Papua New Guinea was then a Trust Territory administered by Australia and was first prospected for The Salvation Army in 1953 by Colonel Hubert Scotney and Major George Carpenter. In September 1957, Major Keith Baker was appointed as regional commander to 'open fire' in Port Moresby, then in 1958, Captains Ruby Dalrymple and Dorothy Elphick started a clinic in Kainantu in the Highlands. These two nurses built up a maternity hospital and commenced the training of assistants. The New Zealander, Dorothy Elphick, soon moved on to Onamuga, where, with a compatriot, she ran a small modern hospital of 12 beds. Here the team expanded to include Mrs Captain Gates and Captains Beulah Harris and Bette Sampson. In the south, in Papua, with half a century of exposure to

Western ideas, a clinic was opened in 1964 at Sogeri, on the notorious Kokoda Trail of World War II. Mrs Major Bev Mole, Mrs Captain Jean Evans and Sister Gwen Peterson made up the staff. Poverty and malnutrition were rife throughout the whole area so the government introduced coffee growing at local village level. The Salvation Army bought the beans from the villagers and with the increased income per capita, Kwashiorkor, a disease of malnutrition, became rare.[162]

Dorothy Elphick opened the most remote centre, at Misapi. It was in the Gimi area, many miles of narrow, treacherous, unsurfaced road from Onamuga. The headman met her when she could go no further and, carrying her bags and walking with her for several hours, brought her eventually to a piece of land which he immediately offered for a church! They wanted the gospel even before they received her as a nurse. The land was accepted and a small building was given to her for a clinic. She built a hospital of local materials, bamboo and thatch.

Dr Harry Williams flew in by helicopter in 1973 and was greeted at the small levelled patch on the steep hillside by a silent crowd gathered around the one white uniform. There were near-naked boys whose grass-skirted mothers with flaccid infants over their shoulders looked dejected. It was a measles epidemic, lethal in such an unprotected community. The area was said to be 'full of difficulties and dangers, as much from the people as the terrain. Some tribes in the area (were) cannibals. The fact that there were more men than women was said to be due to the women having caught a deadly infection from eating human brains.'[163] Australian Salvationist Rotarians persuaded their district to adopt this village, and provide a better hospital. A pre-fabricated building was flown in and the men took their annual leave to erect it. It was a brilliant idea and a great boon to the whole region. Dorothy Elphick was guru to the villagers and a corps flourished.

The headman's desire for Christianity proved to be a widespread phenomenon, so the suggestion was made that villagers should donate land, complete with a bamboo hall and quarters and choose a young man to be their spiritual guide. The Salvation Army would train him as an envoy. The quarters provided should include a garden in which the envoy could grow his own vegetables. The Salvation Army duly trained him, not only theologically, but also as a 'barefoot doctor', sending him back with a tiny allowance and a simple pharmacopoeia. There were regular refresher courses and the system has worked now for some years. The relevance of this arrangement can be seen in the fact that a few months before the date set for independence, the Australian government called a conference to assess the future of health care. It was confirmed that a large part of health care was in the hands of the Church and revealed that the state budget was one Australian dollar per head, of which half was needed for the embryonic medical school in the capital, Port Moresby. So this is how it was managed by one branch of the Church on 50 cents per head!

The Australian administration made great efforts to improve facilities in Papua New Guinea as it approached independence and found a willing ally in The Salvation Army. Many young men had been committed to the courts for what were quite serious offences in western eyes. They were peccadilloes in the indigenous culture and punishment needed to be primarily in training and education, so The Salvation Army accepted a grant and opened a remand centre at Togatia. An officer nurse was appointed and a dispensary opened. The centre had no perimeter wall and from the first days villagers, from all around, collected for morning clinic! By 1975 a health training programme was commenced at Omborda, funds coming from The Netherlands. Later old enmities surfaced and tribal fighting broke out and the programme was relocated to Kainanta. But the Health Training School continues to produce 25 graduates a year, several of whom have gone on to become Salvation Army officers. The tragic loss of one very promising officer nurse from malaria, and another through a murder, whilst on duty, left a significant gap in the work; but God continued to call others into service. Those who came for training were from an animistic culture but responded enthusiastically to the gospel. They carried the holistic health message as they returned to the surrounding villages.

Papua, in the southern part of the island, had been open to Western civilisation for some years, and clamoured for its share in health facilities. The first was opened in Kwaipo in Rigo sub province. A graduate from Onamuga, who had come initially from the coast, was the pioneer at Kwaipo. A second centre was opened in Meii village in the Gulf province. Other provinces were soon to be included.[164]

Indonesia

Celebes (Sulawesi) in the then Dutch East Indies, in the early 20th century, was an equally primitive area when Leonard Woodward from the UK pioneered for the Army. By 1949 Major Estelle Kjelson, the matron of the Surabaya Hospital in Java, opened a small hospital at Kulawi, in the midst of hills raised on a plateau, a vast area with a population of 20,000. It was soon inadequate, and dilapidated from the intense tropical rainfall, so a new one arose; built largely of local materials. When the sun shone it was an idyllic spot, lush, green and pleasantly cool at an altitude of 4,000 feet. It became the centre from which medical tours were conducted at regular intervals by nurses on horseback. It is not isolated to the degree that Misapi is, for a jeep can drive from sea level in about seven hours. With the approval of the Muslim district medical officer, a base hospital was built at Palu, where the Salvation Army divisional headquarters had long been sited, and a nurse training school opened. Earlier, another hospital had been opened 70 miles away in the mountains at Kantewu but after some years, with political unrest, it was abandoned. Amazingly, 10 years later when a Canadian officer, Major Kjelson, walked the many miles on rough tracks, she found that supplies and equipment were undisturbed and usable.[165]

By 1965 two hospitals in Indonesia and one in Korea were found to be among the 10 largest Salvation Army mission hospitals (50-350 beds). There was a scattering of smaller hospitals and clinics, two in Pakistan, one in Malaysia, five in Hong Kong, five in Haiti, two in Uruguay and one in Cuba, a bonny handful for International Headquarters to keep up in terms of variation in health problems, staffing and finance. From 1998 an integrated community development programme, including health services, spread throughout many Salvation Army territories and commands in Asia and the Pacific coordinated by a Salvationist physician, Dr Mirriam Cepe, based in The Philippines.

Pakistan

Busy health clinics in Pakistan have functioned for many years at Faisalabad, Hyderabad, Khanewal and Lahore, with two additional clinics at Saddar and Azam Town in Karachi, under the direction of nurses. The Sunrise Institute for the Blind was established in Lahore in 1958 and by 2004 rural rehabilitation centres served the physically disabled in Lahore and Karachi. The Salvation Army's response to the needs of Afghan refugees in Pakistan commenced in August 1982 in the Ghazi refugee camp. By 1986 a total of six basic health units were in place, providing health care services to approximately 80,000 refugees in the Ghazi and Haripur camps.

Bangladesh

In 1973, shortly after independence, the government of Bangladesh provided The Salvation Army with a building in the 'New Town', which became the base for mobile clinics to village areas. One of these locations was Kholadanga, which has become a centre for community health and a training resource for The Salvation Army and other organisations, as well as having a maternity unit and a good operating room. A community development and rural health project was commenced in Dumuria in 1989. It now has a clinic and nutrition centre with a sizeable staff, which provides village health education and tuberculosis screening and treatment. The

Mirpur medical programme began in the Dhaka area in 1989, with the acquisition of the clinic site in the Bihari Camp. Previously a mobile clinic had operated from a bus, providing maternal and child health services and tuberculosis and leprosy screening and treatment for refugees from Pakistan. The clinic developed a multipurpose building, used for worship, education, home health services, loan schemes and leprosy work. In 1993 HIV/Aids work was integrated into all programmes, and in 1996 following the violent destruction of one of the largest brothels in Old Dhaka,[166] The Salvation Army opened an office close by to provide help to the women who had been thrown out and forced to ply their trade on the street. This has generated alternative employment opportunities and adult literacy training for the 'commercial sex workers' and education for their children. The Salvation Army operates a counselling centre in the Jessore brothel district as well, offering Aids education and opportunities to adopt a new way of life. The Rural Health Project in Jessore commenced in 1980 has focused on primary health care in 15 villages surrounding Jessore. As part of a larger vision of spiritual and physical wholeness, the Bangladesh Command has developed an integrated health services programme which links corps to four main clinics, five village clinics, three child nutrition centres, a maternity unit and other health projects in Jessore, Dhaka and Khulna.

Sri Lanka

Health services in Sri Lanka are limited to outpatient physiotherapy clinics for individuals with physical disabilities. However, from 1991 onward these clinics in Colombo, Hikkaduwa and Rambukkana have extended their services to include HIV/Aids education, counselling, home visits and training.

The Congos

Health services in the Congo Brazzaville Territory are organised under a health services coordinator at Territorial

Headquarters, and include a community health/health education/Aids awareness programme, five dispensaries and a dispensary and maternity training centre. Working out of the dispensary at N'Kayi, extensive mobile programmes reached remote villages.

A year-long programme in practical obstetrics at Yangui trained maternity staff for all Congo Salvation Army clinics. Across the mighty Congo River, when a cholera epidemic threatened Kinshasa in 1979, The Salvation Army and Catholic Health Services were co-opted into a national strategy and have subsequently accepted responsibility for specific health zones. Thus the Democratic Republic of Congo Territory has become an integral part of a national primary health care programme in the former Zaïre. The Salvation Army's health services accompany educational, agricultural, developmental and evangelistic work. The Kasangulu Community Development Project is a major programme. This includes a rural health centre at Kavwaya, where basic preventive medical skills are shared with the community. In addition there are three clinics operating in as many urban locations. The government's territorial medical advisor is Dr David Nku Imbie, who is a product of The Salvation Army's educational system.

East Africa
Again the health programme in the Kenya Territory, apart from a short period in the 1950s at Kolanya, has not followed a hospital pattern. Rather, it has concentrated on meeting community needs, beginning with work among the schools for the blind and physically handicapped at both Thika and Kisumu and extending to community health education. The Afya Ya Jamil (Family Health) Project began in 1985 with SAWSO consultation and USAID assistance to fund a two-year child survival initiative through the Home League, the women's section in every corps. In 25 courses conducted over three years, 75 home league members were certified as trainers, with another 808 certified as home visitors.

In 1992 when still a part of the East Africa Territory, the Kwetu Programme, in what is now the Tanzania Territory, emerged as a response to the needs of women forced to work in the sex industry in Dar-es-Salaam. In order to create alternatives for these women, who were at high risk of contracting HIV infection, The Salvation Army developed a variety of revenue-generating projects under the direction of Captain Seth Le Leu.

Ghana

Medical work in the Ghana Territory commenced in Begoro in 1950.[167] This was enlarged in 1954 to include a maternity ward and an outpatient clinic. In 1975 a rehabilitation centre was opened on the Begoro compound to accommodate disabled children and their mothers. The next opening was at Boso, which operated from 1953 until 1981, when it was taken over by the government. During periods of severe national hardship from 1970 to 1984 Salvation Army clinics proliferated and expanded rapidly, because they were able to import foreign drugs freely, and had regular supplies of relief food. After 1984 there was a steady decline in clinic attendance, although by 2004 Captain Christiana Odura supervised about 1,000 deliveries a year in The Salvation Army's maternity clinic in Accra, and eight other clinics remain up-country. In keeping with a 10-point health policy, the Ghana Territory has focused on community participation, programme development in response to changing local needs, cooperation with government and other agencies, and integration of health services with the spiritual ministry of the local corps.[168]

Nigeria

The Nigeria Territory has four health centres. In addition there are village clinics attached to corps. The success of simple medical care at corps level in both Ghana and Nigeria should set a pattern for the rest of the world.

[142] Williams, H. *Booth-Tucker, William Booth's First Gentleman* Hodder & Stoughton, London 1980

[143] The author followed him as CMO at Dhariwal when Burfoot resigned

[144] Cook, H. *White Gujaratis (Bramwell and Dorothy Cook)* Christchurch, New Zealand 2007

[145] The author watched these on numerous occasions

[146] Richards, M. *It Began with Andrews* SP&S, London 1971

[147] Ibid

[148] Ibid

[149] Ibid

[150] Rader, H. in *Historical Dictionary of The Salvation Army* John G. Merritt (Ed), Scarecrow Press, Lanham, Maryland 2006

[151] Ibid

[152] Richards, M. *It Began with Andrews* SP&S, London 1971

[153] *The Year Book of The Salvation Army* 1941

[154] Williams, H. Personal communication 2008

[155] *The War Cry* Brazil 1953

[156] Watt, J. *Howard Beginnings* 1998 Unpublished

[157] Mortimer, K. 'The Sick African' *All the World* 1946 p. 167

[158] Gauntlett, S. Personal communication 1969

[159] This a section of every Salvation Army corps concerned with hospital visitation and home care.

[160] Kirby, L. *Led and Protected by the Omnipotent God* – autobiography of Isabel and Leonard Kirby

[161] Dunster R. 'Drought and Hunger in Matabeleland' *The War Cry*, Australia 14 January 1984.

[162] Mack, L. *History of Health Services in Papua New Guinea* 2005

[163] Williams, H. *The War Cry* Australia 1970

[164] Mack, L. *History of Health Services in Papua New Guinea* 2005

[165] Kjelson, E. Personal communication 1967

[166] Brekke, Bo *Sally Ann – Poverty to Hope* The Salvation Army UK Territory, London 2005 pp. 34, 35

[167] *The Salvation Army Year Book 1952*

[168] *The Salvation Army Year Book 2004*

Chapter five

All round the world the Army chariot rolls

A hospital for every territory – developing sophistication

(Focus on the UK, USA and Canada)

FINANCING medical care has always been expensive, but until the third quarter of the 20th century, Salvation Army hospitals had certain advantages. The quality of service, particularly nursing, was excellent, due to staff being highly motivated. Costs were comparatively low, for the majority of the senior staff were officers, who received a cost of living allowance rather than a salary, and those allowances were the same for all. There were no additional professional emoluments.

The attraction of such a service meant that while many patients had free treatment, others paid modest fees entitling them to private accommodation. It started quite early in this story, with maternity care which was in demand everywhere.

Then too, as the level and scope of medical expertise grew, laboratory tests, X-rays and more complex investigations, commanded fees which patients expected to pay. So, until the state created a free health service, medical institutions could be self-supporting. Hospitals continued to increase in number and size in Western countries. There was even the commencement of specialisation in terms of the disease treated.

The obstetric programme grew in volume and sophistication and there was an increasing development of training schools for midwives. This provoked the provision of district services, particularly from the Mothers' Hospital in London. Starting with Hoxton in 1914, six district posts were operated. Dagenham, Becontree and Downham followed in 1927/8 and finally Bellingham and Ilford in 1938. A remarkable 7,661 deliveries were recorded.

The Mothers' Hospital had superseded Ivy House in 1913 and was a prominent landmark consisting of a row of large houses, fronting on to the main road in Clapton. There were more modern buildings at the rear. A satellite mother and baby home called Cotland increased the capacity. High standards were maintained and The Mothers' became an important midwifery training school, not least for those contemplating Salvation Army service overseas as well as prospective missionaries for other churches.[169]

The franchise of the services provided by Ivy House/Mothers' Hospital evolved gradually. Starting with unmarried mothers, during World War I it expanded to include the wives and widows of all service personnel. Between the wars continual improvements were made in the service and it was opened to all women. In 1921 the new Nurses' Home and Theatre were opened by Queen Mary. By the 1930s the number of births had risen to 2,000 per annum.

World War II prevented fuller development of the hospital. It was bombed on 30 December 1940, destroying two of the 'bungalow' wards. Alternative accommodation became available at Willersley Castle, near Matlock in Derbyshire, and Bragborough Hall, Northamptonshire.[170] After the war and even during the war reconstruction was speedy.

Doctor Margaret Braden pioneered new policies. Mothers were made mobile on the second day after delivery to ensure that transfers to air raid shelters were orderly. This also allowed more space as fewer beds were taken down. This was contrary to nursing techniques at the time, but is a method now widely practised.[171] There were 18,000 births during the war.

As early as 1918, five years after the opening of the Mothers' Hospital, The Salvation Army secured a grant of £2,000 from local government, an acknowledgement of the quality of its maternity and child welfare work.[172] It set an important trend of state subsidy, which was to increase dramatically with the creation of the British National Health Service in 1948. By then 100,000 children had been born at the Mothers' Hospital and 2,600 midwives had been trained there.[173]

Section 61 of the National Health Service Act provided that the character and associations of any voluntary hospital transferred to the Ministry would be preserved through appointments to the administration of the hospital and its board. During this period of transition the matron was Colonel Christiana Knott, who served for 20 years until, in 1951, she was appointed as chief nursing officer to facilitate liaison between The Salvation Army and the state health services. The hospital developed strong links with the Queen Elizabeth Hospital, strengthening its capacity in neonatal care.[174]

Lorne House, opposite the hospital, was acquired in 1952, and used as a training centre and home for 24 nurses. Some of those trained there not only acquired a midwifery qualification, but also became Salvationists and officers. One such was Janet Cooper. During her Mothers' Hospital training she discovered that it was in the Army where she felt at home. She soon felt called to become a soldier and an officer. She sought the counsel of her Congregational minister uncle who gave his blessing to the move. Janet was ready to answer the call to serve as a nurse in Africa but God had other plans. After her commissioning she was appointed to India, where she served her whole career.[175]

In 1919 the Mothers' developed a satellite obstetric hospital and midwives' training school in Manchester. It had been set up by the philanthropic automobile manufacturer, Frank Crossley. Together with the wartime addition at Willersley Castle in Derbyshire, it helped considerably when the Mothers'

Hospital was bombed. Between 1948 and 1974 the Mothers' Hospital belonged to the Hackney Group Hospital Management Committee, and on 1 April 1974 the Group became part of the City and Hackney Health District. The Mothers' Hospital was closed in 1986, and all obstetric services were transferred to the Homerton Hospital.[176]

USA

If Booth-Tucker managed to cultivate good contacts with political and business leaders, his successor, Evangeline Booth, did even better when, in 1904 she began what was to be a 30 year command in the USA. At the end of World War I she assessed the Army's assets in the USA and found them seriously depleted.[177] She embarked on an aggressive plan to redeem the position, building up the 'auxiliary league', which enabled supporters to contribute regularly to the Army. She oversaw the territorial administrative structures, which came with the establishment of territories, four of them by 1926.[178] Recognising the value of professional advice, the first Advisory Board was established. Evangeline Booth also encouraged acceptance of Community Chest funding for Salvation Army operations and established the annual 'Christmas Kettle Appeal'. It was in this atmosphere of growth and organisational development that the Rescue Homes were restyled in 1920 as The Salvation Army Home and Hospital.[179] It was a time for consolidation and growth of social programmes generally, health services among them.

There was a growing international momentum favouring the development of health services. An International Conference was held in London in 1921 under the chairmanship of Commissioner David Lamb. The discussion was wide-ranging and germinal. Colonel Percy Turner, the newly-appointed Chief Medical Officer at International Headquarters, proclaimed 'the gospel of sanitation as a necessary adjunct of the gospel of salvation'.[180] Lieut-Colonel Margaret Bovill, Women's Social Secretary in New York, saw a hospital as a practical response to urgent need, often a homeless baby. It was also a place where special gifts could be applied; she saw it as a complementary adjunct to the soul-saving ministry of the Army. It provided a way to establish rapport during times of crisis and to provide life-changing influence for good. At the conference she made an impassioned plea for a hospital in every territory. With hindsight, it is clear that much profit would have come from regular conferences of this type.

The gradual decline of maternity hospitals in Britain and Australasia was largely the consequence of financial pressure with reduced demand for services. However, services in the USA grew rapidly because of popular demand. In 1914 The Salvation Army had responded to the citizens of Covington, Kentucky, and begun a general hospital in its newly-acquired Shinkle Mansion. The new general hospital would compete with Covington's Roman Catholic St Elizabeth's hospital. Besides this Protestant/Roman Catholic rivalry, the history of Booth Memorial includes a constant struggle for financial survival and administrative integrity. Tension between its administration and the honorary doctors, and its dependence on mercurial goodwill were additional factors. All in all, it is the history of a humanitarian institution buffeted by urban political, sectarian and other cultural winds. It meant a chequered career. Demand for democratic control was high and input in staff and money too uncertain. Although the property was originally gifted for use as a home of rest for officers, the benefactors readily agreed to its use as a Rescue Home. But the strong desire for a Protestant hospital in a Roman Catholic-dominated community prompted a local doctor, Meek, to persuade Margaret Bovill, former corps officer in the area and now Women's Social Secretary in New York, of the need for a General Hospital. A pamphlet on the Army's Grace Hospital in Winnipeg, Canada, persuaded the benefactor.[181]

In the USA Southern Territory, medical work began in 1914 in El Paso, Texas, with the general care of women and children. In Louisville, Kentucky, maternity services were available from

1919 onwards. The home and hospital in Richmond, Virginia was opened in 1923. Commander Evangeline Booth dedicated a new hospital property in Birmingham, Alabama in 1927 and a year later maternity facilities opened in Tulsa, Oklahoma. In 1930 existing services were rehoused in a new building on Marine Avenue, St Louis, Missouri. The following year a home and hospital opened in Tampa, Florida. At Des Moines, Iowa, in the Central Territory, the Home and Hospital was destroyed by fire in 1918 but new premises were promptly built on the old site. In 1921 the Booth Memorial Hospital in Omaha, Nebraska occupied a new building, but another move was made in 1928 to what had been the Swedish Covenant Hospital. The east wing was converted in 1943 into a convalescent hospital for geriatrics, anticipating what would become a common pattern 50 years later. In Chicago, Illinois the Army's medical services had to be content with rented premises until 1924, when a modern building was again opened by Evangeline Booth. A modern hospital was erected on the site of the original Salvation Army home in Detroit, Michigan. Maternity services opened in Wichita, Kansas in 1921 with a new property constructed in 1926. The Martha Washington Home and Hospital was dedicated in 1922 in Milwaukee, Wisconsin.[182]

In addition to the Booth Memorial Medical Centre in New York, developments continued in the USA Eastern Territory. In Boston, Massachusetts, the Home and Hospital was enlarged in 1920. A year later the 'Door of Hope' maternity home and hospital opened in Jersey City, New Jersey, with a further annexe being added in 1925. There were further extensions in Cleveland, Ohio, when another new building was opened in 1928. A new hospital building was erected in 1941 in Buffalo, New York and both Philadelphia and Pittsburgh, Pennsylvania had their Booth Memorial Hospitals. The care of sick officers was a concern which was addressed in 1935 by the opening of High Oaks convalescent home. Another, at Omaha, Nebraska followed in 1943.[183]

The work also expanded in the USA Western Territory. In Portland, Oregon the one-time 14-room wooden-frame building was vacated in 1920 on the purchase of the Army's White Shield Home from the E. H. Wemme Endowment. Social services for women and girls were housed in a large wooden-frame structure on Beulah Heights in Oakland, California, but in 1922 a modern hospital building was erected and the programme was limited to maternity work. Service to unmarried mothers in Los Angeles dated back to 1890, but the first unit of a modern hospital was only completed in 1925. Similarly, in Denver, Colorado, a hospital was constructed in 1926. A new unit to house existing services was completed in Boise, Idaho in 1928. The Army took over the existing social services for women in San Diego, California in 1931, subsequently developing both the property and the work. In Spokane, Washington the maternity facilities, which started in 1893, were provided with a new building in 1931.[184]

In summary, though they did not all exist at the same time, there were 44 medical institutions in the USA, including the general hospitals in Cleveland, Ohio and Florence, Kentucky and The Salvation Army's single largest institution, The Booth Memorial Medical Centre (BMMC), located in Flushing, Long Island with an annual budget reaching $200m in 1992. By the turn of the century 17 of these facilities had been established. In 1942 there were 36, in 1977 there were 26 and by 1999 the last remaining facilities had been closed or were being put to other uses. The financial strain was too great for a voluntary organisation such as The Salvation Army, though there were other contributory factors. Cleveland, Florence and Flushing were part of this situation for several reasons including concerns about financial liability with a lack of Salvationist administrators. Government regulations, other alternatives, changing standards and new social perspectives combined to force the Army out of one of its premier services. The Catherine Booth Home, Cincinnati, closed in 1969, as did its sister institution in Pittsburgh in 1971. Two years later it was Jersey

City, NJ and in 1974, Buffalo. By 1976 it was closure for Boston Home, the hospital having closed in 1958. Cleveland followed suit in 1980.

The maternity hospitals, which had generally been supervised by the Women's Social Services Departments, gradually closed because of financial pressures and reduced demand. This was accelerated by the 1973 judgment by the US Supreme Court in the Roe vs Wade case, which outlawed anti-abortion legislation. The number of abortions increased with a corresponding decrease in the number of young women needing the Army's specific maternity care services.

The New York State Legislature legalised elective abortions in 1970, a move which was accepted by the BMMC Board including THQ leaders. That was three years before the Roe vs Wade judgment which deemed abortion a fundamental right under the United States constitution, subjecting all laws attempting to restrict it to the standard of strict scrutiny. Large numbers of abortions were performed every week until 1984, when the policy for the hospital was rewritten (and later adopted by the Army) permitting abortion only for statutory rape, proven incest, life-threatening maternal illness and foetal anomalies incompatible with life. The policy seemed reasonable to the medical staff and the outcome was that abortion was soon eliminated from the hospital.[185]

The Booth Memorial Hospital at Queens, New York, was by far the largest of the American hospitals of The Salvation Army, indeed the largest in the world. When the Booth in New York had reopened its doors in 1919, it was as a general hospital. For the next three decades it earned respect for providing quality medical care to low- and middle-income families. By the time the 1950s arrived a pressing need for more hospital beds in Queens prompted local planning authorities to ask the Army to relocate there. In its infancy the BMMC in Queens had 210 beds and 375 employees. By 1992 it was a 487-bed voluntary teaching hospital, employing a staff of more than 2,000. The hospital's comprehensive diagnostic and treatment services included sophisticated radiology, advanced anaesthesiology, clinical laboratories and an oncology centre designed to co-ordinate all cancer-related services. The hospital had a 10-room operating suite and 41 intensive care beds, along with 'step-down' units and a medical oncology nursing unit. It also provided comprehensive outpatient care and its Department of Dentistry helped meet a community's need through 11,000 annual patient visits, 1,600 of which were for emergency dental care.

The BMMC developed a broad range of services. The Trude Weishaupt Memorial Dialysis Center had 22 chairs set aside for nephrology, hypertension and dialysis services. In addition, BMMC was the only hospital in Queens to become an Aids-Designated Centre. Its emergency room was one of the largest in the borough of Queens and it was designated a Trauma Centre. Booth Silvercrest, a 320-bed skilled nursing facility, sponsored by BMMC, opened in December 1990 in Briarwood to help ease the critical shortage of nursing home beds in Queens. Its Home Health Agency, often referred to as a 'nursing home without walls', enabled the elderly and chronically ill to receive professional nursing and support services in their homes. BMMC had entered into a prestigious medical education agreement with the New York University School of Medicine in 1991. By that time it had affiliations with Columbia University School of Dental and Oral Surgery as well as a connection to Albert Einstein College of Medicine. Vast medical resources abounded at Booth by its 35th anniversary of service in the Queens community. They ranged from physical medicine and rehabilitation to psychiatry and alcoholism services; from ambulatory surgery to maternity and paediatric services. The Army's final contribution at Booth was to lay the groundwork for open-heart surgery. The year before its closure it launched a programme establishing the hospital as the premier cardiac care institution in the borough of two million people and with the annual budget reaching $200m in 1992.[186] Booth Memorial's staff believed that its progressive development would act as an inspiration to propel the hospital into the future with confidence. But shadows had been looming on the horizon for some time, which would soon eclipse the Army's involvement in this and other medically related institutions and services. Concerns regarding financial liability related to malpractice became significant. Beyond these, many questioned the need for the Army to maintain hospitals in the USA, where excellent medical facilities already existed. In addition, many felt that the Army's funds should be used for programmes more directly related to its stated mission. After a long series of private negotiations carried out by the executive director and chairman of the board, BMMC was handed over to The New York Hospital in September 1992. The transaction involved $45m. The name was changed, Army crests and portraits were moved to the Officer Training School and all officers were retired or transferred. The one exception was the officer medical director, Lieut-Colonel Herb Rader, who was seconded to the New York Hospital.

Booth Memorial Medical Centre had sometimes been criticised because so many faiths were represented on the staff, but the presence of people of many nations and languages and faiths also afforded an opportunity for witness and service in a world of increasing cultural diversity and religious pluralism. The hospital was, in many senses, a genuine 'mission field' where the Christian life was observed at close hand and the Christian message was supported, as will be discussed in Chapter 7. The last quarter of the 20th century witnessed a major global review of Salvation Army activity and structure. In the USA, administrative changes were made at headquarters and Advisory Boards gained in importance. Social ministry, emergency assistance and rehabilitation were stressed. It was difficult to see quite where health services in a hospital base would fit.[187]

Canada
Canada has an illustrious record in Salvation Army medical history. What happened initially was a reflection of patterns

which had emerged in England, where The Army had become involved in the 'Maiden Tribute' issue in 1885. This exposed prostitution, especially of under-age girls. Booth's shift of emphasis towards a social gospel had culminated in 1890 with the publication of *In Darkest England and The Way Out*. It was well received in Canada. Based on this favourable climate of public opinion, the Territorial Commander, Thomas Adams, travelled extensively, promoting the Army's willingness to meet social need. When Evangeline Booth succeeded him in 1896 she, undoubtedly influenced by her father's thinking at that stage, continued the emphasis. Her biographer, Margaret Troutt, regards her support for the Army's social work as one of her greatest contributions to Canada. [188]

Several other women added their influence and support. The wife of the territorial commander was responsible for social work in earlier days.[189] Mrs Blanche Read was to become the first Women's Social Secretary, and was destined in later years to address influential women from coast to coast, winning them to the cause of the unmarried mother. She and her husband had been appointed to the command of the North-West, with headquarters in Winnipeg. Immediately throwing herself into the work, then only in its early stages, she helped to develop it. A spacious home and children's shelter were soon established and from then on the move forward, culminating in the Winnipeg Grace Hospital, was guaranteed.[190] Another woman recognised for her support was Lutie DesBrisay. As Social Services Secretary from 1912 to 1916 she encouraged the development of health services.[191]

By 1900, within a decade after the growing Salvation Army ventured into full-scale social work, the Social Wing had become a distinct and independent branch of its Christian mission. From a simple 'soup to salvation' concept, where there was a clear aim of securing the conversion of clients, it had developed into a major rehabilitative programme, where the emphasis was subtly changing to the slogan to be adopted later 'saved to serve'.[192]

In the early decades of the 20th century, the launching of new programmes saw a dramatic change in the pattern of Canada's social work. The Manitoba Government passed an Act of Incorporation in 1904, transforming the Winnipeg Rescue Home into the first Grace Maternity Hospital in Canada and in 1919 student doctors from the University of Manitoba began to intern there.[193] In time almost every major Canadian city had its 'Grace'. In 1965 the Army accepted the invitation of iron ore companies in Labrador City to open the Captain William Jackman Memorial Hospital, named after a local marine hero who had rescued a score of seamen in a storm. This was later taken over by the State.

The origins of the name 'Grace' are uncertain. 'Grace' means 'unmerited love' theologically and it would have contrasted appropriately with 'mercy', the name of some Roman Catholic hospitals in Canada.[194] The word 'mercy' was incorporated in a Salvation Army outreach programme, designed specifically for lay people, especially women, as the 'League of Mercy'. Individual, and often corps-based, programmes expanded. League of Mercy members visited jails, hospitals and other such institutions. The League of Mercy therefore marked a growing dichotomy within the Army's structure. Differences between officers and soldiers were negligible in the early days, but within a decade, when the role of the officer became more clearly defined, and when the social officer gained a certain amount of expertise in that field, the difference became greater. As in other established churches (the Army fast becoming one) the roles of clergy and laity were being separated. Professional responsibility for running the social institutions would be increasingly in the hands of officers as time went on, while the lay people would simply remain church members, their participation restricted to helping raise money for the social work, including the health services, or participating in the League of Mercy.[195]

In 1905, a Salvation Army officer became the first Dominion Parole Officer appointed by the federal government, and the Army's contribution to penal reform, its police-court work and parole supervision soon won the admiration of penal authorities across Canada. Also in 1905 the first shipload of Salvation Army-sponsored immigrants arrived from England.[196] By means of such enterprises the Army's social outreach, and its image in the public's mind, took on a national character. In the early days, Canadians who had no reason to encounter the Army's urban work, its hostels and refuges, were only infrequently confronted by reports of these new endeavours through newspaper articles and parliamentary debates. However, their success, particularly the effort to increase the tide of new immigrants, gradually made them a matter of national concern, and the large sums of money contributed to each programme by federal and provincial governments alike, more than ever transformed the Army's Social Wing into a public welfare agency. The Social Wing became the better-known half of the Army's dual mission by the end of World War II. Some Canadian Salvationists were concerned that the evangelical ministry had been relegated to a secondary role, if not to relative obscurity. The Salvation Army was well on its way to acquiring its now familiar 'Sally Ann' image.[197]

The Grace Hospitals had become an integral part of the Army in Canada, needing a significant investment of Salvation Army resources. They had been kept functioning through the Great Depression in the 1930s with funds that might well have eased the hardship of other branches of the work. Leaders questioned the extent to which other services might have been compromised by such investment.[198] The dilemma facing territorial leadership did not decrease with the years, as hospital budgets outpaced other Salvation Army programmes.

In the Canadian setting, by training and appointing officers in hospital administration, chaplaincy and pastoral care, the role of officer-doctor never really materialised within the Salvation Army health services. Blenos Pedersen, Bent

Hougesen and others moved out of officership into professional medical careers. The role of officer-nurse also declined, and some took administrative roles. Notable among these was Grace Dockeray who, after years as administrator at the Windsor Grace, headed up the Health Services Desk which had been established in 1984.

Structures of governance were important in securing the denominational presence. Each hospital was under the direction of a board to which the province allocated funding. Membership and board leadership reflected local community interests and the chair was invariably an influential local person. The deputy chair was usually the local Salvation Army divisional commander. Provision was made for the balance of membership to be weighted in the Army's favour should the need arise. Cooperation between the Army and the community, as represented by the board, was a major task for the administrator. Public opinion seemed to be fully in favour of the Army's administration of its Grace Hospitals.

Salvationists, and especially local officers, were keen that the Army should benefit from professional experience and advice, health professionals among them. They pressed for establishment of what became the Advisory Council of Salvation Army Laymen (ACSAL) in 1966. Developments continued unhindered. Typical of these was that in Ottawa. In 1969 Governor-General Roland Michener dedicated the fifth-floor addition, which increased capacity to 202 beds. The 'Grace Maternity' became the 'Grace General' with the first male patients admitted. The Ambulatory Care unit opened in January 1987 and a new Childbirth Centre was opened in 1992.[199]

In Winnipeg, after 61 years at Preston and Arlington as a 240-bed hospital, the move was made to the 302-bed Grace General Hospital in St James in 1967, where steady growth continued.

The only Salvation Army Medical College hospital was the Grace Hospital in St John's, Newfoundland. It had a great influence throughout the island. As with the Booth Memorial Hospital in New York, it eventually became too great a financial liability to the Army and was taken over by the Federal Government in 1999. The same transition occurred with the Halifax Grace Hospital, although three Salvationists remained in the administration.

The Grace Hospital in Vancouver had a very large obstetric programme, but it was taken over by the State when it refused to perform abortions. This was a pivotal event in the history of the Army's hospitals in Canada. The Scarborough Grace Hospital in Ontario, The Salvation Army's most modern hospital, was merged with another city hospital, with Lieut-Colonel Irene Stickland heading the joint board.[200] Another 'Grace', the Hotel Dieu in Windsor, was administered by a joint Salvation Army and Roman Catholic health board.

The remaining hospitals have set a new pattern with the changing fortunes of a state health system. Their titles vary, but they provide hospice or geriatric care, representing a type of health care for which The Salvation Army is peculiarly suited in its concern for the whole person. It is wide open to lay cooperation in the League of Mercy and will be considered again in a later chapter.

Australia and New Zealand

The work in Australia and New Zealand mirrored that in Western nations, with an emphasis on maternity work. There were nine maternity hospitals and one general hospital in Australia in 1953, but by 1977 there were only three. The last remaining 'Bethesda Hospital', which had become a rehabilitation facility, closed in 1998. Between 1914 and 1946 six maternity hospitals were operating in New Zealand, but all followed the contracting pattern of Australia and the West.

One venture in Australia, which started with the concept of a community health project, failed in its initial purpose, but led to the establishment of the best and most enduring of general hospitals. On 1 February 1903 the Samaritan Nurses' Home was opened at 111 Hotham Street, East Melbourne. Mrs Commissioner McKie made this a pet project and wrote in her *War Cry* column: 'I am glad to say the Samaritan Home is nearly ready. Staff-Captain Cowden has the leadership and she will be supported by several nurses. I intend to start with six or eight. ... The house itself is in the best part of Melbourne'. 'We will welcome those who are able to pay, so that we can admit those who are unable ... the sick and poor and lonely (with) nobody to nurse them.'[201]

However, the Bethesda hospital, which opened in Melbourne in 1907, catered more for the middle-class than the poorest, although it did develop a nurses' training school which included district nursing in the worst slums of the city. The Bethesda nurses were involved, not only in caring for the sick, but often in scrubbing floors and cleaning their patients' rooms, similar to slum services in the UK.

Although between 1982 and 1991 the total number of Salvation Army hospitals declined from 60 to 48, the actual capacity increased from 5,458 to 5,869. There was also a change in the type of institution, the shift being from obstetric facilities to community health programmes.[202]

As previously mentioned, International Headquarters launched the Overseas Planning and Development Department in 1978. Seminars were held at strategic centres around the globe to raise awareness of local needs in health, education and agriculture and to launch schemes which could be financed by the many governmental and private agencies which had sprung up in developed countries. Within three years nearly 1,000 projects were launched, costing a total of $30m. Many were in primary health care.

'It would be a misconception,' said Commissioner (Dr) Harry Williams, the first International Secretary for Planning and Development, 'to think of the whole impetus as primarily concerned with sharing money and know-how. That is but one aspect of the Army's spiritual purpose. It is still our primary purpose to teach that true riches are found in the Lord.'

There was a call for greater simplicity in health care delivery. It needed to be closer to the people. The inevitable call for national leadership was sounding far and wide.

---

[169] Fairbank, J. *Booth's Boots – Social Service Beginnings in the Salvation Army* UKT, London p. 38

[170] Sandall, R. *The History of The Salvation Army Vol III* Nelson, London 1955 p. 205

[171] Ibid p. 204

[172] Fairbank, J. *Booth's Boots – Social Service Beginnings in the Salvation Army* UKT, London p. 39

[173] Sandall, R. *The History of The Salvation Army Vol III* Nelson, London 1955 p. 206

[174] Ibid

[175] Pope, R. Personal communication

[176] St Bartholomew's Hospital Archives

[177] Troutt, M. *The General was a Lady* J. Holman Co, Nashville 1980 p. 190

[178] McKinley, E. H. *Marching to Glory* (Second Edition) – *The History of The Salvation Army in the United States, 1880-1992* William B. Eerdemans Publishing Company, Grand Rapids, Michigan 1995 p. 177

[179] Coutts, F. *The Better Fight – The History of The Salvation Army Vol VI* Hodder and Stoughton, London 1973 p. 63

[180] Ibid

[181] Murdoch, N. 'A Protestant Hospital for Covington: Booth Memorial Hospital 1915 – 1985' *The Journal of Kentucky Studies* 3 October 1986.

[182] Coutts, F. *The Better Fight – The History of The Salvation Army Vol VI* Hodder and Stoughton, London 1973 p. 267

[183] Rader, H. *Historical Dictionary of The Salvation Army* John G Merritt (Ed), Scarecrow Press, Lanham, Maryland 2006. p. 207 ff

[184] Ibid

[185] Ibid

[186] Ibid

[187] McKinley, E H. *Marching to Glory* (Second Edition) – *The History of The Salvation Army in the United States, 1880-1992* William B. Eerdemans Publishing Company, Grand Rapids, Michigan 1995 Chapter 7

[188] Troutt, M. *The General was a Lady* J Holman Co, Nashville 1980

[189] Wood, H. *They Blazed the Trail* The Salvation Army, Canada p. 64

[190] Wood, H. 'A Ministry of Compassion and Healing' *All the World* September 1975

[191] Wood, H. *They Blazed the Trail* The Salvation Army, Canada p. 66

[192] Moyles, R. *The Blood and Fire in Canada* AGM Publications, Edmonton 2004 p. 119.

[193] Ibid p. 56

[194] Brown, A. *The Gate and the Light* Bookwright Publications, Toronto 1984 p. 176

[195] Moyles, R. *The Blood and Fire in Canada* AGM Publications, Edmonton 2004 p. 64

[196] Ibid p. 58

[197] Ibid p. 129

[198] Brown, A. *The Gate and the Light* Bookwright Publications, Toronto 1984 p. 177

[199] Robinson, B. 'The Revival of Parish Nursing' *Horizons* The Salvation Army, Canada May-June 1997

[200] Rader H. *Historical Dictionary of The Salvation Army* Merritt, John G. (Ed) Scarecrow Press, Lanham, Maryland 2006 p. 207ff.

[201] Bolton, B. *Booth's Drum – The Salvation Army in Australia 1880-1980* Hodder and Stoughton, Sydney 1980

[202] Rader, H. *Historical Dictionary of The Salvation Army*

Chapter six

Winds of change

WARS have usually facilitated a rapid growth in knowledge, training and equipment for medical services. The Second World War was no exception. In particular, it witnessed the advent and multiplication of antibiotics, but it also led to a radical rethink of economics and priorities in communal health needs. The first major result was to place community health schemes before hospitals. It also marked out certain epidemic diseases, which needed special treatment, a process which has continued as new challenges have appeared.

In India, new ideas were coming from Vellore Christian Medical College. Dr McGilvray wrote a report for the Christian Medical Association of India (CMAI), recommending a shift of emphasis from curative medicine to community health. In days when 20 per cent of hospital beds and three medical colleges were provided by Christian organisations, the CMAI had some clout. But the changes would have to be implemented by individual churches, and here was the rub, how to finance the new scheme? Economic difficulties harassed the church in India because most of the missionary societies, which had built the hospitals, had by now handed over property and administration. Gone were the days when consultants' fees could underpin a whole hospital of high quality.

When Dr Turner took over the infant Catherine Booth Hospital in Nagercoil from Harry Andrews, he had naught but a few lightly built wards. His first thoughts, prompted no doubt by his qualification in public health, were of a health service for the district. The Maharajah of Travancore soon heard of this new portent at the southern tip of his state, and made Turner a Durbar physician with wider outlook and scope. The Medical School, which was eventually opened, was basically to provide doctors to staff a medical service for Travancore, particularly to staff the branch hospitals, which Turner quickly established. The hospital at Nagercoil was the necessary hub of a large wheel.

By the 1960s this concept had been largely forgotten in India. The base hospital had become all-important and when the new community health emphasis was urged there was considerable misgiving about the cost. However, a start was made in the curriculum of the nursing schools.

In the early 1990s, at the Harry Williams Hospital in Cochabamba, Bolivia which, as we shall see below, was itself a new general hospital in a city shanty-town situated at 9,000 feet up in the Andes, a team helped found a community health programme with a training capacity for community health volunteers. The goal was to care clinically, but within the context of counselling, pastoral care, interaction with community leadership and enhancement of community capacity to make decisions.

Indonesia

In Indonesia, there had been a small hospital in the highlands of Sulawesi (Celebes). It was destroyed in 1977 when an old kerosene refrigerator exploded and sent the wooden building up in flames. It was rebuilt, only to be damaged by an earthquake in 1989. Swedish and British officer-nurses, Eivor Rosengren and Cynthia White were committed to the more basic approach of primary health care. The local district medical officer supported their position. Important decisions were being taken.

Look at a cameo of those days. The dust of the day washed off with a dipper-shower back at the base hospital; in the evening there is time for a Bible study and prayer meeting. It would rightly include a time of special praise for news just to hand that 'Islamics' need no longer be taught in a Christian Nurse Training School. 'He (meaning God) won this for you', was the remark of the government official who had relayed the news. But the hospital was facing other challenges: a 25 per cent annual deficit on running costs, setting up a new computer system and right-sizing staff levels – they too needed prayer. But the concerns of the day can fade in the joy of a capping ceremony for nurse trainees.[203]

It was a proud moment for the staff when, in 1995, they learned that they had won Sayang Bayi, an international award presented by the World Health Organization. Reflecting on this, Cynthia White says: 'To go out as a health team does not mean going out with a bag of medicines. It means working together with the villagers to understand the meaning of health. Digging rubbish pits, helping to make water closets, bringing clean water into the village are all part of health care. The creating of a healthy environment is essential for the well-being of the whole family.'[204]

In North Sulawesi it's a day's journey from the capital, Manado, due west to Makasili, set among clove fields high in the mountains. 'It's the end of the world, here,' remarked New Zealand officer-nurse, Win Ferguson. She had spent more than 20 years in Indonesia. Now she was based at the small clinic at the back of the Makasili Corps hall. There were on average just 10 patients a day, and just three beds reserved for the few inpatients over a year. By 1989 it was facing closure. Relations with government were strained. Ferguson was threatened with imprisonment if she did not comply with immigration and employment rules and leave Indonesia. A meeting with the village head made no difference. Rules were rules. A Palm Sunday morning meeting in the hall led to a movement of the Spirit with tears and rejoicing, reconciliation and restoration. Surely things would work out, and Ferguson should be able to stay. Back in Manado, even the Salvationist head of the North Sulawesi Health Department failed to achieve a stay. Ferguson had to leave. 'It's important for us to maintain cordial relations with government,' he explained, 'and we must be prepared to follow government policy.' Ferguson left Indonesia but continued effective missionary service in Kenya and Ghana.[205]

The hill tribes in Indonesia were animistic, but the Indonesian government was Muslim, and there could be tensions. In 1989 the territorial commander, Commissioner Adiwinoto, pointed out that 'Pancasila', the philosophical basis of the Indonesian state, provided both challenges and opportunities for The Salvation Army's health services in the country. It covered belief in the one and only God; in just and civilised humanity; in the unity of Indonesia; in democracy and in a unanimity arising out of deliberation, with social justice for all.[206]

Papua New Guinea

In the highlands of Papua New Guinea the culture was completely traditional and pre-European when The Salvation Army started to meet health needs. Even under Australian administration, although The Salvation Army did not have enough staff with the technical know-how needed to keep pace with the expanding work, recruiting began through 'Australian Volunteers Abroad' and the Peace Corps. Many volunteers gave excellent short-term support. A story which needs to be told is that of 'Chris', a woman from Adelaide who arrived to work for The Salvation Army on a two-year term with Australian Volunteers Abroad. An excellent worker, she had no idea that God was about to break into her life in a miraculous way. Chris had an encounter with Jesus in her first year of service and this led to a spiritual journey. Some 14 years later she is still in Papua New Guinea, having been commissioned as an officer and holding a position of leadership in the health services. Her special gift to the work has been her capacity for writing proposals and getting Government backing for health services.

In the early 1970s taboos still prevented most women from attending a clinic during pregnancy and very few were delivered at the centre. There was great excitement in Onamuga when the first baby was delivered. Then more began to arrive, albeit in dribs and drabs. What brought about this change? It was the slowly-developing trust between the villagers and the Australian nurses who were serving them. The love of Christ in the hearts of those officer-nurses won the confidence of the women and gave them courage to trust these outsiders and, little by little, they threw aside taboos.

A graduate from the first group at the school was pregnant with twins. When the twins were born, instead of leaving one hidden somewhere in the bush, exposed to the elements to facilitate a quick death and allow her to return home with one child and without shame, the young health worker and her educated husband loved and cared for both boys equally. They knew that everyone in their village believed that to have multiple births you needed to have had multiple husbands. This was clearly not the case for her and we see this young woman talking bravely about her twin pregnancy. This and other false beliefs were gradually being broken down because of the courage of one young health worker.[207]

Another challenge in that era was one common throughout the developing world – the mistaken belief that a person had only been treated properly if given an injection. This situation was usually handled sensitively, avoiding the loss of patients. There were some unexpected rewards. One was from the clinic at Kainantu. The nurses came into contact with a young boy in desperate circumstances. Two of the sisters took the child in and cared for him. In Brisbane, many, many years later, a reunion took place. That child, now grown up, had moved to Australia and become a successful business man. He heard that Beulah Harris[208] was living in Brisbane and sought her out. That was exciting enough, but to hear him witness that he was now a mature Christian was icing on the cake.

In the early 1990s a Salvation Army officer nurse stepped in to help a young three-year-old who had been badly burned in a fire in Onamuga. There was little hope for him, but the nurse knew that a plastic surgeon in Melbourne, who was a Salvationist, had been interviewed in *The Musician*. He had stated that he 'believed that every person had the right to hold their head up high and to walk with dignity'. Contact was made and help requested. Wesley's story took on a new dimension. The new corps at Cranbourne, outside Melbourne, took responsibility for Wesley and engaged with the community to assist him. There are many stories of community members reached through the project, which had become known as 'Operation Wesley'. Wesley had undergone many operations and there had been pain and suffering, but he became a healthy young man.

Independence for Papua New Guinea was not as profitable as had been expected. Leadership in the clans deteriorated and problems with law and order became part of everyday life. The introduction of beer houses into the villages contributed greatly to the breakdown of society. In the following years The Salvation Army saw centres closed because of disorder. Some, particularly those in the Highlands, were completely razed to the ground during tribal fighting. Others were relocated to ensure safety for staff and patients and to allow the work to continue.

Money continued to be raised to build more centres and run new programmes. Even more important, Salvation Army health services staff remained hard at work, demonstrating their love for God through their care of patients and fellow workers. Reflecting on those busy years it is possible to see the impact the health services made. They had commenced with mobile clinics, followed by the establishment of permanent centres. New opportunities were born in the 1990s with the introduction of projects which had a new and stronger community base. Healthier and safer lifestyles came through the introduction of good water supplies, sanitation and other essential services. Opportunities increased to share the gospel, as staff members needed to stay overnight in the communities; a good opportunity to sit and share around the fire.

The training of health workers at various levels was to play a significant part in allowing The Salvation Army to expand operations into different provinces. The use of envoys has already been described, teaching and preaching the gospel but also caring for the sick.

Disastrous events such as the tsunami which struck Sepik Province in Papua New Guinea in 1997 have showed the value of existing services. For instance, out of that tragedy a young woman was selected to come into the training school. She was sponsored because, having lost everything in the disaster, she was unable to pay her way. Following graduation, she returned to her own village in the Sepik, the northern tropical plain, which had never had a health worker. She worked tirelessly, often without pay, to help her own people. During training she took a strong interest in corps activities and understood that the mission of The Salvation Army was to reach out in love to the world. The Salvation Army was then asked to work in the Sepik Province permanently.

Despite the dangers when tribal fighting broke out, The Salvation Army continued to witness. Captain Avee Keiree an officer who was a dentist by profession was appointed to Onamuga, as tribal war was smouldering. He was a stranger to the area, having come from the coast many miles away, so he had no relatives nearby, nor did he speak the language. His wife and children were confined to the quarters when heavy fighting broke out and the arrows and bullets flew. The fighting went on for weeks and the death rates were rising. The captain, with the corps officer, went down to where the warriors had fallen, picked up their shattered bodies and, using the ambulance, delivered the dead of both sides back to their own ground.

Philippines
In The Philippines, community health projects have spread rapidly. In 1995, the corps in General Santos City became involved in discussions about the problem of HIV/Aids, called

a meeting and decided to commence training volunteers in counselling and education. One was headmaster of a school who introduced HIV/Aids education into his school and campaigned for it to be on the school curriculum nationwide.

The government was impressed and a working relationship built up with The Salvation Army. This resulted in funding for a nutrition programme in the city, and house to house visitation with nurses, hospital admissions and follow-up. One volunteer said, 'It's tiring and tough along the way of this service, but the transformation in people's health, lifestyle and behaviour inspires and encourages us'. She described a regular client, who later developed breast cancer. When the team visited her in her tiny room, they found Scripture verses written on the walls. She eagerly opened her home for Bible study. Before she finally went home to be with the Lord, she mentioned that through her contact she met friends who shared the news of God's love with her.

No rigid format can be given for primary health care. Local needs and resources dictate. In The Philippines a mobile team was set up in 1996, which incorporated dentistry and with the inclusion of HIV/Aids counselling included circumcision operations. Dentists and doctors have themselves been volunteers. The area was politically restless and clinics were often broken up by gunfire between the Philippine military and Muslim irregulars. These experiences did not dampen the mobile clinic team's spirit to carry on serving the needy in the remote areas in Mindanao. One such village, Wali, lacked sanitation. Through consultation with the village people and the Barangay Council, it was resolved that the people should dig their own bore-hole latrines and the council provide the water-sealed toilet bowl.

Bolivia

South America has had a very limited medical programme. However the story of The Harry Williams Hospital high up in the Andes at Cochabamba, Bolivia is inspiring. It started in

1978 with an inauspicious community centre on the edge of a shanty town suburb of the city, but soon burgeoned into a much larger health programme. Swedish officers were stationed there and SIDA – the Swedish government's overseas aid authority offered to pay for the addition of a clinic if staff could be found. It was part of Commissioner Harry Williams's responsibility as Medical Adviser to International Headquarters, to interview all nurses and paramedics entering the International Training College in London, and to be consulted on their appointment at commissioning. That year, a nurse from the Regent Hall Corps in London, became a cadet. She had a most positive manner and told him she felt so strong a call to serve in South America that she had commenced to learn Spanish. It clicked in his mind, but still left the big problem of finance. Then the General called him privately one morning to ask for suggestions on what he might do with a personal donation for a scheme 'outside the normal programme'. The amount would cover all the expense of sending and maintaining a missionary nurse for five years! So Captain Janette Davies soon had an out-patients clinic running at Cochabamba in Bolivia and by 1989 the Chief of the Staff was opening a 30-bed hospital with honorary consultants.

Ten years on, an outreach activity had been so successful that a mobile clinic with dental facilities, dispensary and a small operating room, was being driven to specific villages on a rota basis. It developed into a separate community extension programme, providing a simple health scheme over a wide area.

Much of the success of this venture is due to its community orientation and wide local support, but there was another factor not always present, it started with adequate facilities. This was largely due to help from Home Leagues (women's groups) in the United Kingdom Territory of The Salvation Army. The Territorial Home League President was Commissioner Ingeborg Hughes (née Clausen) born in Bolivia! The Silver Jubilee of the Cochabamba venture was held in 2003 and Janette Davies (by now a Salvation Army soldier at Oxford) and Commissioner Williams were guests of honour. They found a very busy outpatient department well staffed and equipped with enthusiastic townsfolk. There were medical students from the city college receiving clinical experience and there were now three separate programmes covering hospital, mobile clinic and district services.

Zimbabwe

Captain (Dr) Stephen Dale served at Howard Hospital from 1989 – 1995. He outlined some of his frustrations about lack of support, both conceptually and financially. It started with the observations of a new arrival that his practice was old-fashioned and out of date. He observed:

> *On continued reflection, the feeling of benign acceptance was replaced by disquiet, anger and frustration. These feelings were engendered not by the comment of the new arrival, but by the dawning realisation that it might well reflect a subtle, but fearfully potent change in attitude by the parent church towards the concept of medical mission . . . One feels that a strong thrust is required from leadership, at IHQ and in more affluent territories, in order to create a lively awareness of the need here – and in other similar situations . . . An obsession with finance is not the prime motive for this article. Howard is a stronghold of faith and Christian witness . . . Spiritual warfare is often evident, and Christ is seen to be triumphant in the conflict . . . If we believe that the true meaning of mission is the passionate presentation of the gospel to the spiritually needy, and we believe that medical ministry is one legitimate way of fulfilling that mission then our international pockets should give adequate support to that belief. If however we confess that we are mistaken, then we will eventually have to say to the people of Chiweshe that once we loved them, but that due to rising costs that is no longer true, and that we may be seeking a divorce – with honour, of course.*[209]

It was a poignant plea echoing the feelings of more than one over-worked medical officer in earlier years. Dale's article provoked an outpouring of financial support, but failed to provoke long-term debate on the fundamental question about the value of medical services in the furtherance of the gospel. 'The donors,' he mused, 'obviously are in our favour.'

However, two nurses well experienced from other parts of the world did reply. From her background in Indonesia, Lieut-Colonel Cynthia White[210] reflected on the dilemmas. 'Showing our love has meant bringing about change – helping both team members and those we serve to realise their potential'. From Ghana, Captain Mary Capsey put in a plea for greater commitment to community development. She appealed for experienced workers to give a year or two to national staff training programmes. A few years later she was to take up appointment in Zimbabwe as medical secretary. Now, some 14 years later, Major Capsey is the Director of International Development Services in the United Kingdom Territory, putting into practice that same plea for greater community development.

A glance at *The Salvation Army Year Book* is revealing. Where at one time The Salvation Army recorded a million inpatients and two and a half million outpatients worldwide, the 2006 figures are 158,971 and 989,574. Whilst there are only 20 general hospitals, there are 181 clinics and more than 331,000 beneficiaries of health education schemes scattered round the world, mostly in rural areas. A trend has emerged, with new challenges and even the potential of conflict between different aspects of health care.

---

[203] du Plessis, P. Personal communication.
[204] White, C. 'International Award for Salvation Army Hospital in Indonesia' *All the World* September 1995
[205] du Plessis, P. *Report on a Visit to Indonesia* The Salvation Army IHQ, London 1988
[206] du Plessis, P. 'Journey Across Indonesia' *Medical Bulletin* The Salvation Army IHQ, London May 1989

[207] Mack, L. *History of Health Services in Papua New Guinea* 2005
[208] Later Commissioner Beulah Cairns, at one time a Salvation Army nurse in Papua New Guinea
[209] Dale S. 'The Cost of Loving' – *The Officer* May1994
[210] The Colonel is now Mrs Major Cynthia Dalziel

Chapter seven

The people have their say

THE winds of change described in the previous chapter were in terms of a shift to simpler, less-institutional programmes. But there was a more violent wind blowing. Colonial administration was now long past. Salvation Army health programmes had flourished under such rule, usually with substantial subsidy. It had encouraged the provision of hospitals with highly trained personnel, which served mainly an urban population. The overseas Salvation Army staff then available attracted private patients whose fees helped to finance the whole. Independence challenged this concept.

In the Dutch East Indies, the Governor, having seen the quality of a Salvationist servant, invited The Salvation Army to take over the government's own leprosy colonies. In two areas in India, Bapatla and Ahmednagar as already mentioned, existing Christian missions were unable to continue their service and asked The Salvation Army to take over.

Yet another impetus had produced the Army's hospital at Dhariwal in the Punjab in 1926. The town's largest employer, The New Egerton Woollen Mill, hearing that The Salvation Army was contemplating building a hospital in Batala, 12 miles away, offered land and a contract to provide care for its covenanted staff.

However, primary health care needs to cover the whole population, involving basic but adequate preventative and curative services using the skills of community health workers, with a referral system to hospital when needed. The people must have their say.

An early rumble occurred in 1976, when Commissioner Arnold Brown, the Chief of the Staff, was informed by the government of Zaïre, that unless the Salvation Army territorial commander was a Zaïrean national, The Salvation Army would be proscribed.

The United Nations consultation on health, held at Alma Ata in Kazakhstan in 1978, issued a statement *Health for All by 2000*, emphasising the role of the people in their health services.[211] The Alma Ata Declaration was a spur to Salvation Army thinking. Although it had not been represented there, the Army issued its own statement. The concept of primary care proved broader than was at first appreciated. It included both social and political interests. The Salvation Army particularly modified its teaching programmes, including the provision of specially trained nurses.

The need for change varied widely, for even existing hospitals had started from different needs. At Mountain View in South Africa, The Salvation Army had bought land to provide a service for its people. The wind of change challenged its ownership of the land.

The Salvation Army held a Hospital Administration Consultation at Delhi in 1984. Dan Isaacs, the General Secretary of the CMAI was invited, and pushed the delegates to think beyond hospitals. 'We need to be willing to keep contact with people so that discharge from hospital is not the end of a relationship,' he declared. Another delegate was Major (Dr) Hazel Scott, who stressed the need for community medicine. 'The key task of management,' she said, 'is not to find the right way of doing things; it is the art of finding the right thing to do.' Tension over medical administration became evident. One delegate was a typical Senior Medical Officer of the day, who found his primary role as a surgeon compromised by the administrative emphasis. But the consultation did stress both the importance of community orientation and 'presence' evangelism in health care.[212]

The question of how medical administration should operate became a matter of worldwide tension as the 20th century progressed. Slowly Chief Medical Officers were replaced in the UK by specially trained Hospital Administrators.

In the USA, university faculties were set up in the subject. Very late in the piece, through the influence of Major (Dr) Hazel Scott in Madras (now Chennai) the Salvation Army Health Services Advisory Council was set up, then developed in Ahmednagar by Major Theodore Marr, especially to provide officer hospital administrators through its capacity-building training programmes. They have proved a great success and SAHSAC was given a wider remit, under the direction of Major John Purshottam Macwan.

Health education was to be another major component of community health. This gave an opportunity both to provide information and to help people to explore values and attitudes and thus to make good choices. Sometimes this operated formally and at others through congregation-related units such as the Home League or the League of Mercy. This is capable of even wider development at corps level.

In 1987 SAWSO, which from the USA supported The Salvation Army social programmes worldwide with USAID grants, appointed Dr Mona Moore to strengthen the health component of the service. Two years later, The Salvation Army collaborated with UNICEF in the production of the booklet *Facts for Life*.[213] These educational principles were tried out by Captains David and Jean Burrows in the Afghan Relief programme, operated from Pakistan, and the booklet was translated into Pushto and Dari, the two main languages of Afghanistan. In 1986 the paediatric GOBI programme[214] was introduced first in Lahore under Elisabeth Fazel, and then extended nationally, especially as a component in the training of traditional birth attendants, by Nasreen Zia Ul Haq.

We can now look at some of these changes occurring around the world.

In Africa the story often differed from the examples already given. Just five years after the 'pioneer column' arrived in Rhodesia in 1891, Captain Edward Cass was killed at Pearson Farm. His death in the first revolt against colonial rule did not deter Adjutant Fred Bradley from establishing The Salvation Army in Mashonaland. Bradley's simple, friendly approach and his command of the Shona language endeared him to the villagers, as he cycled around, staying in their rondavels.[215] Particularly in the 1918 flu epidemic, he cycled round carrying medicines and wise counsel. Even though many died, it was felt that Bradley's prayers had made a difference.

The popular demand was primarily for education rather than health and it was for this that the villagers gave the land that became the Howard Institute. The people's wishes for the name to be 'Bradley' were overruled by The Salvation Army in favour of the then Chief of the Staff! The spot was chosen by Major Len Kirby, on a plateau near the confluence of three rivers. It was 1923 when they marched from Pearson farm, the procession led by the Kirbys in a donkey cart, followed by flag-carrying cadets.[216]

In 1927 a further station was opened at Ibbwe Munyama on the escarpment north of the Zambezi. Salvationists had first appeared in the Zambezi valley as migrant workers returning from the mica mines at Urungwe. By 1933 a small clinic was opened by Captain Mary Adams.[217] The village elders began to see the advantages that could accrue from the presence of a mission, and vied with each other in invitations, coupled with the offer of land. Ibbwe proved difficult of access, so the divisional commander, Major Alf Erikson chose the 200 hectares offered by the headman at Chikankata. It was easily accessible, had the blessing of the government and the climate was mild. Captain Janet Watson, an experienced nurse who spent many years service in isolated situations in various parts of Africa was in charge at Ibbwe Munyama in 1945 when the clinic was moved to Chikankata. Then, by 1947 the governor, Sir John Waddington, was opening a 30-bed hospital. The locals had their say, insisting on the slaughter of a cow, whose blood was allowed to flow into the soil and appease any spirits that might be angered by deaths in the hospital of those coming from other places.[218]

After the mission moved from Ibbwe Munyama to Chikankata, training of national staff became one clear focus, leading eventually to the development of three training schools at the hospital: nursing, midwifery and laboratory assistants, the latter started by Captain Jean Fardon.[219]

In 1970, the General sent Colonel Tom Lewis to make an 'African Survey'. To him, Captain (Dr) Paul du Plessis, then chief medical officer at Chikankata, suggested that the time was ripe to invite the government to take control, making officer staff available for wider deployment in the country. However, such a move would have been costly for the government, as grants paid for qualified missionary personnel did not match the salaries that government would have to offer for non-missionary staff. Also, the Salvation Army administration was not yet ready to give up ownership of the venture. It was a similar reaction in 1972 when a request came for the hospital's laboratory supervisor, Major Jean Fardon, to become Paramedical Coordinator of courses at the Evelyn Home College for those involved in laboratory work, pharmacy, physiotherapy, and X-ray and at the University Teaching hospital where she was already teaching.

When Zambia launched its Third National Development Plan in the 1970s, health programmes were still dominated by doctors. So Paul du Plessis was appointed to the Plan's committee. He viewed his participation as that of a representative of the people and took every opportunity to widen participation in shaping direction of the health service nationally.

Chikankata became such a flagship for other health schemes of The Salvation Army that it is useful to trace its further development. A new Maternity unit opened in 1986 replaced an earlier facility, and at the same time 'under five' clinics were commenced which were soon opened to all children in the district, whereas previously only those born in the hospital had been treated. Within a short while mothers were attending in their hundreds and preventive inoculations were in full swing. At the same time a Hospital Advisory Committee was set up with a local councillor, John Mwiinga as chairman. A fence was erected around the whole mission property, but du Plessis assured the local community that the hospital motto was unaltered: 'to serve God and the people' and that everything in the mission is there for the people.

The Chikankata leadership felt that the presence of so many expatriate staff (inevitable at first because of the low number of qualified nationals) could separate the mission from the local community. New arrivals were coached in the local language (Citonga) notably by Kenneth Maguswi, a Zambian Salvationist teacher. There were also seminars on cultural matters.

In 1970 there was a great disaster for the whole community when five children died in the hospital from accidental poisoning. The understandable local anger erupted into a riot. But next day Chikankata, the village headman, came to settle the peace. 'I must apologise for my people', he said, emphasising the confidence in the hospital which had grown out of years of quality service. The tragedy led to IHQ establishing insurance cover for all its medical work. The parents of the children involved were compensated, but it was moving for the staff to receive one of the mothers, bringing another child, named after his deceased brother. 'How can you trust us?' asked the admitting doctor. 'Where else could I take my child?' she replied.

In 1971 Dr Blenos Pedersen had spearheaded the establishment of mobile clinics throughout the neighbourhood. Their visits included the rural health centres (as they later became known) at Chaanga and Syanyolo. Later a new centre was built at Nameembo. The Army needed its ambulance! By 1980 teams were visiting 15 centres, supervised by officer or Salvationist nurses, Margaretha Erlandssen and Esther

Girsperger among them. Drs Graham Calvert and Theo Loef took over some of the clinics.

When Commissioner (Dr) Harry Williams visited the hospital in December 1975, he recognised the tenuous nature of The Salvation Army's ownership of the site, but recommended even greater commitment to the health service. However, finance remained a problem for The Salvation Army, and accounting and financial management became even more complex. Fiscal economies had to be applied and in later years staff redundancies occurred. Medical staff, including Elijah Cheela, sought posts that were more stable for them. A patient listener, he was much respected by his colleagues.

When the Zimbabwe liberation struggle broke out and spilled over into Zambia, at first it made no difference to the mobile teams. Activities were limited, however, after 2 October 1979. On this day three hospital vehicles, two pick-ups and a Range Rover ambulance, were driving back to the hospital from the Zambezi valley. Fortunately, before starting the journey, the patients in the back of the ambulance had been transferred into the other vehicles. On the journey the ambulance struck a landmine which destroyed it. Its two front seat occupants, Mike Reagan and Alan Slator, managed to escape with minor injuries. Headman Chikankata was soon on the scene with heartfelt wisdom: 'It was God who saved you.' His words were echoed in the staff meeting held that evening in the nurses' training school.

The Chikankata leadership felt that the presence of so many expatriate staff inevitably led to a degree of 'separateness'. New arrivals had always been coached in the Tonga language, notably by Kenneth Maguswi, a Zambian Salvationist teacher. There were also seminars on cultural matters. But the arrival of Ugandan doctor, Julius Okello and his wife Jane to join the staff marked new beginnings for the hospital that were to multiply in later years. Paul du Plessis was the first African doctor to serve at Chikankata, Elijah Cheela the first Zambian and Julius Okello the first black non-Zambian doctor.

The hospital buildings, programme and staff changed regularly in an attempt to meet new demands and needs.

In 1980 Lesley Baker, who had been working in the hospital pharmacy, was appointed to establish a programme for school leavers unable to continue their education or find employment. Young Farmers' Clubs grew into a full Community Development Programme with a wide influence on all aspects of health.

There are touches in the story which emphasise the style of rural Africa. A New Zealander, Rex Wong Too, joined the local Salvation Army corps. After sitting patiently for a meeting to commence, he again asked 'What time does the meeting start?' *'Bantu basika'*, was the reply, 'when the people arrive'. In the late 1970s Gloria Reagan, wife of Mike, and Jonah Simaanya established an outpost at Kaunga, one of the places which the mobile clinic teams visited. Ruth Schoch had been a ward sister and a clinical instructor at the school of nursing and by 1978 had become matron. In 1985 she opened Bethany ward for Aids, but in 1988, feeling she should spend more time on evangelism, she also devoted time to regular tours in the valley with a Jesus film. In 1997 she was admitted to the Order of the Founder.

The debate on leadership at Chikankata led to the training of Elvis Simamvwa, a one-time laboratory assistant, in the UK. His parents were teachers in the Zambezi valley when his mother gave birth to quadruplets. The Salvation Army supported the family so well that they determined that one of their children should serve at Chikankata Hospital.

As the call for community participation became a global demand, The Salvation Army held conferences in the 1970s and 1980s to explore possibilities. Two of The Salvation Army's workers in South Africa, Potgieter and Nxumalo, highlighted the tension for The Salvation Army. 'Autocratic management styles have resulted in building up of a dependency syndrome and lack of initiative. The newer style is towards consultative participation and social agreements.'[220] Some lessons were learned the hard way. Dr Ian Campbell recalls an incident at

Nameembo, a rural health centre 30 minutes by road from Chikankata. Some children had died following inoculations. He arrived to find the nursing staff locked in the clinic and besieged by a crowd of several hundred angry relatives and friends. After three hours of negotiations, the doors were unlocked and the nurses came out. A police car, its staff armed with rifles, arrived and was amazed to encounter no violence. The people had had their say, Campbell had listened and understanding resulted. Appointing community health workers (CHWs) was another step in decentralisation. At first regarded as inferior to doctors, they gradually became accepted, many new programmes being developed by them. It was Harry Andrews all over again! Choice of such workers is all important. Experience shows that the community must define the criteria and choose candidates. Criteria are commonly, residence in the village, compassionate nature, and often literacy and suitable age. Salvationists do not have a monopoly of the required qualities but do figure prominently in the community health workers around the globe.

Against the picture of growing numbers of primary care programmes, several large hospitals were reporting great financial strain. The challenge to Western-style professionals was often painful. We have already noted Captain (Dr) Stephen Dale's question in *The Officer* of May 1994, 'Do we say to the people of Chiweshe we once loved you, but due to rising costs this is no longer true?' His question did not go unanswered. In 2003 a new hospital was under construction at Howard, the gift of the USA Southern Territory, but the debate, and the potential for conflict remains.

Contributing to The Salvation Army's Poverty Conference in 2001, Ian Campbell summarised approaches that were emerging relative to community capacity development. He emphasised the importance of believing in people. 'We come with a spirit of generosity, of looking for strengths, of helping people to find a hope from tradition and from present day experience because God has created this capacity. We are required to be alongside people within their situations. We need to participate, not only in word, nor just on our terms, but from within the experience of people in poverty. Our framework for response is based in belief in people, their capacity to be whole and in disciplined practice of participatory action and reflection.' [221]

Post-colonial strife occurred in Rhodesia following Ian Smith's unilateral declaration of independence. By February 1973 the Howard Institute had its first visit from the security police, insisting not only on closure of the institute, but also the hospital. Captain (Dr) Jim Watt was determined to continue. Gathering war clouds did not inhibit further development of the hospital programme. What could have been nightmares, turned to dreams. There were plans for a new outpatients' department, maternity and paediatric outpatients, a nursing school, staff accommodation and the university's Julius Robinson Centre. The Howard dream was materialising. Work began on a nutrition village. In a traditional setting, mothers of malnourished children would grow vegetables, cook them and feed their children from vegetables available at home. Importantly they would see their children recover at their own hands. The supervisor, Mrs Brigadier Nahari was not only 'queen mother', but in old clothes, traditional badza (heavy hoe) in hand she said, 'I will give all my love to this village,' as she started to break the ground for its gardens.[222] It was the people of the village she loved. She had rondavels built in the hospital compound and in this setting, in which women felt at home, she taught any who were staying at the hospital, sound nutrition from the food that could be produced around any village home.

During this period of conflict hospital staff did what they could to provide medical care but could not ignore the inhuman treatment of people in the nearby camps. The government was assuring the world that people in 'protected villages' were being supplied with houses, running water and food. The *Rhodesia Herald* reported a woman doctor working in

Chiweshe who praised the health benefits of the new villages. Captain (Dr) Pat Hill, based at Howard Hospital wrote to the *Herald* as the only woman doctor working in Chiweshi, telling the truth. People were not being given houses. They were being dumped on the bare ground. Not permitted access to Howard, reporters arranged to interview Pat Hill at nearby Glendale. The district commissioner attended. 'What do you mean saying these people were dumped on the bare ground' he fumed. 'I said dumped and I meant dumped,' Hill replied firmly and courageously.[223]

Journeys into the community continued in spite of danger. August 1974 witnessed the arrival of a second-hand Land Rover truck, specially fitted with examining table, sink and refrigerator.

To this was added armour plate under the cab, reinforced rubber belting behind the seats and the large tyres half filled with water, all in case of landmines. It was christened 'the white elephant'. The Army had an ambulance with a difference! As the war continued there were other developments at Howard. The teaching that Mrs Brigadier Nahari had given to women was now also provided for men. A programme in a backyard butcher's shop was started in February 1975 with Benjamin Bofu as leader, its object to train young men in small plot agriculture, raising small animals whose droppings would act as fertiliser for gardens that in turn would feed the animals.

Though they had some difficulty convincing the guerrillas that the 'white elephant's' radio antenna did not communicate with troops or police, staff travel into the community was normally covered by freedom fighter protection. They were advised against travelling in convoy but always to wear Salvation Army uniform. Suspension of The Salvation Army's membership of the World Council of Churches in 1978 compromised that protection. But even then divine providence seemed to intervene as the Howard mobile clinic vehicle drove safely into a protected village, although the car behind exploded at the gate.

The liberation struggle had a dramatic effect on the hospital. When a truckload of armed soldiers tried to enforce the closure order, the patients jumped out of the windows and ran for the hills. Sister Rebecca Mungate, Staff Nurse Gloria Hurudza, Dr Pat Hill, Major Evelyn Munn (matron) and other sisters stood firm but following the deaths of two Salvationist teachers at nearby Usher Institute in 1978, THQ reviewed the safety of the Howard staff. All mothers and children and expatriates were ordered to leave. For three months, Howard Hospital reverted to being a nurse-led hospital as it had been 50 years earlier. Captains Robin Dunster and Ann Andrews and Auxiliary-Captain Betty Moone moved to Salisbury and, in cooperation with the Evangelical Alliance, trained senior student nurses from Howard Hospital and other Christian mission training schools that had been closed by the war. At the same time Captain Eileen Parkin moved with pupil midwives to Mpilo Hospital in Bulawayo. Captain (Dr) Jim Watt, Captain Dunster and Auxiliary-Captain Moone traversed landmined roads to visit Howard at least once each week.

When the Lancaster House agreement was signed and the war suddenly ended, representatives of government and donor agencies looked for ways to help and The Salvation Army was ready. Community aspirations and needs became the first consideration in planning.

Also in Zimbabwe is Tshelanyemba with another medical saga. Writing to the *Officer's Review* from Mbembeswana, close to the Kalahari desert, Major Wackernagel, a Swiss officer, said, 'There is nothing thrilling to tell but much toil, many difficulties and disappointments. There is a continuous need for greater patience, deeper love, and a wider wisdom. The water problem is ever before us … we continually fear the well may run dry.' On the other hand she rejoiced in the success of the community health approach. 'What we might call "district work" has proved to be both satisfactory and encouraging. We have never regretted one weary step.'[224]

In 1971 Robin Dunster, an Australian officer-nurse, joined Major Brenda Smith, spending many years in building the

126

hospital and its programme. Staff recrutiment presented challenges, so the opening of a nurses' training school was a priority in the remote rural area where there were extremes of temperature and where wild donkeys ate the sparse vegetation. With the escalation of the war of liberation the hospital sustained mortar attack and all missionaries were withdrawn by 1977. The hospital had to close and did not reopen until 1981, when Captain Robin Dunster was reappointed to give oversight to the rehabilitation of the mission. With the reopening, the USA Western Territory, together with SAWSO provided funds and despite many hindrances, General Wahlström opened the nursing school and a maternity wing in 1985. It was notable that most of the grants were routed through government.

The same concern for local input was evident in the preventive health care which was recommenced. Infant feeding, protective inoculations and health education were prominent. Training for pre-school 'teachers' was established. Over a six-month period in 1984, Captain Betty Moone, travelled over 5,000km, listening to villagers and giving 12,000 inoculations. District administrators attended many of the meetings. By 1987, 80 pre-schools were being given supplementary food programmes. This excellent work was maintained against a background of continual unrest, whilst security forces were allegedly dealing with 'dissidents'. Robin Dunster recorded the imposition of curfews, frequent searches, intimidation and political rallies with forced attendance. She instanced beatings, rapes, disappearances and murders, with a marked increase in hospital admissions. On the positive side, a strong community sense was engendered with which Salvationists were identified. Her writing is vivid. 'Has someone rescued the baby? Its mother fled into the bush with the young school teachers to escape the gunfire ... Has the little boy's mother stopped crying? He was a typical seven-year old; he giggled when spoken to in an unfamiliar tongue. Now he is dead, booted to death. Without a faith to sustain them, suffering people are so lost. To tell them about a caring God, the Christ who shares in their distress seems so meaningless ... we can, however, show them.'[225] In 1986 Robin Dunster was recalled to Australia, but she was to return as the Chief Secretary. Meeting with old colleagues, it was remarked: 'When the young people see us sitting together under the tree, they will say: what friendships they made when they were together in those (bad) old days.'

When Captain (Dr) Philippe Huguenin, a graduate of Geneva University, was sent to Brazzaville in 1992, he found a network of clinics. In 1994 he attended the Health, Healing and Wholeness Conference in Sri Lanka, where he spoke quietly of his calling to be a medical missionary. His conviction was clear. His best service to the people would not be in administration but in community consultation with corps and divisional leaders. In 1995 he was made Director of Community Health, but he contracted a malignant form of malaria, and despite heroic treatment he died, leaving a widow and four young children. However, his emphasis on primary health care, and enabling community members to take more responsibility for staying healthy, was not lost. Captain Mary Capsey was preparing to take her MSc and had chosen for her dissertation, a study of Huguenin's work. *Mirabile dictu*, she was promptly to assume the same post!

Some talented expatriate nurses had been involved in establishing the Salvation Army health services in the Congos. Major Eva den Hartog, with Heidi Braun, Captains Andrée Dudan and Josianne Decosterd were among the forerunners. Andrée Dudan established the system that is currently practised. Their planned strategy was to train nationals to replace overseas workers. There were equally striking personalities among the nationals. One was a petite widow, a soldier of the local corps, Citizen Ndona. At Masina, on the outskirts of Kinshasa she understudied the Swiss nurse, Rosemarie Ravall. Staff of the clinic quickly named her, 'La Maréchale' and were delighted to have her in charge. Although she was active in discussions with others in community health, she accepted leadership of her team as her primary responsibility. 'Go on Ndona,' they urged, 'the whole team is with you.'[226] The nurse-run clinics were a great success and the envy of the government.

'The 2001 'War of Aggression' in Congo continued and encouraged the emphasis on 'integrated mission'.[227] One of the dreams of Kinshasa Salvationists had been the creation of a medical college. Hopes were lifted when a Salvation Army University opened in 1997. By 2004 the excellence of The Salvation Army's medical work was recognised when it was contracted to manage the King Baudouin II Hospital. Funding came from the Belgian Chapter of The Knights of Malta, and the Ministry of Health.[228]

The government had increasingly sought the help of The Salvation Army. In 1979 a cholera epidemic saw Salvation Army and Catholic Health services working together in specifically designated areas. Under the 'Ray of Action' policy, families in a community were registered and health record cards maintained for subsequent care. It was largely due to Dr Sidney Gauntlett's visits in 1974/5 that the programme developed preventive care, such as under-five clinics.[229] From the 1980 International Planning and Development Department's initiative and SAWSO funding, the centre at Kavwaya developed a small hospital and a community outreach. At Kasangula, and later at Kavwaya, the centre had a dental clinic, established by Captain Eva Marseille, with a programme for the treatment of gum disorders. By 1982 there was a complex development in Kinshasa, including a new dispensary, maternity wing, and extended teaching sessions in nutrition and agriculture.[230] In 1995 the only Salvation Army foot clinic in Africa was established by Lieut-Colonel Edna Williams, who had been serving in teaching and administration appointments since 1964 and went on to obtain qualifications in podiatry.

Perhaps the most outstanding development was the creation of a chain of rural centres run by experienced nurses. They had daily outpatient sessions with as many as 200, and included teaching and demonstrations in community health and nutrition. The government then approached The Salvation Army with a request that it take over three of its clinics in central Kinshasa. In 1993, a former Salvation Army high school student who had qualified as a doctor, David Nku Imbie, was made director of all the Salvation Army Health Services. Later, in 2002, he became the governor of Kinshasa.

The Salvation Army's nutritional programme was widely acclaimed with coverage on radio and TV and at the National Exhibition.[231] It is noteworthy that the stability of this programme was assured by undertaking contracts with employers to look after the health of their employees.[232]

In 1952 the creation of a clinic was reported from Begoro on West Africa's Gold Coast.[233] An expatriate nurse was appointed and welcomed by the entire town, with the beating of drums.[234] The people were glad to welcome the Army.

Throughout the civil war in Nigeria in 1970, The Salvation Army had been involved in relief work. But at the end of hostilities the territorial commander, Colonel Len Kirby, felt that more should be done for the wounded of Biafra. Brigadier (Dr) Sidney Gauntlett made a month-long assessment and an Australian doctor, Chris Schull, and his wife Judith were sent to the Oji River district, where a former leprosy hospital was turned over to them. There were great problems to overcome, not least ruined buildings. Many government and non-governmental organisations were involved, but The Christian Council of Nigeria was responsible for coordination. Save the Children Fund, War on Want and UNICEF joined forces as well as benefiting from the worldwide relief appeal following the end of the Biafran civil war. Doctor Schull was succeeded by Sidney Gauntlett himself, who wrote, [235] 'To have no financial worries was a new experience ... I had to liaise closely with the government health department, sometimes challenging policy. I was asked to assist in the training of dispensary assistants and final year medical students in the rural setting. What surprised me was the enthusiasm of the students. But they were going to insist on improvements if they were to be involved after qualification.

'I learnt a great deal from this unusual assignment in Nigeria, from which I draw a number of lessons with wider application. The Salvation Army had undertaken to help restore the rural health service in Eastern Nigeria which had been the focus of the civil war. The only hospitals were in the main cities and we came to restore and operate six rural dispensaries no longer operational which represented the government's medical service to the rural population in that area. Nigeria is probably the most densely populated country in Africa. In the country as a whole there was one doctor to 32,000 population (in the UK there was one doctor to 700 population). We had a specially designed vehicle (Land Rover) to act as transport for our medical team, ambulance, laboratory and health education facility. Having restored the war-damaged buildings and replaced stolen equipment and reassembled and retrained staff we sought to provide basic medical care for the people. But their need was far greater than this. The people in general were traumatised and demoralised by the war and considering the privations to which the whole population here had been subjected most of the adults were reasonably well in body though low in spirit. We had to prioritise and concentrate upon the children. The dispensary staff were told that I would only see adults if they were quite ill. Vague symptoms would be treated by hopeful cheerfulness plus multivite tablets three times daily and antimalarial drugs! They were told that I would concentrate upon the children who caused the greatest anxiety. This worked well. Hopes were raised, symptoms disappeared as the Under Fives Clinics got under way. These were places of miracles. Many children were barely alive, suffering with severe starvation, dehydration and anaemia. The latter seemed to arise mainly from untreated malaria. At first every symptom was treated with a different drug – a usual practice I found in such clinics. However, we taught staff that if the main underlying condition was dealt with the body had the power to heal. Anaemia did not call for iron, but for cure of the malaria which was causing the iron deficiency, as iron was stored in the body. Some children had a haemoglobin level of 10 per cent or lower with signs of heart failure. It was impractical to hospitalise them, and blood transfusion was even more impractical. We took a chance, having made sure that the nurses had sat down with the mother and gone through carefully the safe handling of the tiny child, emphasising correct feeding and especially fluid replacement using sugar-salt solution, as well as taking anti-malarials. At first there was some scepticism at the dearth of drugs and the extent of teaching but miracle upon miracle occurred. From our point of view the miracle was the devotion of the mothers who came regularly, often walking many miles with two or more little children beaming with hope and feeling that this they had achieved – which was, of course, true – with the help of God! I personally had never seen such a degree of anaemia survive and certainly not outside of hospital. At first when we explained that we wanted the mothers to bring their children to come even if they were not sick – for checks of weight, blood tests and so on they were sceptical. In time they streamed in nearly 200 children at a time, and the women were encouraging others to come who had given up hope for their child to recover. It was truly healing of body, emotions and spirit and as I reflect back this has applied to so many others with whom I have been involved who have been deprived of some of the essentials of life – love, security, hope, self-respect, faith. Our attitude to people to whom we relate is an important ingredient of the remedy – the value we place on people and a holistic approach.'

An early example of patients' and communities' desire to participate in the control of their affairs occurred at the Evangeline Booth Leprosy Hospital (EBLH) in Bapatla, in Andhra Pradesh, India. In a desire to have a say in their own affairs a large number of the residents of the leprosarium moved across the railway to set up Bethany, and become independent. They had been the victims of the social stigma of their disease. And even cure did not lead to rehabilitation. So in the 1950s, Bethany became a self-run institution for 350 patients and their families. Without income to purchase land, they settled on wasteland, built up shanties and went out begging. By the 1960s they formed the Bethany Colony Leprosy Association and set up a small clinic and school, lobbying the Indian Government for support. They developed industries such as hand-weaving and tailoring and their own programme for the sick and elderly, persuading some of those who had previously cared for them in EBLH, such as Gill and Graeme Griffiths, to help in setting up The Bethany Leprosy Society in the UK. Serving people rather than an institution can be a strong motivator.

Securing national staff for Salvation Army hospitals was not easy. In 1968 Australian officers, Captain (Dr) and Mrs Walter and Olive Lucas, with their two young children, were in charge of the Salvation Army hospital at Dhariwal in the Punjab and commenced their own plans to increase the role of the institution by community work in the district, using a mobile clinic. They included a chaplain in the team and the children flocked to hear his stories and songs. Staff workload increased rapidly but morale was high. Walter's vision was of the hospital under national leadership. Walter and Olive tired themselves out as they blended tradition with change and novelty. Walter's biography is titled *Man in a Hurry*. He managed to move quickly without causing friction. It was not an easy time. The Indo-Pakistan war affected them and both staff and money were short. Even more crippling was a strike of nurses which closed the hospital for two months. By the end of the strike both Lucases were exhausted. Olive determined to seek spiritual renewal while on holiday. At the same time the Spirit was moving in Walter's life. One night after an officers' meeting he was unusually distressed. The Holy Spirit convicted him and he surrendered his doubts, fears and human reasoning. He stepped out in simple faith. He was able to witness to fresh baptism by the Holy Spirit. That was just three months before his tragic passing, whilst undergoing surgery.[236]

The need for national leaders has already been mentioned. There was some response. A notable recruit was John Syamkutty, who joined the staff of the Evangeline Booth Leprosy Hospital at Puthencruz in Kerala, South India, in 1977, when there were 170 patients. He had prepared himself well. Syamkutty sought training under Paul Brand, the pioneer leprosy reconstructive surgeon at Vellore's Christian Medical College. In 1988, he obtained the Diploma in Tropical Medicine at Liverpool. For much of his decades of service he ran the Rural Health Centre and did it without subsidy. He has slowly changed the concept of the hospital to become the hub of community health schemes. Leprosy care was integrated into general hospital services, and later HIV treatment was added. It is not surprising that in 2004, Syamkutty was awarded the Gandhian Puraskaram for his special contribution to the development of leprosy care. Here is his own comment: 'When I joined Evangeline Booth Leprosy Hospital, I was not certain how long I would stay, but I gradually discovered that God wanted me here. What inspires me to work among the inmates, each with a burden of suffering, is the words of our Lord Jesus, "inasmuch as ye have done it unto one of the least of these my brethren, ye have done it unto me"' (Matthew 25:40).

Reference has already been made to the establishment of the Salvation Army Health Services Advisory Council at Ahmednagar. The Hospital Administrator's Capacity Development Programme has been a marked success. The first of the two-year courses was completed in 1999.

In earlier days all indigenous health systems were regarded as inferior to western ones, but this has slowly modified and traditional herbs and methods have been incorporated where effective. Dr Paul du Plessis reported the effectiveness of traditional eye-remedies.[237] Another modification has been the adoption of Intermediate Technology in rural communities. Such simple machinery as can be manufactured by local carpenters and blacksmiths has been advocated in seminars. Notably, Major (Dr) Jim Watt developed the 'Tippy Tap' to save water in hand washing. And a few traditional methods have been taught. For instance, at Howard Hospital Major Joan Gibson used the upright posture in delivery; whilst Dr Clarry Pratt at Chikankata advocated the kangaroo method in the care of low birth-weight babies.

Whilst officially The Salvation Army has stressed its non-political stance, most of its personnel have regarded it as vital to cooperate with governments, serving on committees and councils whenever possible. It was, therefore, difficult to decide when to criticise and resist government dictates. The Zimbabwean liberation war challenged Salvationists but Jim Watt and his colleagues weathered the challenge and The Salvation Army medical services continued.

---

[211] *WHO Alma Ata Declaration of Primary Health Care* World Heath Organisation, Geneva 1978

[212] *Report of Hospital Administration Consultation, New Delhi 1984* The Salvation Army IHQ, London

[213] *Facts for Life – A Communication Challenge* UNICEF1989

[214] Growth monitoring, oral rehydration, breast feeding, immunisation

[215] Traditional round thatched hut

[216] Watt, J. *Howard Beginnings (1998)* Unpublished

[217] Johnson, D. *Mufwa Cibuka (The Story of Ibbwe Munyama)* 1989

[218] McInnes, B. *Flag Across the Zambezi* The Salvation Army, Zambia 1997

[219] Jean is now Mrs Colonel Sidney Gauntlett

[220] Potgieter, S. 'Family Health Programmes in Rural South Africa' in *Rays of Hope*, Knowles, G. (Ed) The Salvation Army Australia Eastern Territory 1998 p. 103

[221] Campbell, I. *Voices of Our Global Family* The Salvation Army IHQ, London 2001

[222] Watt, J. *Howard Beginnings. (1998)* Unpublished

[223] Watt, J. *Vaenzi Vauya – The Strangers Have Come* 1988 Unpublished

[224] Wackernagel, G. 'Glimpses of Medical Work in Africa' *Officers' Review* 1937 p. 113ff

[225] Dunster, R. 'Drought and Hunger in Matabeleland' *The War Cry*, Australia. 14 Jan 1984

[226] du Plessis, P. *A Miracle of Change – Zaïre's Ray of Action Policy. All the World* 1984 p. 84

[227] *The Salvation Army Year Book 2002*

[228] *The Salvation Army Year Book 2005*

[229] *The Salvation Army Year Book 1975*

[230] *The Salvation Army Year Book 1983*

[231] *The Salvation Army Year Book 1980*

[232] *The Salvation Army Year Book 1971*

[233] *The Salvation Army Year Book 1952*

[234] Barnes, C. *The Salvation Army in Ghana* 1978 International Heritage Centre, London

[235] Gauntlett, S. Personal communication

[236] Rusher, L. 'Man in a Hurry' *The War Cry* Australia 1978.

[237] du Plessis, P. 'Some Traditional Tonga Eye Remedies' *Zambia Medical Journal* 1978 p. 94

Chapter eight

Specialisation

BEYOND the provision of a general health service at institutional or community level, The Salvation Army has, from the earliest days, responded to special medical needs, notably in emergency situations such as epidemics.

In the early years the most common of these was cholera. Booth-Tucker lost his wife, Louisa Mary, and also Colonel Arnolis Weerasooriya, the talented Singhalese who was his deputy, who both succumbed to the disease in Bombay. In South India outbreaks of cholera were so frequent that Dr Percy Turner sent out teams of medical students and nurses from the Catherine Booth Hospital, Nagercoil, and built a separate ward for victims, which could be accessed from the main road at the front of the hospital. Many years later when cholera broke out in Zambia, in 1990 and 1991, the Army provided clean water, blankets and powdered milk to affected areas. It sent teams from the mission hospital at Chikankata and together with the support of corps officers and League of Mercy members, supplied medicines, food, water and comfort to the afflicted people.

TB and leprosy

The Salvation Army has also responded to those affected by the two chronic infections, tuberculosis and leprosy. The causal bacilli for these diseases are so alike, they're almost indistinguishable from each other under a microscope. Both are greatly feared, but whilst the presence of tuberculosis is usually well hidden, it is quite the other with leprosy, where deformity is quickly apparent and since biblical days the disease has led to isolation, exclusion, stigma and hardship.

In 1909 the Indonesian government asked The Salvation Army to undertake the management of tuberculosis and leprosy hospitals. The first of these was at Pelantungan in the Prouw Valley of central Java. Five colonies for leprosy care were established within a year.[238] In the era before dapsone and other anti-leprotics, care was the only 'treatment', providing some sense of worth when depression and despair overtook those confined to isolation with an incurable and chronic infectious disease.[239] A wealthy Bandung benefactor, Mr K. Bosscha, left a sizeable legacy to The Salvation Army for Pelantungan in 1928, allowing for further development. There was great joy when lighting was installed, but disappointment when a trial, using radiation from the newly-installed X-ray machine for leprosy treatment, did not succeed. Captain Bridson, an officer with long years of experience with leprosy work in Indonesia, was sent to India for six months to advise on the establishment of leprosy work there. A home for children born to patients with leprosy was opened near the entrance to Pelantungan, parents having to part with their children shortly after birth, this being at that time the only known way of preventing them contracting the disease.

The Army had also been responsible for the leprosy colony at Palau si Tjanang in Sumatra since 1914 and this was still in effective service in 1973.[240] Situated on an island in the estuary of the Langkat River, it was the largest of the colonies under the Army's administration. Surrounding forests provided plenty of scope for hunting and fishing, the occasional crocodile or snake supplementing the daily rations.[241] The leprosy colony had begun through the efforts of a group of benevolent Medan people who approached the Army's public relations officer. This group, not the government, bore the substantial financial burden and supported in many practical ways. A Chinese patient at Palau si Tjanang remarked, 'Thank God I became ill, because if I had not come to this hospital I would never have known the Lord Jesus. Here I got to know him as my Saviour: my diseased body will be changed some day to a better one as the Lord has promised in his word.'[242] In countries like Indonesia where family solidarity is strong, or in India with its rigid caste system, leprosy, by permanently breaking the tie has made it easier for patients to become Christian when they choose.

Kundur, Sumatra, was another colony situated on an island in a river delta, the Musi, in South Sumatra. Local benefactors supplemented government financial support, helping it become another paradise, developed from a muddy swamp.[243] Semarang, situated on the outskirts of Surabaya, was another of the leprosy colonies under Army administration. A happy spirit in the Army meetings, with singing accompanied by a brass band, was a feature. There were plans to close this, and to merge it with Pelantungan (Broekhuis). However, the navy pre-empted the move by taking over the complex for their operations in 1941.[244]

There were 1,200 leprosy patients under the Army's care when the occupying Japanese forces officially proscribed The Salvation Army in 1942. Fear of infection meant that leprosy work suffered little interference. However, food and medicine ran short and many of the more able-bodied patients roamed the countryside, living by looting.[245]

Madge Unsworth documented the story of 'Sister', an unnamed Salvation Army officer, who had served at the William Booth Hospital, Semarang, with the Army's maternity and preventive work for young girls, and also at one of the leprosy colonies. It was the personalities of the patients in the colony, personalities illumined by the love of Christ, which left the deepest impression on her. 'She, like so many other devoted officers, saw fear transformed into calm triumphant trust, even with the youngest; an evil disease losing its power to affright and embitter.' In the colony garden grew a flower which opened only in the darkness, blooming for one brief night. The

Javanese call it the 'Evening Queen'. Salvation Army officers, their patients in mind, renamed it 'Faith in the Night'. [246]

In 1928 the Baptist-run leprosy hospital in Bapatla, Andhra, India, with 80 patients was handed over to The Salvation Army. It was renamed after Evangeline Booth and the first superintendent was Major C. N. Senaputra. The eponymous general hospital was only 13 miles away at Nidubrolu, and provided medical cover. The leprosy hospital is noted for the outstanding service given by missionary nurses. Brigadier Hilda Plummer (with the Indian name Jiva Ratnam) from the USA, refused to give up at retirement and settled in a nearby leprosy village, Bethany, attending the discharged patients in childbirth and illness. At a later date a husband and wife team, Captain and Mrs John Vincent from Australia, served when reconstructive surgery had commenced at the Catherine Booth Hospital, Nagercoil. The jeep ambulance would be loaded with suitable patients and driven the 700 miles. No hotels would give a night's hospitality, so they camped out together at the roadside.[247] Bapatla was central to government planning as the one inpatient facility in a large area. The hospital compound was divided in 1982/3, with the William Booth Junior College being developed in the larger section.

The Salvation Army's leprosy work in South India was extended in 1931 after the Cochin State health services asked it to assume responsibility for 200 patients with leprosy, who had been moved by Kerala State health authorities to a new 160-acre jungle facility at Koratty, near Adoor. Staff-Captain (Dr) William Noble from the USA Southern Territory took responsibility that year and appointed Captain Edwin Francis, an Australian, as the first superintendent, with Dr Margaret Round, from the United Kingdom, as medical officer. Captain Francis established a Salvation Army chapel in this government facility and soon had a 35-piece band. This highly regarded Salvation Army medical centre continued to care for 350 patients until it was absorbed by the government in 1955.

In 1936 Dr Noble established a temporary dispensary for leprosy patients near the village of Puthencruz in South-West India. With funding from the USA and a land purchase grant from International Headquarters, the dispensary was enlarged to a hospital, officially opened that year by General Evangeline Booth. Major Herbert Murray was appointed as manager. Two years later it was moved to a nearby 100-acre site and became a self-contained community, with a balance of complementary tasks performed by the patients, including gardening, rubber-tree management and crop cultivation. Through 28 years of service by Lieut-Colonel K. C. Joseph, the medical superintendent, and his wife, this leprosy facility was, by 1969, able to accommodate 200 patients. Since then, the small but busy Evangeline Booth General Hospital has been established on the edge of the estate.[248]

There is a happy tail-piece to this story of disability and isolation. In the 1960s Paul Brand adapted operations, designed for the treatment of polio palsies, to reanimate paralysed hands and feet of leprosy patients. Lieut-Colonel (Dr) Williams opened a ward in the Reconstructive Surgery Department of the Catherine Booth Hospital, Nagercoil and transferred patients from both Salvation Army leprosy hospitals. Soon other bodies with leprosy patients were sending them for similar surgery including the repair of facial deformity and ulcers of the feet.

It is pertinent to add here that there were so many convalescent patients from this type of surgery, as well as those treated following accidents in the home or on the road and even from congenital deformities, that a Vocational Training Centre was established at Aramboly, in a former branch hospital, eight miles from Nagercoil. In Nagercoil itself and at Trivandrum, two more Vocational Training Centres were opened for women. Aramboly became a factory under the brilliant management of Sundar Egbert, a polio cripple who had been a Catherine Booth Hospital patient himself.[249] It produced a variety of hospital metal furniture, whilst Nagercoil taught office skills and

Trivandrum compositing and printing. Sundar Egbert himself recognised that it was the fact of his own disability which made him so profound an inspiration to others. His romance, leading to a wheel-chair marriage to Saguntham, who had become the office manager of the Vocational Training Centre for women in Nagercoil, was itself an encouragement to all those engaged in the surgical programme at Catherine Booth Hospital.

It was a most rewarding enterprise as this personal reminiscence of Harry Williams records.

The acorn from the Catherine Booth Hospital, Nagercoil, planted eight miles away in an old branch hospital, had become a sapling, a vocational training centre. Now it was a fully-grown oak. I was asked to open a new section of the factory, which made all kinds of hospital furniture. With delightful self-effacement the manager deputed the foreman to show me round. As he moved to the first lathe he paused and silently held up his hands. At the wrists and the sides of each finger were fine white scars, almost invisible. I looked at the beatific smile on his face and then to those scarred hands and recognised him as one of the first leprosy patients I had operated upon. In that first batch of young men was a mix of backgrounds, of which leprosy was foremost. Initially, like the guests in Christ's parable, all except the leprosy patients found a pressing need to go home first. But we persisted and slowly a mixed family settled down to learn skills, which would make them creative once more. I learned that men who had been on the scrap heap did not have to be coaxed or cajoled to work. In that short pause I also remembered making those incisions in the first experimental operation. An active tendon from the finger was divided and brought out through the wrist incision. I ran a scalpel up that tendon three times, wondering whether the thin slips would be strong and smooth enough to provide a grip when re-routed to each finger. What a miracle it was to the patient when the plaster was removed and he learned to grasp, first

142

a tennis ball, and then tools. It was a happy day when 100 wheelchairs, made at Aramboly, were shipped to Ghana for its government's plan to give a free wheelchair to any who would thereby be able to earn a living.'[250]

This story can be rounded off with a brief review of other attempts to relieve disability by vocational training. Some of the earliest attempts in rehabilitation were for the blind and deaf, especially in the Caribbean and Kenya. In the latter there were three primary schools, with a total of 650 pupils and a high school with 163 more. The Salvation Army made provision for patients with orthopaedic disability, providing 50 places at 'Joyland', Kisumu, and 'Joytown', Thika, the latter with a high school. Another three centres catered for youth with multiple handicaps.

An unusual instance of specialised hospitals was instituted at the end of World War I, when the worldwide influenza epidemic broke out in the USA. Hospitals to care for influenza patients were established in 1918 within corps buildings at Roxbury, Massachusetts, and Charleston, West Virginia, and were maintained by a local physician and with community support.

One area in which The Salvation Army might have expected a role is psychiatry, but this has not evolved. However, it is interesting to find Dr Turner's interest in psychiatry blossoming during his years at IHQ. He accepted a post at the Tavistock Clinic, a pioneer centre. He was a Vice President of the London Medical Missionary Association and he and Mrs Turner paid regular visits to the Association's hostel in Highbury, to keep an eye on any Salvationist students.

The oldest of Salvation Army programmes to cover specific conditions or diseases, is that to combat alcoholism and other addictions. Alcoholism was such a common problem facing those who knelt at penitent forms in Salvation Army halls that it led to the opening of hostels for 'drying out' and rehabilitation. When 400 'saved drunkards' were marshalled on the platform at a meeting at the Exeter Hall in the Strand, the comment was made that 'it could easily have been 4,000 if space had been available!' Of course, much of the violence and brutality against Salvationists in the early days was from mobs stirred up by brewers whose trade was being ruined.[251]

A century later The Salvation Army in Sweden launched a campaign with the motto 'Down with King Alcohol' and Salvationists were on the streets with a petition urging better government policy to prevent or control addiction. Posters and brochures were everywhere and 15,000 people signed the petition.[252] It was, of course, in Sweden, that one of the earliest programmes was launched, at government behest, on the island of Kurön, with 25 per cent of its patients sent there from the courts.

Colonel (Dr) Sidney Gauntlett became an authority on the subject in London, where he published *The Salvationist and Alcohol* in 1985. Slowly, growing expertise and knowledge led to a comprehensive programme with good results. In a condition in which relapse was almost normal, a sustained recovery rate of 35 per cent was achieved. Some of these continued to serve others in the programme. Christopher Cook writes '… alcoholism is an unusual area of psychiatry … in that it deals with a group … who are not 'mad' but have often been thought of as bad!'[253] There is no definite boundary between normal social drinking and addiction, which led to The Salvation Army making abstinence a requirement for its members. In the transition to deliverance from dependence, sought and achieved, religious conversion was common.

Salvationist medical personnel participated with other international agencies in the formulation of new strategies for their treatment, care and rehabilitation. Alcohol was long regarded as a significant problem affecting those under the care of the Army. The need for greater emphasis on prevention, and the early treatment of those with an alcohol addiction became apparent. Among new programmes was a model in holistic treatment started in Costa Rica. North America broadened its programmes, often involving health, with social and counselling personnel. When the International Christian Federation for the Prevention of Alcoholism was formed, The Salvation Army became an inaugural member. Colonel (Dr) and Mrs Sidney Gauntlett, who had responsibility for the Army's response to alcohol and drugs, made a significant contribution. A study group also met and redrafted and strengthened the section on abstinence in the Army's manual for all Salvation Army soldiers: *Chosen to be a Soldier*.

In the large programmes developed in most Western countries, detoxification (detox) units were the first stage in treatment. The detox unit's primary purpose is to manage its clients' health risks and physical discomfort. Detox may be the entry point for early recovery for many individuals. For others, detox is the only service they desire. However, staff make every effort to encourage involvement in the full continuum of treatment offered.

USA

By far the largest treatment programme for alcoholism is in North America, where Harbor Light centres have been familiar for more than a century. The first recorded 'Inebriates' Home was opened in Toronto in 1886, which is not surprising, as the opening meeting of The Salvation Army in Canada recorded the conversion of 'Ash-barrel Jimmy' who was dragged feet first from a trash bin, profoundly drunk. He was sobered up and converted. He became a soldier and then served as an officer until his death 15 years later.

The Salvation Army developed a very large system of industrial homes throughout the USA, their purpose being to provide employment for homeless and workless men. In time it proved that the majority of those who applied for admission were heavy drinkers. At a great social congress in London in 1911, William Booth declared that the distinction between Army industrial homes for the unemployed, and 'homes for inebriates' or 'drunkards' had never existed in the United

States. In 1912 one experienced manager estimated that 80 per cent of the men who came to the Army industrial homes were 'victims to some extent of the drink appetite'.

Many managers took it upon themselves to direct special religious appeals to the heavy drinkers in their institutions. Officers counselled those working with drunkards to show kindness, patience and understanding in explaining religion to them, and advised that those who became converts and tried to renounce the 'foam of death' required still more kindness and patience. Special meetings were held to encourage new converts by the example of saved drunkards who had persevered. Industrial officers participated enthusiastically in the annual 'Boozers Parade' in Manhattan, which began in 1909 and continued until Prohibition became law in 1917.

The most exuberant warrior in the war against the 'Moloch of Drink' was Major W. W. Winchell, who organised the 'Drunkards Brigade' in the Jersey City Industrial Home in 1911. Winchell, with his assistant and five or six converts from the home, roamed the streets well into the early hours of the morning, collecting drunken men and carrying them back to the home in an industrial wagon, another type of ambulance! There they were sobered up with hot coffee or the major's famous 'cocktail', Worcester sauce, a raw egg and Epsom salts, and given solid food and lodgings.

Prohibition was introduced by the 18th Amendment to the Constitution when the USA entered World War I in 1917. In every country where The Salvation Army works, it is known for its specialisation amongst alcoholics and drink-related offenders. Such an organisation must be listened to, as in this report from late 1932, when the agitation for repeal of Prohibition was at its height:

'In New York before prohibition The Salvation Army would collect 1,200 to 1,300 drunkards in a single night and seek to reclaim them. Prohibition immediately reduced this number to 400 and the proportion of actual intoxicants on the day selected from 19 out of 20 to no more than seven in all. In

1920, the first year of prohibition, The Salvation Army took charge of the Bowery Hotel. For two years there was co-operation between the Army and the police but despite that fact, there was much trouble with the lodgers owing to vice and drunkenness. Every night and especially on Saturday night, men had to be ejected for creating disturbances and owing to the intoxication of the occupants, the bed linen was often left in a filthy condition.'[254]

The change in treatment, which occurred with increasing knowledge of the nature of alcoholism, was worldwide. This can be illustrated by a glance at the process in the USA. The Salvation Army has always regarded alcohol as its particular enemy. In the 1930s the conviction that the Army had a special divine calling to rescue the drunkard, was combined here and there around the country with a new spirit of professionalism, which recognised that alcoholism is caused by special factors, physical perhaps, certainly mental and emotional and that understanding these things will help officers to guide the drinking man to a permanent solution.

Despite the energetic sincerity of the 'great-hearts' of the Boozers' Parades and not gainsaying the real conversions from these efforts, some had come to the conclusion, in the 1930s, that simply sobering a man up with prayer did not cure him of what was in most cases an addiction. In 1937 Adjutant Roy Barber was appointed to a special committee comprised of leading social agencies in Boston to study the problem of the homeless alcoholic. The Army was the only private agency represented. Programmes specifically designed to deal with alcoholism in a thorough manner were formed within the Army. In 1939 the Detroit Harbor Light Corps opened its doors. It was the first Salvation Army facility in the territory specifically designed for the treatment of drunkards. There was also a small, family alcoholic programme in the Army corps in Holland, Michigan. In that same year, 1939, in Philadelphia, Major R. E. Baggs started the first Alcoholics Anonymous group in any Salvation Army centre in the country.[255]

In 1942, George Purdum, divisional welfare officer in Philadelphia, joined the Research Council on Problems of Alcohol, part of the American Association for the Advancement of Science. The first issue of its *Bulletin*, two years later, noted that Brigadier Chester Brown, head of the Army's social welfare department in New York City, chaired a discussion in that city in June 1944 on 'The Church and the Alcoholic', part of a national symposium on alcoholism. At the second symposium, held in Cleveland later in the same year, Major Peter Hofman contributed to a discussion on group aids in therapy. The association that allowed the largest number of officers to develop an understanding of alcoholism and its treatment was the Summer School of Alcoholic Studies of the Yale University Laboratory of Applied Bio-dynamics. The famous 'Yale School' was a major influence on the developing alcoholic rehabilitation programme within The Salvation Army.

In 1954, General Albert Orsborn confessed that though he had seen many individual drunkards set free by the power of God, until he visited the USA he had not seen the problem *en masse*, involving hundreds of derelicts.[256]

The Harbor Light Centers became most sophisticated in the variety of their treatments. One of the most unusual is recorded at the Harbor Light in Cleveland Ohio, where Captain Edward Dimond used music in the programme, clients being taught to play a variety of instruments. He even drew the famous composer, Emil Söderström, into creating a Harbor Light Music Library.[257]

Converted alcoholics sometimes became involved in running programmes. One of the most memorable was transformed alcoholic Walter McClintock, who became an envoy and then Superintendent of the Chicago Harbor Light Center for 14 years. He was admitted to the Order of the Founder in 1988, a year before his retirement. The citation for this honour reads: 'Envoy McClintock, a compassionate, tireless worker in a challenging and sometimes desperate part of the

Lord's vineyard, has inspired hundreds of alcoholics to forsake the old life and find salvation'.

The Detroit Harbor Light has networked with the City of Detroit Health Department to provide confidential testing and assessment of clients on site. Harbor Light case managers administered a health risk assessment to clients and an educational orientation for those entering the residential programme about HIV/Aids and other sexually transmittable diseases. The physician under contract and nursing staff could follow up with those who needed, or were already taking, medication. Nursing staff could attend to special dietary needs as a result of treatment for HIV/Aids and other diseases. Similar medical services were provided for residents of the Harbor Light Center in Indianapolis, where a medically supervised sub-acute residential detoxification programme developed '24/7'. In addition to the medical supervision provided, there was a doctor on call 24 hours a day and clients were newly admitted daily.

In 2004 alone, 1,270 persons were served in the detox programme associated with the USA Central Territory. The majority of staff were committed Christians who encouraged the addicted people in their care to commit their lives to Jesus Christ. This evangelical approach was supported and aided by the corps through an active church and chaplaincy office located in the centre.

Detox Unit staff see many individuals in various states of drug- and alcohol-induced impairment. Some are unresponsive to care for a time, while their systems are cleared of the intoxicant. Clients are frequently anxious and suffering from depression. Staff can feel challenged by negative attitudes until the addicted individuals are able to think more clearly. All unit employees have to respond to each individual in a kind and caring way, demonstrating the love of Christ in every case. At the same time, many addicted persons have learned to manipulate people and must be dealt with in an atmosphere of 'tough love'. This is sometimes very hard.

The physical condition of some of the people coming in for treatment presents another difficult challenge. Some addicts enter detox violently sick, with vomiting and severe nausea. Staff have to work through these situations, demonstrating a loving attitude toward all the persons they served; they need to remain non-judgmental, regardless of an addict's habits or attitudes. During their stay in detox, clients are coached on fundamentals of nutrition and other necessary skills such as finding employment and positive inter-personal relationships. One common outcome of alcoholism is marriage breakdown. Once a person is ready to be released, a case manager helps him or her find a place to stay in the community.

Response, both from those served and from the community is usually overwhelmingly positive. Feedback from former clients often refers to staff as 'angels of mercy', who were frequently credited with helping to save their clients' lives. The staff members receive great satisfaction from seeing the success stories from some of the clients.

At the end of the 20th century there were 92 Harbor Light Centers in the USA and Canada.

New Zealand

In New Zealand, the Army pioneered in the field of alcoholism in 1908, when the government asked it to provide an institution suitable to receive inmates, under the Habitual Drunkards Act of 1906. The work on Rotoroa Island, in the Hauraki Gulf, had some success, and Colonel Walls claimed in his evidence to the Royal Licensing Commission of 1946 that 70 per cent of men committed to the island did not return a second time. However, under the appropriate legislation, committals to the island were largely penal. Unless a client committed himself, or a relative did so, he had to be sent from a court for some legal offence such as drunkenness, indecency, obscene language or vagrancy and the minimum term for a man committed by the courts in those days was one year. With the growing realisation that alcoholism was a disease rather than a crime, this penal approach was subject to criticism. There were complaints that the inmates were not receiving adequate treatment other than enforced separation from alcohol and that they were merely being dried out before going back to the pubs on their eventual release.

In the early 1950s, Commissioner Hoggard, who had some experience of the new approaches to alcoholism developing in the USA, recognised the need for change. He pushed ahead with the upgrading of buildings and equipment. He sensibly urged cooperation with Alcoholics Anonymous and, in an inspired choice, sent Captain Robert McCallum to Rotoroa as manager. McCallum is a good example of the picturesque characters who have often come under the influence of the Army and found in it a remarkable sphere of service. He had served in both the Merchant Navy and the Royal Navy in two world wars, had been a champion boxer, had seen service in every continent and had himself become an alcoholic. He was converted in a meeting of the Richmond Mission, Christchurch, and the good folk there referred him to The Salvation Army when he was transferred to Devonport. He was accepted for full-time service in The Salvation Army as an officer on his discharge from the navy, and had several successful terms as a corps officer before going to Rotoroa. He did outstanding work on the island with the help of an equally devoted wife. Their evangelical zeal was tempered by sound common sense, great practical ability and an instinctively right approach with men. In this context, the value was shown of a non-medical, purely pastoral approach.

Brigadier A. 'Scotty' Grant, McCallum's successor at Rotoroa, was just the right man to carry on the work. He came from a very poor family in the north of Scotland, and his father was an alcoholic. On the way to becoming one himself, he went out to New Zealand as a young man in 1931, under the Army's immigration scheme. He was converted and became an officer, serving for many years in boys' homes. His work on Rotoroa won for him, to his own surprise and embarrassment, the vocational service award of the Auckland Rotary Club in 1973.

First in New Zealand, then in Australia, the approach became more medical under the direction of Lieut-Colonel (Dr) Bram Cook. He became Chief Secretary in New Zealand in 1954, after nearly a quarter of a century of medical missionary service in India. Deeply interested in the medical aspects of alcoholism and able to write authoritatively on it, his expertise was recognised nationally. He was one of the founders of the National Society on Alcoholism and was asked to be a member of the Government Co-ordinating Council on Alcoholism.

At a government-sponsored conference on alcoholism, held in August 1956, the contributions of both McCallum and Cook were convincing proof that the Army was now fully alive to the most up-to-date methods of tackling the problem of alcoholism. With the full backing of Lieut-Commissioner Harewood, the Territorial Commander, Cook was able to embark on a new development, quite unprecedented in New Zealand. This was the establishment, in 1959, of a residential clinic, appropriately called 'The Bridge', situated in the centre of Wellington within walking distance of a score of hotels.

Here again Cook's medical expertise and administrative drive needed to be backed up by the right manager on the spot. Envoy Bernard Mitchell, another converted alcoholic, was the man. A down-to-earth figure with a tender heart but a practical outlook, Mitchell was well qualified to distinguish the true alcoholic from the itinerant in search of accommodation and to deal with men from all walks of life who came to the 'Bridge' for help. His work was consolidated and extended by Captain David Brinsdon.

Major Noel Manson, who was an energetic president of the New Zealand Association of Social Workers in 1954 was a recipient of one of the coveted Churchill Fellowships, as well as a Nuffield Scholarship for the study of alcoholism overseas.

Out of the experience gained from the Wellington 'Bridge' there developed a nationwide Bridge Programme, officially recognised under the Alcoholism and Drug Addiction Act 1966, comprising an extensive network of clinics, hostels and rehabilitation centres, utilising the services of as many disciplines and professions as are able to contribute to the diagnosis and prognosis of the disease. Commissioner (Dr) Harry Williams, the TC, with his own medical background, was able to give impetus to the programme in the early 1970s, and also arranged for the secondment, for six months, to New Zealand, of Brigadier Joshua Monk of Canada, a graduate of the Yale University School of Alcoholic Studies.

By 1980 a total of nearly 700 alcoholics was passing through the programme annually. Its underlying philosophy is expressed in this statement of belief: 'We welcome all that scientific research has contributed to the understanding and rehabilitation of alcoholics. Our programme needs the services of doctors, psychologists and social workers, and welcomes the successes obtained by various approaches used by other organisations. It would, however, be denying our experience, and therefore unscientific, if we failed to give a distinctive witness to the power of God to transform people's lives, and this includes the alcoholic.'

The Salvation Army Bridge Women's Auxiliary (SABWA) was founded by Mrs Major Winifred Manson, and run by trained volunteer women helpers to provide a strong supportive service to the wives and families of men under treatment and also to those families where the suffering alcoholic has not yet come forward for assistance with his problems. This has become an integral part of the programme. At the Arawhata Recuperation Centre in the Akatarawa Valley, provision is made for wives to visit husbands. Women alcoholics, too, are now benefiting from the programme in both Auckland and Wellington. The widespread ramifications of the present Bridge programme stand as a tribute to the many devoted officers and lay people involved in the work, and to the way in which The Salvation Army has adapted to fulfil a pressing need.

Australia

A Bridge Programme began in Sydney in August 1964 with the opening of the Nithsdale clinic at the back of the territorial headquarters building. The clinic was managed by Captain Cedric Bedwell, who reported 327 enquiries in the first three months of its existence. Group therapy classes were held daily, using the 12 steps of the Alcoholics Anonymous programme. Medical care was provided for men in the hospital ward of Foster House.

The programme was later extended to include a residential clinic, Bridge House, in Redfern and a country centre, Selah Farm, at Chittaway Point. In the quiet and peace of country life, surrounded by everything that was natural and good, it was felt that the men could rediscover themselves and their real desires and expectations. A larger farm, Miracle Haven, was purchased in 1969. Originally a country club, it could accommodate 100 men. Selah Farm was then used for women alcoholics and drug addicts. A further step was taken in equipping the Bridge programme, by the transformation of the William Booth Hostel for working men into the William Booth Institute, the heart and headquarters of the Bridge Programme. It replaced both the Nithsdale Clinic and Bridge House. The Booth Hostel was a rather bleak, institutional-looking building in Darlinghurst, but when the architects and painters had finished, it was startlingly different. Lines flowed, spaces opened out, colours shouted triumphantly. It asserted faith in the future and recognition of people as individuals of worth. The Institute included three service centres: the treatment floor where alcoholics and drug addicts received hospital care, the half-way house where male participants in the programme could live and the youth floor, designated the John Irwin Hostel, which provided accommodation for boys who had been in trouble in the courts. Women clients of the Bridge Programme were accommodated on the Bridge Floor at nearby Samaritan House. There was a carefully worked-out programme. The majority of alcoholics and drug addicts suffer from malnutrition by the time they seek help but in all cases they had to realise and admit that they were ill. The clients were first admitted to the hospital floor of the William Booth Institute for assessment of their medical condition. There was need for urgent medical treatment in some cases, a need for physical building-up in most cases.

When ready to leave hospital, clients were considered for admission to Miracle Haven or Selah Farm. Sometimes they preferred to go back to life in the community and to attend regular group meetings at the Booth Institute. Each individual patient needed to make a personal choice. Treatment at the farms was slow. Usually the clients were in poor health, needing a high protein diet and the quiet balm of caring for animals and plants. It was here that group therapy, later applied in other settings, proved effective. When a patient had gained confidence and felt able to live alone, he or she could return to the city and rejoin the work force. During this time accommodation was provided at the Booth Institute or Samaritan House until confidence to move out into the community was established. Contact with the Booth Institute was maintained, with clients attending chapel and group therapy meetings as they felt necessary.

A great number of people have gone through the Bridge Programme each year, some of them young, others growing old. There are professional people and those with little education but a comradeship develops among them because they have known despair together and then hope. The Bridge Programme is only part of the Army's work for alcoholics in Australia. Virtually every corps has its history of quiet personal work with alcoholics and their families.

South Africa
In South Africa, The Salvation Army developed a certified retreat for alcoholics on an 800-acre farm 26 miles from Cape Town. This was used by government, with court referrals. Martin, driving a powerful sports car was driving too fast to

take a sharp bend and crashed into an oncoming vehicle, killing a boy. He was devastated and gladly downed the brandies his friends offered him. He was soon an addict. A wise magistrate gave him a year's sentence, not to jail, but to The Salvation Army's Mulder's Vlei, where there were no high walls or locked gates. He found himself with 80 others who swapped similar sad stories with him as they worked in the orchards, kitchen garden or main farm. Slowly, good food, medical care and Christian grace brought more than half the company to triumph over drunken failure. Conversion gave a new purpose to life and Martin was one of those happy men. [258]

United Kingdom

In the United Kingdom, the most recent extension to the Alcoholism and Addiction Service was located in the shadow of Canary Wharf in London's Docklands. Riverside House became a specialist hostel, providing accommodation for 40 men in en-suite single room accommodation. Each room was located in a cluster of four or five, with a shared kitchen and lounge available in each cluster. In addition, the hostel provided a number of communal areas, including a recreation area and an IT suite. Matthew House, adjacent to the main building, was constructed as a block of 20 one-bedroom self-contained flats.

Riverside House became owned and maintained by the Salvation Army Housing Association (SAHA). The Salvation Army, as managing agent, was responsible for the day-to-day management of the centre and for the delivery of the programme, with specialist staff providing support and assisting with the transition into a long-term drug/alcohol free lifestyle. Admission policies defined the target group: single homeless men dealing with drug/alcohol issues and who are 'dry', some being referred direct from detoxification or rehabilitation. Others would have been released from the prison system, having been involved in a drug/alcohol prison service programme. Each referral was interviewed and risk-assessed prior to admission. Whilst each was considered on individual circumstances, issues such as those using non-prescription drugs or alcohol remained.

In summary, The Salvation Army has had marked success in treating alcoholics. Though reports vary, they record success of up to the 77 per cent recorded by a visiting committee to the Rotoroa centre. Results have been poor with other addictions. The 'World's End' centre which opened in London in 1967 closed in 1970, reporting that each addict needed a personal assessment and adaptation of programme, whilst relapse was common. It must be remembered that for each addict saved from dereliction there was commonly a spouse, children and community with a problem solved.

Disaster

Sporadic medical relief in disasters has always been attempted but in recent years The Salvation Army has responded to the needs of victims of disaster worldwide on a regular basis. The 'knee-jerk' response has always come from Salvationists on the spot in all parts of the world. Here are some examples from New Zealand.

A pattern of service, which the Army was to adopt, had its beginnings in the bush fires, which devastated the area around Raetihi in March 1918. Freak gales, combined with the annual burn-off by dairy farmers wanting to increase their acreage, led to uncontrollable fires, so extensive that the smoke caused a weird yellow pall to appear over Wellington, more than 320km away. Nine sawmills and several farms were destroyed, as well as 58 houses in the township. Three people lost their lives. Captain Griffin of the Raetihi Corps, together with the Anglican priest, organised bands of volunteers to save a few houses and provide temporary relief. Immediately the news reached Wellington, Commissioner Hodder despatched a relief team under Major Andrew Carmichael and Staff-Captain John Dixon, and the team was entrusted by the authorities with the task of setting up a relief centre in the large drill hall which had survived the fire. Food, clothing, blankets and bedding and other necessities were procured from all over New Zealand and distributed by the Army team. Even while many of the stricken inhabitants were still living in tents, sheds and other makeshift shelters, they had to endure some of the worst snowstorms and one of the harshest winters on record. The Army team, in co-operation with government and local authority agencies, continued its emergency relief for as long as possible, with generous financial assistance from the general public.

Another example of emergency relief work was at the Hawke's Bay earthquake in February 1931. A relief team was sent from Territorial Headquarters as soon as the news of the disaster came through. The Napier Corps building and the Salvation Army Maternity Hospital were wrecked, fortunately without casualties. The Army relief team helped with the many homeless people, and the nurses organised house-to-house visitations to find and assist those needing first aid. Brigadier A. Greene was food controller for the whole area and Major Annie Gordon of Auckland was chairman of a committee which arranged accommodation for refugee families from Napier. Ensign Philip Norman, the corps officer at Napier, played a big part in the relief measures and later was succeeded by Ensign and Mrs Goffin, who helped greatly in the rehabilitation of the corps.

Along with other religious and social service organisations, The Salvation Army was called on to undertake a great expansion of its relief activities during the years of the great economic depression. A commentator of this period in New Zealand's history, A. J. S. Reid, has written: 'No church responded to the need for charitable relief as wholeheartedly as did The Salvation Army. It has always regarded its mission as particularly to the poor and consequently it was better prepared both organisationally and in mental attitude to cope with the crisis. In every centre it had homes for men, women and children.'[259]

Over the years, and throughout the world, refugee crises have mushroomed, with more than 20 million refugees worldwide, the majority being women and children, fleeing terror, famine, and genocide; often having seen their loved ones suffer violent death. Medical aid, both preventive and curative, became one of the Army's major components in responding to the world's worst suffering.

Disturbances in Cambodia in 1985 led to a major movement of refugees into Thailand. A consortium of Christian relief agencies, including World Relief, World Vision, World Concern and Christian and Missionary Alliance, approached the Army requesting the services of Major Eva den Hartog to head up a medical team in southern Thailand. The Army joined the consortium and success in the joint venture led to further collaborative efforts in other refugee situations.

One of the most recent of these was the 2004 tsunami in the Indian Ocean. Rehabilitation work, including rebuilding villages and providing fishermen with boats; community health and counselling training were significant programmes which continue still. The people have been helped to find their own solutions. Corps and individual soldiers have found a new ministry.

Training

Finally, there is quite a different type of specialisation; medical education of many kinds. The Salvation Army's programme for training nurses at five of its hospitals in India is flourishing. The state has taken control of the curriculum and even introduced standard fees, for nurses can travel the world and earn good salaries. Indian nurses, mostly graduates of Salvation Army schools, began taking diplomas in teaching and administration. This led to the appointment of Brigadier Sugantham as Nursing Superintendent at Nagercoil and to Major Grace Punjalal taking over at Anand.

Reference has already been made to the development of dentistry in South America. In India, an efficient dentistry department was brought into being at Nagercoil with the arrival, in the 1930s, of Captain and Mrs James Kennedy from the UK. She had been a Sister at the Glasgow Royal Infirmary, whilst he had a successful practice in dental mechanics. Mrs Kennedy took over the European Nursing Home, whilst he opened a well-equipped Dental Department. His ability in dental prosthetics brought a stream of patients to the Nursing Home. An Indian dental surgeon took over when the Kennedys were transferred to district evangelism.

The Salvation Army hospitals gradually gave a lead in the training of paramedics in a variety of disciplines. These were linked by the Christian Medical Association of India (CMAI), which ran the courses, held the examinations and issued the diplomas, which were registered by the government. Even before unified training was started, Major Ruth Woolcott, from Canada, was training laboratory technicians at Dhariwal. Radiography at Anand, with Captain Ken Tutton, and at Nagercoil, with Captain Keith Wylie, was under the CMAI banner. Then there was a first in physiotherapy, which has already been mentioned as Dr Beer's last venture. Lieutenant Jethulal was the first graduate and many more followed and found employment in the physiotherapy departments, which sprang up in the medical college hospitals.

The discipline developed further at Nagercoil, where Mrs Rosemary Collins, MCSP, ran a school from which Captain (Dr) Ruby Samuel was one of the first graduates. Ruby went on to qualify at Vellore and ran obstetrics at Nagercoil in succession to Major (Dr) Hazel Scott who had followed Dr Sarah at Catherine Booth Hospital. Mrs Collins had a constant stream of young orthopaedic patients, who progressed through occupational therapy to the provision of prostheses, from callipers to artificial limbs. At this point, enter Major George Scott, BSc, who had training at the Royal Orthopaedic Hospital at Stanmore in vocational training. Eventually there were three Vocational Training Centres. In this, George had the cooperation of Sundar Egbert, who had been the quality control officer at the Swedish Red Cross Centre at Vellore.[260]

The United Nations proclaimed 1981 as the International Year of Disabled Persons (IYDP). According to their statistics there were at that time 450 million disabled persons in the world. 'The most tragic aspect of childhood disability is its needlessness,' the bulletin explained. 'Most impairments are preventable, and can be eliminated through immunisation, medical care, adequate nutrition and education.' The Salvation Army, motivated by the belief that each person is a child of God, continued to make a frontal assault on disability by aggressive programmes, which promoted health and well-being in order to further the prevention of needless impairments.

Representative of many of the Army's front-line ministries to the disabled around the globe were its leprosaria in India, schools in Hong Kong, schools for the blind in Jamaica and Kenya, a sheltered workshop in Calcutta, homes for physically disabled children at Oji River and Benin in Nigeria, vocational training for physically disabled women in India and a primary school for the physically disabled in Tanzania.

The Army has, in recent years in the 'first world' mandated that new buildings, and major renovations, incorporate architectural provision, such as ramps and other arrangements to make facilities and services easily available for persons with physical handicaps. Mention has been made of the wheelchairs, made at the Army's vocational training centre for the handicapped in India, and shipped to Ghana. As if in anticipation of the International Year of Disabled Persons (IYDP), a new hostel for the handicapped was opened in Adelaide, Australia, towards the close of 1980. Known as Centennial Court, the building accommodated permanent residents as well as an assessment centre for the Association for the Intellectually Retarded.

The opening of an institute for the blind, the first of its kind in Congo, Brazzaville, further marked the IYDP. This was in response to a request from the government, and made possible through financial help from Germany. In Nigeria, the first phase of a new rehabilitation centre for disabled children, had accommodation for 12 with plans for extensions to accommodate 50 children. The first two children walked out of the home with the aid of calipers and returned to their communities. Six children received corrective surgery and learned to walk again.[261]

A significant development was the cultivation of community-based rehabilitation programmes, which developed later in Ghana, Pakistan and elsewhere, which had their beginnings during the IYDP. The Salvation Army's century-long commitment to persons with disabilities placed it in the vanguard of meaningful ministries in response to the United Nations proclamation.

Salvation Army endeavour multiplied around the world as the result of a major administrative advance in 1978, related to the funding of the Army's international projects. Responding to the need for a conduit to link benefactor and beneficiary among the world's 'have needs' people and the 'have resources' public, General Arnold Brown established the Planning and Development Department at International Headquarters. It had a fourfold mandate:

- Handle and stimulate project applications from all needy territories
- Train officers for development projects
- Give technical assistance to territories in formulating new plans
- Publicise what is being done in this field, what help is needed in personnel and finance and liaise with and inform the major donor agencies throughout the world in like manner.

The transforming impact of this programme on countless lives through the following years ranks it as one of the landmark developments of the Army. This department recruited experts in health, agriculture, education, and in project planning and handling. It set up immediate linkages and liaised with major donor and development agencies such as SAWSO, USAID, CIDA, SIDA, NORAD and many others.

Copies of *The Salvation Army Year Book* show how great is the support received annually for new schemes.

---

[238] Bridson, T. *Lightening the Lepers' Load* SP&S, London 1946

[239] Richards, M. *It Began with Andrews* SP&S, London 1971 p. 140

[240] Coutts, F. *The Better Fight – The History of The Salvation Army Vol VI 1914-1946* Hodder & Stoughton, London 1973 p. 270

[241] Brouwer, M. *History of The Salvation Army in Indonesia* The Salvation Army, Australia 1996 p. 118

[242] Ibid p. 119

[243] Ibid

[244] Ibid

[245] Coutts, F. *The Better Fight – The History of The Salvation Army Vol VI 1914-1946* Hodder & Stoughton, London 1973 p. 227

[246] Unsworth, M. *The Flower Called Faith in the Night* SP&S, London 1946 p. 7

[247] Williams, H. Personal recollection

[248] Rader, H. *Historical Dictionary of The Salvation Army* John G. Merritt (Ed), Scarecrow Press, Lanham, Maryland 2006.

[249] Yesudasen, U. *Brokenness as a Way of Blessing* ICSA Books, Chennai, India 2008

[250] Gariepy, H. *Mobilized for God, The History of The Salvation Army Vol VIII (1977-1994)* The Salvation Army, Atlanta, GA 2000 p. 59

[251] Ibid p. 335

[252] Ibid p. 146

[253] Cook, C. *Mad, Bad or Sad* Christian Medical Fellowship 2006

[254] Booth, S. *To Be or Not To Be* p. 11

[255] McKinley, E. *Somebody's Brother: A History of The Salvation Army Men's Social Service Department* Lewiston, NY, The Edwin Mellen Press 1986

[256] Coutts, F. *The History of The Salvation Army Vol VII 1946-1977* Hodder & Stoughton, London 1986 p. 85

[257] Ibid p. 116

[258] Coutts, F. *The History of The Salvation Army Vol VII 1946-1977* Hodder & Stoughton, London 1986 p. 117

[259] Bradwell, C. *Fight the Good Fight – The Story of The Salvation Army in New Zealand* A. H. & A. W. Reed, Wellington 1982 pp. 95, 96

[260] Williamson, V. *The Inside Story* New Zealand

[261] Gariepy, H. *Mobilized for God. The History of The Salvation Army Vol VIII (1977-1994)* The Salvation Army, Atlanta, GA 2000 p. 59

Chapter nine

Paradigm shifts in health services – a new disease appears

AN international conference in 1978 at Alma Ata, the capital of Kazakhstan, produced a major advance in world consensus on priorities in health. Although The Salvation Army was not represented, the resolution issued from the conference had its impact. Its goal, 'Health for all by 2000' was further explained as 'all the peoples of the world should attain a level of health that would permit them to live socially and economically profitable lives'. Primary health care was seen as the way to reach the target. The Army would have to make changes and it did. By 1980, IHQ articulated a policy already developing. Paul du Plessis, the Medical Adviser at International Headquarters in the 1980s, aware of the winds of change, kept a watch on worldwide trends in Salvation Army health services. It was apparent that without a change in policy some hospitals would not survive. There was a growing awareness that health, generally, was a more profound issue than medicine and surgery or even community health schemes.

There was another cry; a plea for a return to the close link between evangelism and health of earlier days. In 1982, Major (Dr) Herb Rader, CMO of Catherine Booth Hospital (CBH) Nagercoil, addressed the Executive Officer's Councils of The South East India Territory on 'Where are we going in medical work?' 'I have a dream,' he said, 'I have a dream of a beautiful hospital where the sick can come knowing they will receive the best possible care, where the love of Christ is demonstrated, where committed Christians explain how to be born again, where the curable are led to the fullness of life, and the dying are gently guided into the arms of Jesus'. He observed that very few Salvationists saw the hospital as a base for evangelism, or for community health. However, he called for a careful examination of the potential dangers of an unquestioning adoption of community health. He feared that the 'healing equals salvation notion' being promoted in the literature could divert the Army from its prime task. Community medicine must be complemented by evangelism.[262]

Captain (Dr) Ian Campbell was Chief Medical Officer at Chikankata Hospital in Zambia when HIV/Aids burst on the world scene, with particularly dramatic effect in Africa. The new epidemic disease was without cure and devastated families and communities. In the hospital, a programme of care and counselling was developed, which proved to be a pilot scheme, capable of being shared internationally. With help from the Federal Government in Campbell's native Australia, teams from International Headquarters led seminars, stimulating the cry for more.

Aids is caused by a virus, which, as its name, Acquired Immune Deficiency Syndrome, implies, opens the victim to every other infection around. As Henry Gariepy stated, it has 'become the new leprosy of the modern world' [263] Every Army territory was asked by General Burrows to make its response to the crisis. Major (Dr) Paul du Plessis, as IHQ Medical Adviser, had convened the 1987 IHQ consultation on HIV. He also wrote an article, published in the Army's international journal, *The Officer,* providing a discussion paper to challenge Army leaders, and assisted the first co-ordinated response at Chikankata, where he had served previously.

One of the participants in the 1987 consultation, Major Trevor Smith of the British Territory had already circulated a document *Aids Care – Pastoral Guidelines* arising from his own care of Aids patients. This was revised, extended and published by IHQ. The demand for this handbook was so great that a reprint was required within months of its publication. The development of Major Smith's own ministry to HIV-positive people, covering two decades, is documented in the UK Territory publication *The Falling Leaf* (2004).

In the same year, 1987, the All-Africa Medical Consultation was held in Zaïre, welcoming delegates from Zambia, Kenya, Nigeria, Ghana, South Africa, Congo and Zaïre, as well as the USA and the UK. The consultation addressed the subjects of primary health care, child survival and alcoholism. Aids was emerging as a major issue, but other important health issues were not neglected. Following the consultation, a manifesto for the Army's health services in Africa was prepared, and this was considered by all the African territories.

Hong Kong was the venue for a South Pacific and East Asia Consultation in 1989, with a focus on the theology of health, healing and wholeness. Human behaviour, as an important factor in the cause of Aids, and the value of corps-based health programmes, was stressed.

Captain (Dr) Campbell was asked to address the 1988 London Conference on the Global Impact of Aids. He spoke of methods the Army used for care and prevention in a rural Zambian community, highlighting the importance of compassionate support and emphasising that, 'the management of Aids at Chikankata Hospital has followed a pattern of home-based care, with hospital intervention where required. It has explored the principle of patient care as being the best method of mounting a preventive programme, as well as expressing appropriate compassionate support. By extending patient care from the hospital into the community, opportunities for prevention through education and community surveillance become more frequent.' He also reported on the specific Aids unit within Chikankata Hospital, which maintained close contact with both patients and their relatives.

Later Alison Rader, Community Development Consultant to International Headquarters, speaking about home and community care, reported on an aspect of the crisis that resists statistical analysis, the hidden toll on relationships in the family and in the larger community:

'Aids is today,' she said, 'a devastating global epidemic, with over 30 million people infected with HIV. There is a need for face-to-face communication, the holding of hands, and the sharing of emotions and deep understanding across cultural, economic and social boundaries. We need to assist people in coping with the relational issues this disease raises, a collective consciousness of guilt and fear, and the implications of a person in crisis. The Salvation Army has been exploring these questions since 1987 in different places around the world, with a facilitation team since 1991. As responses have emerged, our pool of team members has been growing into an increasingly broad-based international group. Technology alone cannot address this issue, because HIV and Aids are fundamentally about brokenness and healing within relationships. As we enter into the experience of suffering, and the search for hope, we must help people face the journey of dying.'[264]

Salvationists from around the world gathered in San Francisco in June 1990 to attend The Salvation Army's Aids Consultation with the theme 'Aids and The Salvation Army: Determining Global Patterns of Response'. Coordinated by Ian Campbell, it was held in conjunction with the sixth International Conference on Aids convened in the city. 'We need to have organised panic in reaction to the Aids epidemic,' urged the captain in attacking the complacency many had toward the crisis. Major (Dr) Herbert Rader, Medical Director of the Booth Memorial Medical Center, New York affirmed: 'We care for the pariahs of society. We are strategically placed throughout the world and I believe, with God's help, we can make a difference.' The consultation made recommendations for supporting and developing Army programmes worldwide, allowing participants to construct action plans for use at local levels. Commissioner Paul Rader, Territorial Commander, speaking at the conclusion of the conference, said, 'Aids ministries are consistent with our mission. If the Army doesn't care, who will?'[265]

The Army's assault on the Aids pandemic continued in June 1991 with its conference on Aids, held in Switzerland. It was attended by 114 delegates involved in related programmes around the world. The theme was 'From Fear to Hope – An Integrated Response to Aids'. The conference defined common goals, ideas and procedures, which could be adapted for use in most parts of the world. 'By keeping the patients close to family and friends,' Campbell emphasised, 'their isolation, stress and anxiety are diminished. Furthermore, there is a better chance that others will adjust their sexual behaviour to reduce the spread of infection.'[266]

Community Health Action Network (CHAN) was launched in Mizoram, North-Eastern India, in September 1991 to facilitate a change in behaviour and environment among those at risk from HIV infection. Major Naomi Lalngaihawmi reported, 'Prior to the International Headquarters Aids technical team coming to Mizoram, the Mizo people had heard very little about Aids and no one took it seriously. From that day onwards, we understood the seriousness of it and the urgent need to educate our people.' A resource centre was erected to provide clinical care and shelter for female workers, as well as counselling, spiritual care and training. The team that was formed reached out into the community, 'sharing in their suffering, bringing about change, revival and hope.'[267]

It has meant a new understanding of inter-faith fellowship and cooperation. Ian Campbell writes, 'Now is it possible for Hindu counsellors in Bombay to train Christians and then together work in Muslim communities in helping change happen … It is not moralistic imperatives that really change people, but facilitation of mutual morality, where values can be shared respectfully.' He adds that, 'often heightened spiritual sensitivity is the result'. [268]

A typical example of the ripples running out from the seminar is from Trinidad, where an HIV/Aids volunteer of General Santos Corps writes:

I have learned how to co-ordinate with the Barangay (village) leaders and other Health Services agencies; learned (how to conduct) strategic house visits (and) also (to run) workshop(s) for team building and actual counselling with HIV/Aids patients. I need to go on as a volunteer and do more to help my community. Some women rent houses in our village because they worked as hospitality girls in various night-clubs and bars in the city. This is their means of livelihood to support their family. As the HIV/Aids volunteers in the Salvation Army, General Santos Corps, we visited these women, and after several visits, friendship was established. The gospel was shared with them, then a Bible-study follow-up was conducted within the neighbourhood. Some of them sincerely wanted to have a changed life, and decided to leave behind the immoral lifestyle, returning to their hometown to earn a decent living. Some have engaged in small-scale business. The number of commercial sex workers in our place has been minimised.[269]

The impact in the USA has been massive. In 1995 a complete nationwide curriculum on Aids education for Army youth and their leaders was written. 'Aids and Adolescents' contained factual information for young people, presented in the context of religious, moral and ethical standards and emphasising the dangers of high-risk behaviour.

The moral, programmatic and financial challenges posed by HIV/Aids remain very great. Unfortunately, a number of health services for both HIV/Aids and other client groups have been reduced or eliminated in recent years due to

LEFT: India Central Territory's School of Nursing, pictured in 2000. BELOW: Commissioner (Dr) Prathipati Devavaram

ABOVE: Evangeline Booth Hospital, Nidubrolu. BELOW LEFT: Commissioner (Dr) Paul du Plessis; CENTRE: Tapping rubber at Puthencruz; RIGHT: Lieut-Colonel (Dr) K. C. Joseph of Puthencruz Leprosy Hospital.

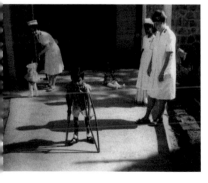

ABOVE: A young patient at Nagercoil learning to walk with the aid of crutches made by Major George Scott, as Major (Dr) Hazel Scott and Major Elsie Hansford look on.

ABOVE: A patient with a reconstructed nose and Nurse Gunvor Eklund in front of a portrait of William Booth at Nagercoil Hospital.

ABOVE: Aramboly Vocational Training Centre.
RIGHT: Women's Training Centre, Nagercoil.
BELOW: Sundar Egbert in his wheelchair.

ABOVE LEFT: Sundar Egbert shows General Frederick Coutts round the Aramboly centre.

RIGHT: Sundar Egbert in New Delhi, receives the Indian Chamber of Commerce Award for Outstanding Achievement in Training and Placement of Disabled Persons, 1984.

ABOVE and RIGHT:
Emery Hospital staff
pictured in 1953 and at
the hospital's centenary
in 2006.

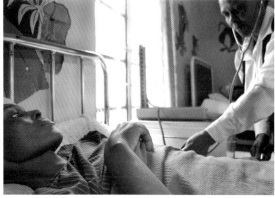

Picture: Thomas Haugersveen

ABOVE: At Mountain View Hospital in Natal, South Africa, spiritual as well as physical comfort is available to seriously ill HIV-positive patients, most of whom suffer with tuberculosis.
BELOW: Carl Sithole Wellness Centre in Soweto, South Africa.

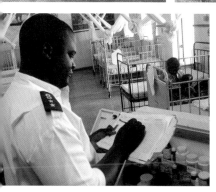

ABOVE: In Zambia, Captain Chilala, a local corps officer, spends a day a week at Chikankata Hospital utilising his professional skills.

RIGHT: On the other side of the Southern Hemisphere, Tetokatu Clinic in Paraguay provides a valuable medical ministry.

South Africa pictures: Southern Africa Territory Health Services

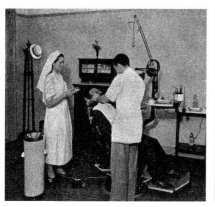

ABOVE LEFT: A Salvation Army dental clinic in Argentina in the early 20th century.
ABOVE RIGHT: A clinic in Democratic Republic of Congo 100 years later.

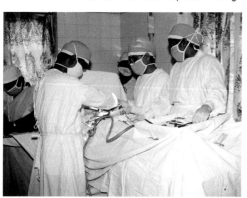
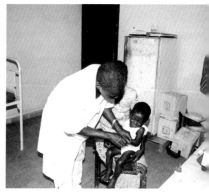

ABOVE LEFT: A modern Salvation Army operating theatre in Democratic Republic of Congo.
ABOVE RIGHT: Basic care is not forgotten.   *Congo pictures by Lieut-Colonel Eva Marseille*

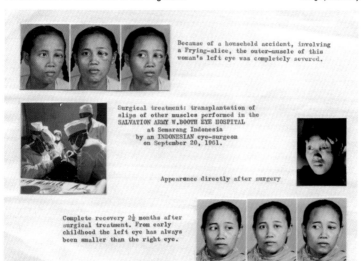

Because of a household accident, involving a Frying-slice, the outer-muscle of this woman's left eye was completely severed.

Surgical treatment: transplantation of slips of other muscles performed in the SALVATION ARMY W. BOOTH EYE HOSPITAL at Semarang Indonesia by an INDONESIAN eye-surgeon on September 20, 1961.

Appearance directly after surgery

Complete recovery 2½ months after surgical treatment. From early childhood the left eye has always been smaller than the right eye.

Sometimes success can be charted, as in this pictorial record from William Booth Eye Hospital, Semarang, 1961.

ABOVE: Dentist Captain Avee Keiree in the garden of his retirement home, with his grandchildren.

BELOW: Major Dorothy Elphick pictured in the 1960s.

ABOVE and BELOW: The work continues in Papua New Guinea.

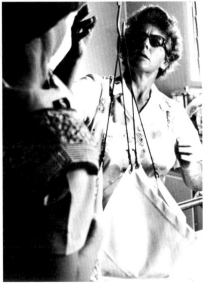

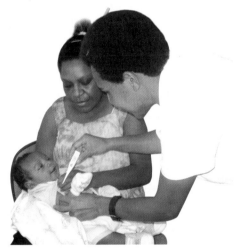

Pictures above courtesy Papua New Guinea Territory

LEFT: Captain Cynthia White in 1960s Indonesia, giving similar care, which continues today (RIGHT).

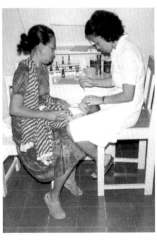

Picture left: International Heritage Centre. Picture right: Major Ann Powell

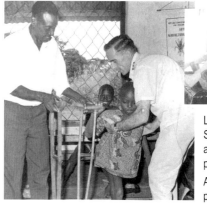

LEFT: Brigadier (Dr) Sidney Gauntlett assesses a young patient at Oji River.

ABOVE: A happy patient.

ABOVE LEFT: Cosmos, an Oji River graduate who now works tirelessly for others like himself, visiting Gudrun Agunwa, his former physiotherapist at Oji River.

ABOVE LEFT: Captain Asoegwu in the children's home at Oji River with a reporter from the *Nigerian Star* newspaper and (RIGHT) in the schoolroom.

All pictures on this page by Gudrun Agunwa

ABOVE: The boy on the right now walks upright with the aid of calipers and lives in his own home.

LEFT: Emmanuel, pictured on arrival at Oji River and on discharge.

ABOVE: The staff of Harry Williams Hospital at Cochabamba, Bolivia, pictured in 1999. LEFT: The building as it was in 1979.

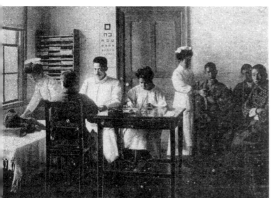

ABOVE: Japan's Dr Sanya Matsuda in his consulting room and (RIGHT) on the streets of Tokyo.

LEFT: Opening the new health centre at Kokorogoro, Papua New Guinea, in 2007.

Picture left: Papua New Guinea Territory

Picture right: Major Ann Powell

ABOVE: Dr Jim Smith with Commissioner (Dr) Harry Williams at the opening of a new block at Turen Hospital, Indonesia, in 1988.

ABOVE: The new Howard Hospital in Zimbabwe, funded by the USA Southern Territory.

Pictures: Captain Karen Lemke

ABOVE: Booth Memorial Hospital New York, once the Army's largest medical centre.

LEFT TO RIGHT: Major Wallace Winchell; Harbor Light Center, Cleveland, Ohio; 'Fighting the demon drink' demonstration, New York, 1910.

funding cuts. There is cause for concern in that an estimated five to 10 per cent of individuals receiving substance abuse treatment in Salvation Army programmes may have HIV/Aids. Help has come from many sources, and programmes differ in detail.

Two of the USA Central Territory's largest HIV/Aids programmes, located in the Northern Division, have been funded primarily through the USA Department of Housing and Urban Development's Housing Opportunities for People with Aids (HOPWA) programme. The Hope Harbor housing programme in downtown Minneapolis is a 96-unit housing facility providing efficiency apartments for a minimum of six individuals. Residents had to be HIV/Aids positive and possess a second disability such as mental illness, chemical addiction, physical impairment or a combination of all three. Targeting the most needy, it was preferred, but not required that clients be homeless prior to moving into Hope Harbor, Housing Opportunities for People to Excel (HOPE). Hope Harbor staff, with many other community service providers, work with persons living with HIV/Aids. The Salvation Army's Harvest Hills housing programme in a Minneapolis suburb, has offered eight three-bedroom apartments of permanent supportive housing for families, wherein at least one member of the household is HIV/Aids positive and has another disability.

For India generally a constitution, linking all the existing hospitals and dispensaries was established and, in Ahmednagar, a permanent centre, the Salvation Army Health Services Advisory Council for administration and training of hospital administrators and other personnel was set up, facilitating HIV/Aids emphases and care.

Bethesda House, in Soweto, South Africa, opened in August 1993 as a home for the abandoned babies of HIV-positive mothers, the first facility of its kind in the country. The Salvation Army opened a second home, with a capacity for 40 babies. Even though the deaths of the children in these two homes were an ongoing tragedy, care continued undeterred. Captain Lenah Jwili related the following story, which emphasises the social and spiritual aspects of HIV/Aids care.

> *Nonhlanhla, aged 18 months, had been abandoned by her mother. She was tested and found to be positive with Aids. When she was brought to us she was malnourished and had to be given intravenous drips because of severe dehydration. As the director of Bethesda House I made a plea through the media to the grandmothers to look for their grandchildren who needed support not rejection. Nonhlanhla's grandmother started searching for her granddaughter. She came to Bethesda House and, overwhelmed to find her granddaughter, tears of joy ran down her cheeks. Nonhlanhla seemed to understand and the sense of belonging was evident as she clung to her grandmother, in a moment of reunion and joy. The grandmother made arrangements to take the child back within her family. When Nonhlanhla's time came to die we were able to arrange a funeral and burial with dignity. On the burial day we expected only the grandmother, but instead families came from both Nonhlanhla's mother's and father's side, and were reunited. We praised the Lord for that coming together and accepting their child unconditionally.*[270]

Even before the government in Papua New Guinea had addressed the problem of HIV/Aids, The Salvation Army was already at work. Services were provided at Government Clinics for support of those being diagnosed; hospital visits and a drop-in centre were arranged, but the Army health workers often went to places where no one else would go. The staff, by involving themselves in the lives of the sufferers, showed compassion through their actions.

If care of those with HIV/Aids is a large programme, care of the elderly is one of the oldest. Geriatric programmes have long been prominent in The Salvation Army's services internationally. The size of the current demand can be illustrated from one of the ventures in Singapore. Called Peacehaven, its 339 beds are always full. 'Most of the residents have multiple diagnoses, including combinations of dementia, schizophrenia, depression and physical disability. Originally established as a nursing home for the aged, now more than 25 per cent of our residents are less than 65 years of age. In 2005 it was the largest nursing home in Singapore. The demands on Captain Ian and Mrs Isobel Robinson were great and continuous. He wrote of a typical situation:

It was one of those moments that was very funny and at the same time quite sad. The speaker at our Sunday afternoon chapel service had just finished her presentation of the gospel. She called on the congregation to raise hands to receive Christ and about 15 responded. As I looked at them and turned to Isobel, 'Didn't we enrol some of them as adherents last Sunday?' I whispered. 'Yes,' she replied, gently admonishing, 'remember, they have dementia!' It is encouraging to note that the chaplain is Anglican, loving, cheerful, and tireless. Such ecumenical solidarity is growing, particularly amongst the Chinese, and the concept of health is increasingly holistic. Perhaps our most tragic resident is 'Adam'. The name card above his bed said 'Unknown'. Found on the streets about three years ago, completely unable to care for himself, he was taken to the hospital and eventually referred to Peacehaven for long-term care. He cannot move, speak or hear. No one knows who he is or where he came from. Despite our best efforts we cannot find any family or friends. We don't even know his nationality or his age, but doctors estimate that he is Chinese and in his 60s. We are Adam's family until God calls him home.[271]

This last report is typical of hundreds from around the world, and emphasises the supreme need of forgiveness, love and the grace of God for full health, and the constant requirement of such love and grace from the staff. It calls for another chapter to consider it in depth.

[262] Rader, H. Personal communication
[263] Gariepy, H. *Mobilized for God, The History of The Salvation Army Vol VIII (1977-1994)* The Salvation Army, Atlanta, GA 2000 p. 337
[264] Ibid
[265] Ibid
[266] Ibid
[267] Ibid
[268] Ibid
[269] Ibid
[270] Ibid
[271] Robinson, I. 'Singapore's Peacehaven Home' *New Frontier*, 3 June 2004 The Salvation Army USA Western

Chapter ten

Health of mind and spirit

SEEN in perspective, the emphasis of the 1970s was community health, in the context of community development. The 1980s saw a search for the meaning and purpose of health programmes in the total mission of the Army, and a quest for a theology of health and healing. The 1990s witnessed an openness to a wider interpretation of health and healing in the total ministry of the Army and greater emphasis on congregation-based healing. It included the relationship of the concept of wholeness to the Army's doctrine of holiness as synoptic, integrative and incarnational.

Building on the work of his predecessors at International Headquarters, in the 1980s the Medical Adviser, Major (Dr) Paul du Plessis, led a series of regional meetings on health and healing strategy, which laid the foundation for two significant trends in health services. The initial issue was the very survival of Salvation Army health services. Towards the end of the decade more attention was being given to the development of a Salvationist theology of health, healing and wholeness. The process continued into the 1990s with significant conferences that aided the development of vision and direction in the Army's health ministries.

The sequence of these conferences culminated in the landmark International Consultation on Health, Healing and Wholeness, held in Sri Lanka from 26 February to 4 March 1994. This first international conference of its kind envisaged by Colonel (Dr) Paul du Plessis and organised by his successor as Medical Adviser, Captain (Dr) Ian Campbell, was presided over by Commissioner Arthur Waters. It brought to fruition a new health paradigm, more diverse, yet integrated. The past and the present were debated before breaking new ground. Topics included the theology of health and wholeness, integration of varied perspectives, guidelines for development, publications, technical assistance, hospital crises, history of the Army's health ministry, accountability, evaluation and ethics. One concept articulated was the need for a 'better, more integrated understanding of the relationship between wholeness and holiness, and healing as a door to evangelism and holy living'.

Guest speakers included Lieut-Colonel Philip Needham (USA) with his perspective on community and mission; Mrs Captain Barbara Robinson (Canada) on pastoral care and chaplaincy in health services; Dr Jim Read (Canada) on bio-ethics; Major Hiroshi Takahashi (Japan) on Aids health services; Gordon Bingham (USA) on shared missions; Colonel (Dr) Paul du Plessis (India) on major themes of philosophy; and professionals from a number of other international health agencies. Four songs composed for the conference by Major Joy Webb (UK) added a devotional dimension.[272]

'The Army was maturing in its expression of the healing ministry,' summarised Captain (Dr) Campbell. 'Our theology of health, healing and wholeness is not only about our expression of Christ's compassion, but also about quality of life, capacity for change and for sharing in community.' Colonel (Dr) Paul du Plessis underlined a willingness to make those fresh discoveries as a healthy sign in a movement wanting to be relevant to the people of the 21st century.

One of the speakers at the Sri Lanka conference was Dr Daleep Mukarji who said, 'Christians must be in a healing ministry, not to make people Christians or to serve Christians, or to give jobs to Christians or even because there is a need in society. Christians are involved because we are Christians — not doing so would make us less Christian, disobedient to the command to preach the Kingdom and to heal the sick. So we do this, not to build our own kingdom, but to build the Kingdom of God.'[273]

Following the conference a selected group met in South India at Nagercoil, coinciding with the Centenary of Catherine Booth Hospital.

Dr Graham Calvert collated the papers and presented the book; *Health, Healing and Wholeness*, published by International Headquarters in 1997. In his foreword, General Paul Rader wrote of the watershed in the nature and scope of Salvation Army health ministries, which 'seemed to most of us an exotic and specialist task … this book puts us all in the picture … We are all at some level or another engaged in the redemptive work of health, healing and wholeness.'[274]

The book introduced the new Medical Adviser's agenda for future action. Captain (Dr) Ian Campbell introduced 'this paradigm shift' as 'a commitment to the diverse, to the difficult, to arduous communication, and yet also a growth process that can be enriching.' He stressed the change as being from provider to participant. It had been the burden of emphasis in his predecessors' terms.[275]

In the meantime, the existing structure of general hospitals was seeking a new role in many countries. Canada led the way as the changing pattern of state concepts and control evolved in the 1960s. The Grace Hospitals at Scarborough, Windsor, Calgary and Winnipeg became class B general hospitals, while that at Toronto was styled 'a complex continuing care centre' and the Catherine Booth Hospital in Montreal, a rehabilitation hospital. But parts of the Calgary and Winnipeg Hospitals had been set aside for a new type of health care, peculiarly suited to the spirit of The Salvation Army, namely hospices.

Dame Cicely Saunders founded the first purpose-built hospice in Britain, at Sydenham in South-East London. This was dedicated to providing 'a good death' to the terminally ill. It became the flagship of many Non-Governmental Organisations (NGOs), with a persistent rejection of the idea of euthanasia. The British National Health Service eschewed it, refusing funding to such institutions. Cost was a problem, but the style of treatment appealed to the public and more and more hospices began to appear, funded by fees and public subscription. Pain relief was the prime consideration, but even more important was the atmosphere created by an organisation which permitted the unhurried time to talk to both patients and relatives. This embodied the ideal of Salvation Army treatment, where the Kingdom of Heaven is realised in awareness of spiritual realities and is encouraged in an atmosphere of loving service. It inevitably demands staff with a sense of vocation.

General Arnold Brown was sometimes asked whether The Salvation Army should be in the general hospital field at all. For the 'Third World' his answer was always a confident, 'Yes!' He was much less certain for the Western world. Hospital services are costly and competitive. Medical equipment has an early obsolescence and the medical staff cannot be blamed for bringing pressure to bear on an administrator to secure 'the latest' in everything if it will enhance the healing process. As hospitals have multiplied, Salvation Army officer staff in them has diminished. Today, it is left largely to the administrator and a chaplain to maintain what is referred to as 'the Army atmosphere', but this is no small task with hundreds of in-patients or outpatients.[276] He visualised opportunities in palliative care of the chronically ill, the handicapped and the dependent geriatric. In the General's home country of Canada, the changing priorities of government health services have caused a continuous review of Salvation Army institutions.

In a strategic planning document, pastoral care was being urged as a service to the sick that was accountable to those it seeks to serve and to advances in understanding in the areas of theology, psychology and social sciences. Salvation Army hospital chaplains were being urged to complete formal pastoral education training. Programmes were to include perinatal bereavement ministry, grief counselling, participation in ethics consultation and training of League of Mercy members.[277]

General Brown knew the work done at St Christopher's Hospice in London, already referred to. In the hope of avoiding the closure of 'Grace' and with the support of all associated with its work, he submitted a brief to the Minister of Health, proposing that the 'Grace' could do the work of a 'St Christopher's'. He advanced the idea that Army personnel would also be able to surround the patients with the spiritual influences vitally necessary to those on the edge of eternity. In the conference which followed, the minister said that the proposal for the Grace Hospital's change of use was accepted. He then added the overwhelming news that the long-sought relocation was also approved. A general hospital was to be erected in the Toronto suburbs with a starting accommodation of 350 beds and an eventual optimum of 650. Hardly able to believe what he was hearing, General Brown hurried back to headquarters to tell the chief secretary that, instead of losing the one hospital, the Army was to have two.[278] Cooperation with government has its problems for religious bodies, including changing political control, financial uncertainty and size. But Canada provided The Salvation Army's greatest challenge, including ecumenical projects. It meant continual change. The story must be told more fully.

The Health Services Department was formed in 1984 to look after the hospitals, merging in 1986 with the Senior Citizen's Department which gave oversight to 21 long-term care facilities. Hospital administrators met on an annual basis, usually following the meeting of the Canadian Hospital Association. In 1986 administrators from the USA joined with their Canadian colleagues. Apart from the recurring theme of the purpose of Salvation Army health services and their sustainability, two other issues were to have been addressed: ethical dilemmas and the theology of healing in a Salvation Army context. Theological issues were shelved in favour of a more pragmatic approach. Nevertheless, participants recognised that health services were under threat, not only because of changing government policies and requirements but also because of continuing uncertainty about the place of health services in the mission of the Army. While citizens might have preferred the ambience of an Army hospital, in some areas a decision to merge, or to close, was made on the basis of Army capacity to maintain leadership by providing trained administrators for multi-hospital systems, for example in Toronto. Sometimes the decision was based on ethical concerns, as in Vancouver. In other cases the Army was more comfortable providing long-term care. Roman Catholic institutions throughout North America were facing similar issues and many Catholic voices were addressing the difficult issues of accommodation to cultural bio-ethical norms, community demands for services, the 'sale' of not-for-profit institutions and the acquisition of secular ones. Many felt that institutions continued to provide a unique opportunity for ministry and that ownership rather than just the provision of chaplaincy services is required to maintain a Christian environment for healing.

Major changes had occurred by March 1999. They included mergers, hand-overs, closures, further redevelopment or diversification. The 250-bed St John's Grace, with a school of nursing, was about to close (2000) and the Halifax Grace had merged with IWK (Izaak Walton Killam) Hospital in 1990 becoming IWK/Grace. Salvation Army officer staff included one administrative assistant and two chaplains. The Captain William Jackman Memorial Hospital in Labrador City had been taken over by the regional health authority in 1996.

The Toronto Grace remained as a long-term care facility, providing continuing and palliative care and the Scarborough Grace merged with Scarborough General in 1998 to become the largest community hospital in Canada, the Army retaining an administrator at the Grace site. The Hospital Dieu Grace in Windsor, Ontario was, from 1999, being run jointly by the Army and the Catholic health system with Salvation Army representation on the board, its mission incorporating sentiments acceptable to both Salvationist and Catholic: 'We are a health care community inspired by Jesus Christ's healing ministry, respecting the sanctity of life. Our compassionate hearts and competent hands will care for the body, mind and spiritual well-being of all.'

Army planners like David Luginbuhl in Canada, asked leadership to value the contribution of the past but to anticipate inevitable change in the future. Community demographics, government funding and professional staff diversity required new thinking. Hospital-based ministries offered opportunities for service, evangelism and community development, but healing ministries could also be corps-based. If the Army was forced to withdraw from traditional institutional services it must not abandon health care and healing ministries, but discover new venues and new approaches. Parish nursing was developed in Ottawa. Long-term and palliative care seemed congenial to Army experience and expertise.[279]

A further response was the establishment, in 1994, of The Salvation Army Ethics Unit to assist with complex decision-making in the moral dimension of contemporary issues. Its director, Dr Read, has special interest in, among others, health care ethics. The various Canadian hospitals had modified their programmes to meet local demands and thereby continued to maintain a varied programme. The Catherine Booth Hospital, Montreal, became well-known for its physiotherapy and rehabilitation programmes as a long-term care and geriatric facility. The Ottawa Grace had been required to focus on ophthalmology and obstetrics and was later converted into a long-term care facility run by the Army.

The Calgary Grace relocated to a new site as the Grace Women's Health Centre. The Agape Manor, the Army's only hospice in Canada, was a second facility. Established in 1992 for the intended care of people with HIV/Aids, it became a home away from home for the terminally ill, offering people a place where they could die with dignity; a place that echoes with the hope of life; giving families spiritual and emotional support at a traumatic time in their lives.[280]

In June 1995 more than 90 participants gathered in Calgary for The Salvation Army Health Care Conference with the theme 'Excellence in Mission: Contemporary Reality'. Participants included Board/Council chairs, Governing Council members, divisional commanders and programme secretaries, together with senior managers from hospital and long-term care facilities. The principal aim was to heighten awareness of the Army's mission and values. The conference provided opportunities for strengthened relationships and cooperation.

October 1996 marked the beginning of an imaginative corps-based community health programme. The Gladstone Avenue Corps, Ottawa, in association with the Ottawa Grace Hospital, hired a registered nurse to work directly out of a congregational setting. The corps was already functioning as an effective 'healing community' under the ministry of its leaders Bert and Kathy Sharp. Officer-nurse Barbara Robinson shared her vision in the corps health committee. The need confirmed and the agreement of health professionals secured, the feasibility of integration into the corps programme had to be tested. It quickly became apparent that the 'corps nurse' concept could greatly expand by becoming known as health care coordinator, and the range of possible pastoral care services of a corps could be greatly expanded. They could include: visits to expectant mothers, facilitating widow support, weight-loss monitoring, organising workshops on the care of elderly parents, study groups on 'stress, prayer and healing', the training of League of Mercy visitors and arranging 'well adult' screening clinics. Helping corps members understand and utilise resources for health and well-being central to Christian faith, prayer, forgiveness, faith, hope and love, had high priority.[281] The nurse became a member of an already vibrant healing ministry team in downtown Ottawa, working with United Church, Roman Catholic, Anglican and Salvation Army congregations. The Social Services Department at Territorial Headquarters actively promoted the concept, providing a resource pack. The programme gathered momentum and by 2005 it had been established in Ontario (Peterborough) and British Columbia (Burnaby, Vancouver, Victoria Highpoint and Richmond).

Writing of her experience as a Salvation Army parish nurse, Toni Surko explains how fear is the most pressing health concern among members of the congregation, fear of dying, fear of ageing, fear of losing independence, fear of being alone, fear of 'not making it'. The response of a gentleman grateful for the corps nurse underscores the richness of the ministry. Her presence, the presence of God and a healing community of faith gave him the prescription needed to turn his back on his fears and make the necessary changes in his life.[282]

In 2002 the Canadian Government set up the Romanov Commission on 'The future of health care in Canada' and The Salvation Army responded, stating both its credentials and track record, but underlining its specifically Christian concept of health. Its credentials were well stated: 'The Salvation Army in Canada provides faith-based health care services that are accredited, award winning, innovative and community based. We have a long history of operating maternity hospitals, general community hospitals, teaching hospitals, chronic and rehabilitative hospitals, community clinics, schools of nursing, chaplaincy services, drug and alcohol rehabilitation programmes, programmes for mentally ill and developmentally delayed adults, parish nursing programmes, palliative care programmes, and hospices for the dying. In recent times, The Salvation Army has moved into partnerships with government and private non-profit health care providers, often forging relationships that have increased the quality of care and services we are able to provide.'[283]

The Salvation Army clarified its own motivation for involvement in the health care debate: 'We are a Christian organisation whose mission is to preach the gospel of Jesus Christ and to meet human need without discrimination. We adopt a holistic vision of health, which includes the physical, emotional, psychological and spiritual aspects of human beings. Our values as an organisation are rooted in the Christian tradition and our principles of healing in the model of Jesus. We are an international organisation with a strong national presence in Canada and represent tens of thousands of ordinary Canadians, be they members of our churches, friends or supporters, employees or clients, all who have a personal interest in the development of health care services in Canada. We believe that our Christian values regarding health, transcend particular religious belief and are generally shared by all Canadians regardless of creed. These common values are what Canadians want to retain in their health care system.'

This submission accepted the five requirements listed in the Canada Health Act: public administration, comprehensiveness, universality, portability and accessibility. It then proceeded to marshal arguments against the introduction of a parallel 'for profit' system, identifying with the marginalised and poor.

There was a powerful statement on spirituality: 'Health has an important spiritual component. We do not mean this in a narrow sectarian sense but rather that humans have a spiritual reality that needs to be nurtured and healed, a reality that holds together the physical, social, emotional, and psychological aspects of being. As a case in point, our pastoral ministries operating in our hospitals contribute to the overall health of our patients. The provision of follow-up pastoral care to the bereaved parents of a stillborn baby is not only valid, but necessary for the health of that couple and consequently for all of society. This type of soul care, as just one example of a wide range of services provided by non-medical professionals, should be valued, with financial support by our health care system. Those who treat the social, psychological, and emotional aspects of being, are equally as valid in contributing to an individual's total health as those who treat the physical needs.'

Similar changes in health promotion were being worked out in the USA. Closure of medical institutions provided opportunity for refocusing energy and resources in new directions. The integration of medical services with other territorial or corps activities and the involvement of communities in planning health services is a recent international trend also being followed in the USA. Health became a feature of a number of Salvation Army Social Programmes. This became apparent at The Salvation Army Bell Shelter in the Los Angeles area, which opened in January 1988. It started as collaboration between The Salvation Army and Harry Pregerson, a US 9th Circuit Court of Appeals judge. Bell Shelter was one of the first programmes to fulfil the objectives of the McKinney-Vento Homeless Assistance Act of 1986, which utilises vacant federal facilities for the benefit of the homeless. It expanded its programme over the next 15 years and by 2005 was providing transitional housing to 345 adults.

Medical needs were provided by several means at Bell Shelter, including individual and group psychotherapy on site provided by a licensed marriage and family therapist. Clients, in need of medical detoxification services, entering the 128-bed California State Licensed Drug and Alcohol programme at Bell Shelter, were referred to Cider House at Norwalk. A mobile medical unit, with a physician, served clients at Bell Shelter twice a week, in collaboration with the Los Angeles Dream Centre. The unit provided a range of services including gynaecological examinations, HIV/Aids testing, various types of prescription medications, health screenings and physical examinations, prostate cancer screening, tuberculosis screening and diabetes testing and treatment.

More flamboyant and one-off medical events were explored in the Community Health Fairs in the USA Central Territory. In 1993 the Appleton, WI, corps co-sponsored, with Midwest Dental Clinic, a day of free dental care at the Army's clinic. Shortly afterward the corps opened a permanent free dental clinic for children, staffed by volunteers and operating once a month. The Metropolitan Division co-sponsored a Community Health Fair for children in May 2005. In cooperation with Rush University Medical Center in Chicago, the day-long health screening provided basic health examinations; clinical services including vision and hearing testing, bone mass scans, dental care, HIV testing, immunisation, Kid Care enrolment (state sponsored low-cost medical coverage for children), health promotion information and aftercare referral services.

An ongoing service was provided by the Lakewood Adult Day Services, located in the Northern Division, developed to provide a supportive environment to help participants maintain the highest level of independence within their current living situation. Safety, wellness, structure and caregiver relief were promoted. Care plans directed physical, social and recreational activity for groups, or specific people. Recreational programming, health care, dietary services and social services became part of the regular programme. Participants have experienced a variety of health concerns such as memory loss, strokes, Parkinson's, brain injury, mental health, physical impairment and social isolation. Staff received specific instruction and training on topics such as Alzheimer's disease, cardio-pulmonary resuscitation and first aid emergency procedures and care of the vulnerable adult. Highlights of the programme were guest speakers, community outings, pet visits, art therapy and gardening. Music, fun, friends, dignity and independence all contribute to a well-rounded ministry, which has served the emotional, physical, and spiritual needs of the clients.

In addition to institutional and community settings, a number of corps social service programmes have included health services. Many have opened and closed during four decades, but in 2005 the Detroit Brightmoor Corps Health Clinic, the Sheboygan Health Care and Dental Clinic, Lakewood Temple Corps Adult Day Services and the Mason City Adult Day Health Center (ADHC) were in operation in the Central Territory. Detroit Brightmoor has developed a medical clinic, which serves a broad array of health concerns, featuring a unique programme in conjunction with AIMHI (African American Initiative for Male Health Improvement).

Mason City, IA, ADHC has provided services to adults with medical and/or social needs in order to maintain or improve their health, promote independence and to assist their primary care giver. In 2004 the centre provided services to 106 people from seven counties. Some of their diagnoses were: Alzheimer's, Parkinson's, chronic heart disease, stroke, diabetes, brain injury, chronic arthritis or, in most cases, a combination. Staff included registered and certified nurses and an activity director/programme assistant. The centre had a management contract with Mercy Medical Centre, North Iowa, for the director and nurse positions. This relationship provided the centre with advantages such as referral sources, support services and educational opportunities for the staff. Most of the people served by the centre would never again have been self-reliant, but participation in the programme had decreased their dependence in many areas. Participants could remain active in communities by interacting with volunteers who conducted recreational or social activities at the centre. In January 2003 the centre earned the distinction of being only the fourth adult day centre in the state of Iowa to be accredited by CARF (Commission on Accreditation of Rehabilitation Facilities).

The Sheboygan Health Care Clinic opened in 1992 in a renovated Sunday school room, providing free short-term medical and vision care for adults and children. The children's dental clinic was added in 1996 in partnership with the Sheboygan Christian Medical and Dental Society. In 1999 the clinics served more than 800 low income, uninsured people in Sheboygan. They were treated by a staff of seven doctors, 23 nurses, 17 dentists and 24 support staff, who volunteered time and skills to provide health care and education. By 2005 the clinics had a referral network of medical, ophthalmological, dental and mental health professionals who provided reduced-cost care by vouchers for prescriptions at wholesale prices. There has been strong financial support from the community

Although The Salvation Army's obstetric programme in the USA had virtually ceased when it refused to perform abortions, there was a new twist in the Army's health service for pregnant young women, which continued beyond the closure of the Booth Hospitals. A continuum of services emerged to pregnant and parenting teens throughout the Central Territory. They included, but were not limited to, prevention, crisis intervention, case management and counselling, outpatient medical clinics, transitional housing, residential services and continuing care. It was stressed that services could be accessed through corps community centres or social/family service units.

Specialised programmes for pregnant or parenting adolescents have been developed in Grand Rapids, Detroit and Omaha. The Denby Maternity Program in Detroit arranged residential and health services to pregnant teens. In Omaha, the CARES programme (Comprehensive Adolescent Residential Educational Services) has provided case management, an on-site medical clinic and residential services for pregnant teens. The Booth Health Clinic in Grand Rapids was established to provide prenatal and family health care and ongoing support to young adults and families in Kent County. Booth Family Services, in partnership with Cherry Street Health Services, has covered X-ray, ultrasound and mammography treatment and other services including dental and optical care. The Booth Clinic has focused on reducing the rates of infant mortality and the incidence of pre-term births, on increasing birth weights and improving the infants' first year of life through medical treatment, health information, education and support and by bringing women out of examination rooms and into groups for their care. The programme was to be a model of group therapy in obstetrics; up to 12 women/couples/teens with similar due dates, meeting together regularly during their pregnancy.

There were unexpected twists to the administrative requirements of the state in relation to health. One was the use of Salvation Army records as a source of information in tracing relatives. This meant that relationships continued to be forged as clients looked to the programme in search of medical information regarding births which took place at Salvation Army Booth Hospitals in the Central Territory from 1887 to 1984. By 1996 a new law regulated electronic transfer and recording of health care transactions. The law included Salvation Army health service programmes, qualifying as 'covered entities'. The Central Territory worked to identify such programmes to meet extensive legal requirements prior to the deadline of 16 October 2002. Adding to the complexity of the new legislation for The Salvation Army was its dual function, both as a 'health care provider' (for client services) and a 'health plan' (for its employees). Under guidance from The Salvation Army's National Legal Counsel, the Territorial Social Services and Risk Management Departments worked with the law firm Erickson and Sederstrom to develop compliance plans and provide training for 18 identified health service programmes by December 2003. Similarly, the federal Occupational Safety and Health Administration (OSHA), largely in response to the HIV/Aids crisis, published new regulations in 1992 for protection against diseases transmitted through human blood and/or body fluids. In order to comply with the new regulations, the Central Territory developed an 'Exposure Control Plan Resource Book', which was adopted by all US territories by April 2003. However, despite such distractions, commitment to holistic ministry remains a central commitment of The Salvation Army in the USA but still includes concern for physical well-being. As developments proliferate in the health care field and national and administrative issues impact on services, the exact nature of Salvation Army health services is bound to change, but the heart of the ministry will continue unchanged.[284]

Earlier reference has been made to St Christopher's Hospice in London, but the idea of the hospice as being peculiarly suited to The Salvation Army's concept of care was being discovered in countries as far apart as Japan and New Zealand. In Blenheim, New Zealand, The Marlborough Community Hospice was custom-built in the grounds of Wairau Hospital, but was intended to serve the whole of Marlborough district. The Salvation Army manager, Jenny Black, described the typical hospice programme as providing specialist care in a safe and caring environment for patients with active progressive illnesses which are life-shortening and unresponsive to curative treatment. Although cancer is the most common illness, patients may also suffer from conditions such as motor neurone disease, end-stage renal failure or Aids. 'Patients came to the hospice for three reasons: they needed relief from symptoms such as pain and nausea, required care during the terminal stage of their illness and a hospice service to provide carers with a needed break (respite care).'

In Japan in 1989 a 30-bed hospice in Kiyose, for the care of the terminally ill and their families, was dedicated by Commissioner W. Stanley Cottrill. The commissioner spoke to the large crowd assembled for the dedication ceremony of the great responsibility of not only assuring the terminally ill of comfort and peace of mind, but also of doing everything possible to prepare them for eternity. The first enthusiast for this new programme was Lieut-Colonel Dr Taro Nagasaki. When on 15 August 1945 the Second World War ended with the defeat of Japan, Taro was a young medical student. He had intended to become a navy surgeon, but the fact that the atomic bomb had not fallen on his home town of Kokura City, changed his whole outlook. He felt that his life had been spared for a purpose. A poster on the university notice board led him to a meeting addressed by Commissioner Mazuso Uemura, Territorial Commander of The Salvation Army in Japan, who spoke of the needs of the sick poor of his country. He became an officer and was appointed to the TB hospitals under Lieut-Colonel (Dr) Rin Iwasa and Lieut-Colonel (Dr) Seamans. He wrote of his vision for a hospice: 'A human being who is the total existence of body, mind, and spirit, needs to bear all sorts of agony and pain when coming to the end of life. The Salvation Army hospice should recognise this, the staff forming a team with his family and the community to share that pain

... helping them to live with dignity until the end, (then) helping them to die in peace. This should be carried out with the spirit of love that comes with a genuine Christian faith.' The reason for the long delay in the realisation of his vision, was that the state, as in the UK, was slow to support the concept and the cost was too great for The Salvation Army to bear alone.[285]

Poverty is universally recognised as a main contributor to bad health. The Salvation Army planned an International Summit on Poverty to be held in Bangladesh in 2001. The terrorist action in the USA in September led to this being held on the internet. Glenn J. Schwartz, Executive Director, World Mission Associates, was a major contributor. He described his search for meaningful ways to help the poor in the words of Christ. He was struck by the frequent association of the provision of healing and deliverance with the blessing that the poor had the good news of the Kingdom of Heaven given to them. In other words, health is holistic and a spiritual approach is vital. Then he turned to his own experience and described a situation in Guatemala. The people there were so demoralised by unemployment and poverty that they turned to alcohol and crime. Before long, jails were full and spiritism rife. At the point of desperation people joined together for prayer. They were surprised by the result! Alcoholics were converted, jails emptied and poverty decreased as 'even the soil was converted' and brought forth greater harvests 'vegetables grew larger'. Again the problem was of how to get surplus produce to market. Denominational differences healed as they joined together in prayer, seeking a joint solution.

From Bangladesh came a testimony from one denomination, which felt that poverty was related to holding Christianity too cheap. Members described how their church was growing, not by financial support from overseas, but by following what they regarded as God's principles, namely:

    1. Every member must pay his debts, Christians being known as those who pay what they owe.

2. Every member must pay his taxes. They must show non-Christians that they are law-abiding citizens.
3. Believers learn from day one that they must tithe. No excuse of being too poor to pay is acceptable. Everyone must give back from what God supplies.
4. And finally, they must learn to save to build a little margin.

Now that church is growing! It maintains that poverty isn't just about money. We must give back to God, '… be it a banana, a cow, or a bag of maize'.[286]

Major P. J. Verstoep responded from 12 years' experience in Port-au-Prince, Haiti, where again there is extreme poverty. She agreed whole-heartedly, pointing out that prayer changes things by changing people. 'When people started to pray instead of asking help from outside, a power was released and was changed into action. They were no longer captives, but learned to think and choose for themselves'. The Salvation Army health services in Haiti had been made self-supporting after 12 years. The interesting confession she had to make is that much of the opposition she encountered was initially from The Salvation Army itself! She had turned the assumption of many years on its head. It was assumed that missionaries from the affluent West should bring the money required with them, that they knew what was best for people, and that they remained in charge of the whole operation.[287] Verstoep's story must be music to the ears of Commissioner (Dr) Paul du Plessis and his successors, who have consistently urged cooperation and open discussion, shared responsibility in place of an authoritarian administration.

A holistic approach to health is more than philosophy: it determines practice too.[288]

---

[272] Gariepy, H. *Mobilized for God, The History of The Salvation Army Vol VIII (1977-1994)* The Salvation Army, Atlanta, GA 2000 p. 341
[273] Ibid

274 Calvert, G. (Ed) *Health, Healing & Wholeness – Salvationist Perspectives* The Salvation Army IHQ, London 1997
275 Ibid
276 Brown, A. *The Gate and the Light* Bookwright Publications, Toronto 1984 p. 178
277 Rader, H. Personal communication
278 Brown, A. *The Gate and the Light* Bookwright Publications, Toronto 1984 p. 177
279 Rader, H. *Historical Dictionary of The Salvation Army* John G. Merritt (Ed), Scarecrow Press, Lanham, Maryland 2006
280 Ibid
281 Robinson, B. 'The Revival of Parish Nursing' *Horizons* The Salvation Army, Canada May-June 1997
282 Surko, T. 'The Role of the Parish Nurse in the Church' *The Standard* Winter 2000 The Salvation Army, Canada
283 Luttrell, W. *A Submission by The Salvation Army in Canada to The Commission on The Future Of Health Care In Canada* The Salvation Army, Canada 2002
284 McCarty, C. *The Salvation Army USA Central Territory Health Services 1970-2005*
285 Yoshida, M. Personal communication
286 Schwartz, G. *Searching for a Meaningful Way to Help the Poor* Paper prepared for The Salvation Army's International Summit on Poverty. 2001
287 Verstoep N. Response to the paper: Searching for a Meaningful Way to Help the Poor. The Salvation Army's International Summit on Poverty 2001
288 Gariepy, H. *Mobilized for God, The History of The Salvation Army Vol VIII (1977-1994)* The Salvation Army, Atlanta, GA 2000 p. 342

Epilogue

IN the years 1903 to 1905 *The War Cry* in New Zealand published articles and photographs of 'The Salvation Army Ambulance Brigade'. This was some years after a medical Department had appeared at International Headquarters and one of its officers had written 'An Army needs an ambulance'. The reports came from most of the main cities. It was a youth movement (from age 16 upward). It appears to have commenced spontaneously and although Lieut-Colonel Gilmour obviously fostered its development, there does not appear to have been any standardisation. The various group photographs show a recognisable, but varied, nurse's uniform for the women, and none for the men. It used the St John's *First Aid to the Injured* as a textbook. There were separate classes for men and women and Lieut-Colonel Gilmour's intention is recorded as being, 'to make our young people more useful and helpful to suffering humanity'.[289]

The New Zealand *War Cry* of 19 March 1904 carried this statement: 'In conclusion, we would like it to be understood that it is neither a fad, a fancy nor a pastime that we are engaged in, but a real effort to qualify ourselves to carry out our Master's command (Luke 10:27-37). The Samaritan must have known something about first aid to the injured. He did not even call for a doctor; he had full confidence in his own skill.' Although it states 'it is neither a fad, a fancy nor a pastime' there is no evidence that an ambulance service developed regular public activities, other than as entertainment in dramatic demonstrations. Did THQ give it a thumbs down? There is no evidence of that, but reports dried up. It was, however, a development, which could have given The Salvation Army a distinctive role amongst the churches.

We saw in an earlier chapter how Bramwell Booth produced an effective Ambulance Brigade in the First World War, and the worldwide response to need which involved ambulances from as far as Australia being shipped to Europe, under the auspices of The Salvation Army.

The St John's Ambulance organisation has long published two textbooks. The second of these, on Home Nursing, has been extensively used for training Salvation Army social work officers and staff employed in local clinics.

The germinal idea remains. A medical service could become a section in every corps, peculiarly suited to present ideas. As mentioned elsewhere, Papua New Guinea has already instituted a 'village health worker' in many corps. The idea of a corps as a healing community has also been recorded as part of Ottawa's Gladstone Avenue Corps, with its 'corps health committee'.

Canada has used the League of Mercy in corps life, chiefly to provide hospital visitors in each corps. But why not extend the scope by training Salvationists as counsellors, available at local level for the needs of hospices, nursing homes and geriatric facilities, as well as a body of trained personnel capable of helping the sick in their own homes? It could involve the Medical Fellowship, which might well provide leaders in corps units.

In East Africa, the Home League has become the channel for health education, whilst in South Africa the Women's Department spearheaded a family health programme. As these pages report, corps medical clinics have operated in the USA and Canada.

Dr Ian Campbell said of the 'paradigm shift' that it was 'a commitment to a process'. He described it as a commitment to the diverse, to the difficult, to arduous communication and yet also a growth process which can be enriching. It was to be a 'major transition in vision and direction from that of being a provider to that of being a participant, with the core concepts of care, community, change and hope'.[290]

The application to the needs of developing countries is immediately apparent. Nutrition programmes in the Congos, Zambia and Bangladesh included growth monitoring, oral rehydration for diarrhoea, breast-feeding encouragement and even immunisation. As already reported, corps in the developing world have been quick to address their local health needs, with village clinics attached to corps in Nigeria and Ghana and to home leagues in Kenya.

The United Nations conference in Alma Ata, Kazakhstan in 1978, gave birth to the document *Health for All by the Year 2000,* which as we have seen had a significant influence on Salvation Army health service policy. The document emphasised the role of people in relation to their own health and health service delivery. UNICEF was the principal protagonist of child survival and development. Its annual publication, *The State of the World's Children,* became a valued resource for Salvation Army health teams.

The establishment of SAWSO in 1977, and the Planning and Development Department at International Headquarters, led to a series of regional and national seminars promoting the concept of community development. A major grant from USAID to SAWSO was used to develop a focus on the issue of child survival. An outcome was the joint publication with UNICEF and WHO in 1989 of the book *Facts for Life,* with a Salvation Army preface and crest added to the Army edition.[291] In the foreword, General Eva Burrows wrote: 'The book is full of prime messages. I hope you will take your part in spreading the word to families who deserve to receive these messages. And act on them yourself for the sake of the child.' There is a need for continuing health education and simple nursing skills at grassroots level, and not only for children. There could be a League of Mercy section in every corps but it would be better with a new title, such as 'The Health Resources Team'.

In 2004 Oslo University, Norway, made it clear that a 'street level' hospital was needed in their city, a hospital for people with severe problems caused by drug abuse and other such social problems, not addressed by the state system. The Salvation Army responded to this appeal, opening a 10-bed facility and 24-hour cover, as a three-year project. The Health Minister has now declared that the hospital with double the capacity is to be permanent, run by the Army, but financed by government.

It must ever be true of The Salvation Army that it is quick to respond to human need, locally as well as internationally. When in 1977 the World Humanity Award was presented to The Salvation Army by Earl Mountbatten, General Arnold Brown in accepting the award, mindful of the words of the Prime Minister, James Calllaghan, said 'Salvationists proclaim with selfless conviction and sincerity that people matter and that there is no greater calling than the service of others, especially those in need.'[292]

---

[289] Bradwell C. *Fight the Good Fight. The Salvation Army in New Zealand, 1883-1983.* A. H. & A. W. Reed, Wellington 1982

[290] Gariepy, H. *Mobilized for God, The History of The Salvation Army Vol VIII (1977-1994)* The Salvation Army, Atlanta, GA 2000 p. 334

[291] *Facts for Life – A Communication Challenge* UNICEF 1989

[292] Gariepy, H. *Mobilized for God, The History of The Salvation Army Vol VIII (1977-1994)* The Salvation Army, Atlanta, GA 2000 p. 14

Looking forward to a faithful future

by Majors Dean and (Dr) Eirwen Pallant,
International Health Services Coordinators,
International Headquarters[293]

IT has been inspiring and humbling to read the preceding chapters by Commissioner Harry Williams. We owe him a significant debt of gratitude for recording the dedication and sacrifice of many faithful, heroic people who, in God's strength, made Salvation Army history. Commissioner Williams has personally played a major part, particularly among the poorest people in developing countries. His energy, passion and lifelong determination are an excellent example to the younger generation – and as he is now 95 years old that includes almost all of us!

It is an honour for us to contribute this final chapter. Since October 2007 we have been given the privilege of coordinating the International Health Services of The Salvation Army. The preceding chapters of this book remind us that we stand on the shoulders of giants. This is a privileged place but also a rather precarious position. It is precarious because Salvation Army medical ministry has scaled great heights over more than a century of service but, as this history reveals, hospitals, clinics and health programmes never stand still. They constantly change. The medical world does not stand still. The communities we serve do not stand still. Christian health ministry needs to be agile, while still being faithful to God.

As Commissioner Williams repeatedly reveals, the history of Salvation Army medical service is one of faithful ministry in the midst of constant change. The future should not be any different – in the midst of chaos and change The Salvation Army must always be faithful to God. How do we know if we are being faithful? Answering this question is of critical importance.

We sense that a God-faithful future for Salvation Army medical work will be different to the past. Commissioner Williams's history has highlighted the ministry of healthcare workers based in hospitals and clinics. However, few Salvation Army hospitals and clinics are thriving today. Almost all Salvation Army hospitals and clinics in Australia, Canada, The Netherlands, New Zealand, the UK and the USA have now closed. During 2008 we visited almost all the remaining large hospitals in India, Indonesia, Africa and Latin America. We can report that every Army hospital is struggling with the pressures of finance, government regulation, a shortage of committed doctors and increasing patient expectations.

As we travelled we were asked many tough questions by concerned Salvationists, employees and community members. Has the time come for The Salvation Army to honourably withdraw from all hospitals? Can the poorest people rely on their governments for health care? Or should The Salvation Army expand its health ministry when government services seem prejudiced against marginalised minorities? Are commercial health providers now able to do the work traditionally done by the Church? What happens to people who cannot access or pay for basic health services?

These questions are difficult and require thoughtful answers. However, as we will show in this chapter, we believe there is a faithful, God-honouring future for Salvation Army health ministry.

We can learn much from history and while it is clear that medical and health needs are constantly changing, Commissioner Williams has provided many examples of leaders willing to trust God and adapt to changing circumstances. Agility coupled with faithfulness to God's direction characterised the early days of The Salvation Army and these qualities will be required for an effective ministry in the 21st century. This is not an agility born of unprincipled pragmatism – which says we do anything as long as it can be funded – rather The Salvation Army is Kingdom-effective when decisions are made with 'principled agility'.

There are many problems in the 21st century requiring an agile, yet principled response. There is no future in living in the past. Equally we do not believe God is calling the Church to withdraw completely from health ministry. This is true in both wealthy and finance poor societies. While some richer countries have adequate government or commercial health provision, there are still many health problems requiring community-based, Christ-centred solutions.

Despite wealthy governments investing vast amounts of money in health budgets, preventable diseases such as obesity, diabetes, heart disease, teenage pregnancy and sexually transmitted infections still affect millions of westerners. As increasing numbers of people in Asia, Africa and South America experience western-style prosperity, the number of people suffering from the 'lifestyle diseases' of diabetes and heart disease are exploding. The solution cannot be found in merely seeking better technology, more drugs and bigger hospitals – relationships in families and communities that help people change their way of life are urgently required. This is equally true for people in the rich communities and those struggling in poorer societies.

Salvation Army health ministry has always been more than just hospitals and clinics. As Commissioner Williams outlines in chapter 10, recent opportunities to expand Salvation Army health and medical services have mainly emerged in community and corps-based ministries. There have been impressive developments in the past 20 years giving cause for optimism and confidence. Lessons have been learnt – and continue to be learnt – by partnering with poor and disadvantaged people. These voices and experiences are

shaping the future direction of Salvation Army health services
– and it is exciting!

The aim of this chapter is to briefly summarise the global
health situation for poor and marginalised people, restate the
principles underpinning Christian health ministry and, then,
describe a vision of a God-faithful future of health, healing and
wholeness for all.

1. The challenge: A changing world yet familiar problems

The health of the world's poorest people attracted much
attention at the start of the 21st century. Campaigns like *Make
Poverty History* captured the headlines and millions of people
demanded change. Philanthropists like Bill and Melinda Gates
and Warren Buffet generously donated huge amounts of their
personal wealth to the fight against HIV/Aids, TB and malaria.
World leaders approved the UN Millennium Development
Goals, set ambitious targets to increase aid to poorer countries
and agreed massive debt cancellation schemes. People
genuinely hoped that progress was going to be made.

However the challenges are enormous and health facilities,
systems and programmes serving the poorest people in the
world are still failing. For at least the past 20 years,
international health policies led by the United Nations, IMF,
World Bank and western governments have encouraged vertical
health interventions (funding for specific diseases like Aids or
polio or malaria) rather than supporting integrated primary
health services (horizontal health interventions). The Salvation
Army fell in line with this trend and adopted a specific focus on
HIV/Aids – one of The Salvation Army International Trust's six
key objectives in the 2007 Annual Report.

This focus on Aids had a positive and significant impact in
focusing Salvation Army responses on this serious pandemic
and the 'vertical' approach had some success. For example, the
accessibility of drug treatment for Aids patients has increased
significantly. Thousands of poor people in Africa are alive today
because they can access free anti-retroviral drug treatments.

We have been thrilled to see the difference in the health of some of our friends in Zambia who now have access to this treatment.

However, despite these glimmers of hope, the health indicators for the poorest people are not improving as planned. Progress towards the Millennium Development Goals (MDGs) is disappointing. The *World Health Report 2008*, published by the World Health Organisation (WHO), found striking inequities in health outcomes, in access to care, and in what people have to pay for care. Differences in life expectancy between the richest and poorest countries now exceeds 40 years. Of the estimated 136 million women who will give birth this year, around 58 million will receive no medical assistance whatsoever during childbirth and the postpartum period, thus endangering their lives and those of their infants.

Globally, annual government expenditure on health varies from as little as US$20 per person to well over US$6,000. For 5.6 billion people in low and middle-income countries, more than half of all health care expenditure is through out-of-pocket payments. With the costs of health care rising and systems for financial protection in disarray, personal expenditures on health now push more than 100 million people below the poverty line each year. The WHO report revealed vast differences in health within countries and sometimes within individual cities. In Nairobi, for example, the under-five mortality rate is below 15 per 1,000 in the high-income area. In a slum in the same city, the rate is 254 per 1,000[294]. The Salvation Army is working in these slum areas – as it does in many of the world's largest cities – and is still called by God to serve poor and marginalised people.

The international health community is recognising that the 'vertical', disease-specific approaches are inadequate. To steer health systems towards better performance, the World Health Organisation is calling for a return to primary health care, a holistic approach to health care formally launched 30 years ago with the Alma Ata Declaration calling for 'health for all by the year 2000'. Unfortunately the targets set 30 years ago were not achieved and poor people continue to struggle to access basic affordable, appropriate health care.

In calling for a return to primary health care, WHO argues that its values, principles and approaches are more relevant now than ever before. Several findings support this conclusion. As the *World Health Report 2008* notes, inequalities in health outcomes and access to care are much greater today than they were in 1978. In far too many cases, people who are well-off and generally healthier have the best access to the best care, while the poor are left to fend for themselves. Health care is often delivered according to a model that concentrates on diseases, high technology and specialist care, with health viewed as a product of biomedical interventions. The power of prevention is largely ignored.

In many countries specialists perform tasks that would be better managed by general practitioners, family doctors, nurses or paramedicals. This contributes to inefficiency, restricts access and deprives patients of opportunities for comprehensive care. When health is skewered towards specialist care, a broad menu of protective and preventive interventions tends to be lost. WHO estimates that better use of existing preventive measures could reduce the global burden of disease by as much as 70 per cent.

Many Salvation Army hospitals are being pressured towards higher level technology and high cost specialisation – and it is a pressure that needs to be resisted because it does not best serve the poorest people. Poor and marginalised people often experience high maternal, infant, and under-five mortality – problems that often indicate a lack of access to basic services such as clean water and sanitation, immunisations and proper nutrition. In contrast, a primary health care approach, when properly implemented, protects against many of these problems. Primary health care, including integrated services at the community level, can help improve health and save lives. It promotes a holistic approach to health that makes prevention equally important as cure in a continuum of care that extends throughout the lifespan.

The *World Health Report 2008* makes the case as follows: 'Primary health care (PHC) brings balance back to health care, and puts families and communities at the hub of the health system. With an emphasis on local ownership, it honours the resilience and ingenuity of the human spirit and makes space for solutions created by communities, owned by them, and sustained by them. PHC also offers the best way of coping with the ills of life in the 21st century: the globalisation of unhealthy lifestyles, rapid unplanned urbanisation, and the ageing of populations. These trends contribute to a rise in chronic diseases, like heart disease, stroke, cancer, diabetes and asthma, that create new demands for long-term care and strong community support. A multisectoral approach is central to prevention, as the main risk factors for these diseases lie outside the health sector.'

Faith-Based Organisations (FBOs), such as The Salvation Army, are being recognised as particularly effective partners in the new Primary Health Care initiative as they are long-term members of the community (and not merely short-term NGOs). Many FBOs also have long-term institutional and technical capacity through mission hospitals and clinics. The Church provides as much as 40 per cent of the health care in some parts of Africa[295] – rising to as much as 70 per cent in some rural areas.

The World Health Organisation published a report in 2008 *Building From Common Foundations* which emphasised the vital role that FBOs can play in Primary Health Care. The Salvation Army is well placed to respond to this renewed interest in Primary Health Care. There is no shortage of poor and marginalised people with health problems! Donors are increasingly willing to work more closely with Faith-Based Organisations. The giants upon whose shoulders we stand have left 21st-century Salvationists a legacy of credibility and opportunity.

Therefore, in the light of this global picture of poor people unable to access adequate basic health care, this is not the time for The Salvation Army to withdraw from health ministry. However, a faithful response will not be achieved by using 19th-century solutions for 21st-century problems. This is a precarious, critical moment for the direction of Salvation Army health ministry. Wise decisions are needed, and courage will be required to implement them. The principles underpinning Salvation Army health ministry will be critically important in establishing a God-faithful direction.

2. Principles underpinning Salvation Army health ministry
Jesus is the model for ministry
During his earthly life Jesus made healing a central part of his ministry. He cured people of all kinds of diseases, even death itself, sometimes by simply touching a person and speaking a word. When Jesus sent the disciples out into the world (Mark 6:7) they were given three tasks: preaching, teaching and healing. In the 2,000 years since then, Christians have been closely involved with health, healing and wholeness. There is an impressive tradition of Christian engagement in health ministry upon which to establish a vision for the 21st century.

However, there are still some Christians who view the healing ministry with a degree of suspicion. Professor Abigail Rian Evans, of Princeton Theological Seminary in USA, summarises the challenge:

> *'The healing ministry of the Christian Church has been sadly misunderstood and often relegated to the fringes of the Church and to various sectarian groups. It is not some occasional activity or special project – nor is it random, breathtaking events that happen at Lourdes or miracle cures that touch only small numbers of people. The ministry of the Church as a healing institution is at the heart of its whole mission and should permeate every part of its mission.'*[296]

Unfortunately many Christians seem to have accepted the secularist approach which prioritises science over faith particularly in matters of medicine and health. The integrated model to preaching, teaching and healing that Jesus practised is viewed with suspicion in 21st-century medical practise. However the Church, and The Salvation Army in particular must resist being squeezed out by the forces of health specialisation and commercialism. Health and healing is much more than the business of doctors, nurses and health professionals and ever increasing technology. The health ministry offers 21st-century Salvationists an opportunity to witness to 'wholeness' – the healing ministry offers a visible, practical and necessary witness to our faith to a world scrambling around for solutions to ever-spiralling health care costs.

An integrated Salvation Army mission
The Salvation Army is a faith-based organisation and not merely a non-government organisation (NGO). Therefore theology must always determine the foundations of Salvationist mission. Christian conviction about the importance of health, healing and wholeness comes from the doctrines and beliefs about who God is and what he wants his people to be and do.

General John Gowans (now retired) helpfully summarised The Salvation Army's mission in a three-point statement: save souls, grow saints and serve suffering humanity. This statement of salvation, sanctification and service is not a menu of three options from which we can choose – rather it is a statement of the essential components for integrated Salvation Army mission. People engaging in only one aspect of mission are missing out and fragmenting the three-fold purpose of The Salvation Army. For example, a corps merely seeking to grow saints and enjoy a holy huddle without engaging with the world for the saving of souls or the service of suffering humanity is not fully participating in what God desires for The Salvation Army. Likewise hospital programmes justifying their existence because they serve suffering humanity are being unfaithful in failing to give opportunity for people to explore salvation and sanctification. In extreme cases we have heard some hospital leaders suggest the purpose of their programme is to make profits and they don't seem to think they need any of the three legs of the stool.

No Salvation Army programme will remain faithful to God's purposes if it relies on one or two legs of the stool – all three are required for a stable, sustainable, God-honouring expression of Salvationism. When one leg is weak, the whole stool is unstable. If two legs are missing, the stool will topple over! The word 'integrating' is a reminder that the task will never be fully complete – it is an ongoing process.

Role of the local church
When Christians get past the incorrect idea that only trained health professionals can be involved in health services, it is possible to see the many opportunities for 'ordinary' people – and particularly people of faith – to respond to God's call to be involved in the work of healing the world. This work of healing the world is a key task for Christians working together in corps and churches around the world. As Bill Hybels often says: 'The

local church is the hope of the world and its future rests primarily in the hands of its leaders.'[297]

Local churches (and particularly Salvation Army corps) are well placed to bring hope to the health needs of the poorest people. There is clear evidence showing that the most effective health care (particularly for the poorest people suffering from preventable diseases) is done in the home. In many cultures this is undertaken by untrained women who are expected to do most of the caring – but often they are unaware of basic prevention, treatment and care information. The Church can play an important role in improving the knowledge, attitudes and practices of women in the poorest communities. It is also important for men to understand their responsibilities and opportunities. The best way for The Salvation Army to improve the health of the poorest members of the community is through the ministry of local corps members because Salvationists live in the community – they are not merely employees of short-term projects.

Some important principles support the proposal to make corps the pivotal point for Salvation Army health care.

Firstly, *theological reasons*: Salvationists believe that every corps is part of the Church and the Church is part of Christ's Body. One of the corps' main tasks is to collaborate with the Holy Spirit in the integration of body, mind and spirit as well as the vital ministry of reconciling individuals, families and communities. Emphasising the connection between health and holiness is a central aspect of Salvation Army health ministry.

Secondly, *missiological reasons.* Christians believe everyone is called by God to build the Kingdom and that God desires people to enjoy life in all its fullness (John 10:10). The corps (and local church) is the closest entry point to the community and health is an excellent entry point for mission. The understanding of 'corps community centres' is at the heart of Salvation health ministry as corps buildings become known as places where any member of the community is welcome whatever their need.

Thirdly, *discipleship/spiritual formation reasons* – Salvationists can testify to the many blessings they receive from serving other people – particularly people in need. Corps need to understand their mission is not just to save souls and grow saints, but to engage in the service of suffering humanity because that experience is good (in fact it is essential) for the spiritual health of Salvationists.

Unleashing the potential of people

Hope, change and a healthier life will not be achieved in corps, churches and communities until the lives of individual people are transformed. Christians believe this best happens through an encounter with God and this is the basis for the impact that faith-based organisations have around the world. Even people with a more humanistic worldview can see the tremendous capacity, resilience and power that is unleashed when people of faith work together.

However, this is not easy to achieve. Institutions can easily become disengaged from the communities they seek to serve. This can happen in Salvation Army hospitals, clinics, hostels and even corps. It is easy to become content with a 'provider' mindset which says, 'You come to us and we will help you'. People then quickly become comfortable within their own walls and just wait for the community to come to them.

This 'provider' mindset has too often characterised the way concerned Christians try to serve communities. It does not allow people to help themselves; it does not allow people to solve their own problems and it increases levels of dependency. It is an unsustainable, unfaithful approach – but it feels less risky and therefore many people and programmes slip into this way of working. In contrast a 'covenant partner' mindset encourages everyone to build relationships of equality; it moves out of the buildings and into the communities to meet people where they are and does not wait for them to come to us. This approach is much more likely to have long-term sustainable success.

Under Dr Ian Campbell's leadership, International Health Services have played a leading, vital and important role in the past 15 years resisting the 'provider' trend by helping Salvationists discover new ways of engaging with their communities. The emphasis on 'Integrated Mission' – and the tools, teaching and experiences encouraged by the international health services team – have been successful in helping many Salvationists gain the confidence to step outside the institutions and get involved in Christ's mission in the world. This is an important, complex and often fragile approach that can easily be trampled on and The Salvation Army must be alert to the risks of losing the significant gains made in recent years.

The renewed focus on Primary Health Care compliments this approach. It offers opportunities to bring balance back to health care by putting families and communities at the hub of the health system. As the World Health Report 2008 from the WHO says: 'With an emphasis on local ownership, Primary Health Care honours the resilience and ingenuity of the human spirit and makes space for solutions created by communities, owned by them, and sustained by them.'

Top-down or bottom-up?
This all sounds good on paper but it is hard to deliver. One of the key tensions for a large, hierarchical organisation like the WHO and also for The Salvation Army, is the 'top-down' versus 'bottom-up' debate. In recent decades there has been a reaction against authoritarian leadership from the top of every organisation and a strong belief that people closest to the problems in the community should be enabled to make decisions.

We believe both 'top-down' and 'bottom-up' dynamics are required. Mobilisation may start with international and national leaders, but any long-lasting sustainability will depend on continuing community participation. Professor Carl Taylor – who like Commissioner Harry Williams is a dynamic, medical doctor in his 90s with a lifetime of experience in health services

211

for the poorest people – argues that both 'top' and 'bottom' must play their part:

> *'Community energy seldom mobilises by itself. Communities need help from officials, who can adjust policies and regulations, facilitate cooperation among factions, and channel essential resources. Communities also need help from experts, who can build capacity and skills by training, introduce new ideas and techniques, and help monitor change, ideally bringing multiple perspectives – academic, business and nongovernmental – to the process. Progress comes from collaborative bottom-up (community), top-down (officials), and outside-in (experts) activity, with no one sector deciding that it alone is "in charge".'*[298]

Professor Taylor's concept can be adapted to reveal the important role that faith-based organisations like The Salvation Army can play in this process.

CHURCHES PLAY A VITAL ROLE IN **COMMUNITY LIFE**

People energy is generated at every level

TOP LEVEL
Policy decision-makers, donors, executives

GRASS ROOTS
local knowledge, most affected people taking ownership

MEDIATOR
Outside-in, making it work, faith-based organisations can be ideal mediators

It highlights the vital impact and role that Faith Based Organisation – with strong connections and relationships in the community – can play as mediators. When these creative relationships flourish, a dynamic 'people energy' is generated at every level. These ways of respectful working together are essential if sustainable health improvements are to be achieved by the poorest communities.

This section has outlined the principles underpinning Salvation Army health ministry: the life and ministry of Jesus is the model; an integrated mission including salvation, sanctification and service must be present in any Salvation Army ministry; the local church and corps is at the heart of the healing ministry for reasons of theology, mission and discipleship; and finally, the community must be engaged in this process as equal partners. The Salvation Army cannot merely deliver health services to people – rather we engage with communities as covenant-partners seeking to find sustainable solutions to change lives.

3. A vision of a God-faithful future full of health, healing and wholeness

This chapter is seeking to emphasise that The Salvation Army is still being called into health ministry and many people are finding great joy and fulfilment in this area of service. This includes those with technical skills (doctors and nurses) but also people without specialist knowledge. All sorts of gifts are needed – people with a pastoral calling to visit the sick, provide basic care to neighbours, learning together with people in communities through stimulating conversations and discussions. Health ministry opens doors into the lives of communities and individuals which would otherwise remain closed. It enables Salvationists to live out our commitment to healthy communities, healthy churches, healthy hospitals and healthy people.

Vision Statement
After careful consideration of the global health challenges and based on the principles underpinning Salvation Army health

services, in September 2008 General Shaw Clifton issued the following vision statement for Salvation Army health ministry:

The Salvation Army will seek to be a significant participant in the delivery of faith-based, integrated, high quality primary health care as close to the family as possible, giving priority to poor and marginalised members of society. The Salvation Army will offer education programmes that equip health workers with appropriate skills and experience as well as developing commitment to holistic Christian health ministry.

Achieving this vision will require a prioritisation of certain health interventions. It is not possible to meet every health need. We recommend a focus on the following health interventions based on community priorities and organisational capacity:

- Addictions
- Diabetes
- Disabilities
- End-of-life care
- Eyes
- HIV/Aids
- Hypertension
- Infectious diseases
- Leprosy
- Maternal and child health
- Mental illness
- Nutrition

This list of health issues may seem rather unconnected but, in fact, they have a common thread. These issues all respond well to community-based health programmes and require long-term relationships to overcome the medical condition. In other words, quality primary heath care as close to the family as possible can make a huge difference in the lives of people experiencing these challenges.

Corps and churches are as close to the family as possible
As we have noted above, Primary Health Care (PHC) requires bringing quality health programmes as close to the family as possible. The Salvation Army is well placed to do this by prioritising corps as the pivotal point of Salvation Army health services. With more than 15,000 corps around the world, The Salvation Army has a significant capacity to be a focus for a ministry of healing and education in thousands of communities across the world. Such an emphasis will help more people discover their wholeness in Christ and in their community.

The following diagram illustrates how different Salvation Army programmes can be integrated into a continuous chain of care from home to hospital and back.

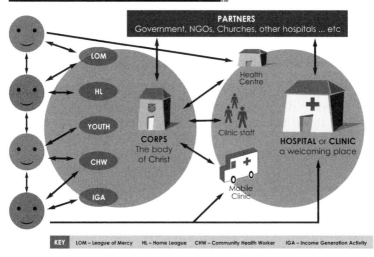

It is important to emphasise that this is not a new model – it is a restatement of an integrated approach that has been characteristic of The Salvation Army throughout its history. It is still working today and can be seen in Democratic Republic of Congo, Ghana and Papua New Guinea, for example, where corps officers and local Salvationists are fully involved in the ministry of healing with the support of mobile clinics, rural health centres and clinics. This strategy takes The Salvation Army back to focusing on the grassroots. An African Salvationist reflected on the above diagram: 'The Salvation Army does not belong to the elite, we belong to the people at the bottom. This concept of integrated health ministry closes the gap between rich and poor by improving access to care.'

Some readers may question why The Salvation Army believes there is still a role for hospitals and clinics. The trend in western countries – influenced by a post-modern suspicion of institutions – has been to delegate as much health care as possible to community-based services. Some argue that only the Government should run hospitals and clinics for poor people and that the Church should withdraw from direct service provision. We want to question this thinking.

Salvation Army health ministry often occurs in deeply dysfunctional societies. Societies ravaged by poverty, war, disease and community breakdown are chaotic places to work. Governments are often incapable or unwilling to deliver health services to all members of society. Such communities still require an integrated health system that links people in their homes with reliable, sustainable health services. It is very difficult to do this without an institutional base. A clinic or small hospital is an essential anchor in these chaotic communities – a place of stability from which the essential community-based health and development work can be sustained and supported. Faith-based hospitals and clinics are often found in remote, difficult locations avoided by government and commercial providers.

The role of the institution in Salvation Army ministry is not limited to hospitals and clinics. Across the world The Salvation Army has significant institutional presence. In addition to 20 general hospitals, 45 maternity hospitals and 123 health centres/clinics, The Salvation Army, working in 117 countries, has many other 'institutional' programmes. For example, 440 hostels for homeless people, 228 children's homes, 116 homes for elderly people, 60 homes for disabled people, 12 homes for blind people, 57 remand and probation homes, 41 homes for street children, 41 mother and baby homes, 77 care homes for vulnerable people, 104 centres for people seeking refuge and 204 residential programmes for people with addiction dependency[299]. Therefore envisioning a faithful future for institutional based care in 21st century society is an issue for more than just Salvation Army *health* services.

As we have travelled to every continent in the past year we have repeatedly been told by Salvationists and community members that Salvation Army institutions are still needed. This is a need particularly felt in countries where Christians are in the minority and often viewed with suspicion. For example, hospitals and clinics offer an important neutral space for Christian ministry to all people, of all faiths and none, without discrimination. The Salvation Army has 2,286 education institutions which offer similar opportunities for ministry.

However, we must admit that it is very difficult to envision a future for large, multi-speciality general Salvation Army hospitals. A few may survive with significant government funding but we cannot see this being a sustainable approach for most territories. However, we do believe that a corps-centred health ministry supported by small hospitals and clinics has a great potential for 21st century faithful ministry.

Educating the next generation
Maintaining some hospitals will also allow The Salvation Army to be involved in the important task of educating health workers. Nursing schools and biomedical colleges have shaped – and continue to – the lives, skills and passions of thousands of health workers around the world. There is a shortage of health workers worldwide. The Salvation Army has a good reputation and can help young people who are excluded due to faith, gender, caste or finance. Families are willing to pay education fees. However, health worker education will require partnerships with other hospitals to ensure adequate clinical experience for students.

Serving everyone

The opportunities for hospitals and clinics to support primary health care are not limited to working with corps and churches – there is also an important role for The Salvation Army to foster good relationships with people of other faiths. The international mission statement states The Salvation Army 'will meet human needs in his name without discrimination'. Therefore while not denying commitment to Christ, Salvationists should still be ever alert to the opportunities to meet human needs without discrimination. Working with people of other faiths is an excellent way of building relationships as partners rather than as competitors. There is also interest by donors in faith centred health care. The Salvation Army could take a lead in supporting other churches and faiths in the delivery of community based health services.

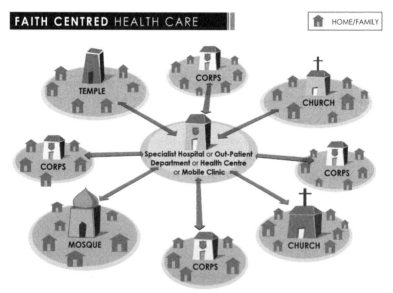

Quality, quality, quality

In every aspect of 21st-century health ministry, quality will be the watchword. It is not just about quantity – patients rightly demand the best. We recently visited an Army hospital in Indonesia and were told that even the poorest patients were expecting air-conditioned rooms. With temperatures in excess of 100F it was understandable but it is a marked change from the quality expected in the early days of Salvation Army medical services.

In order to ensure quality health ministry two important realities must be accepted. First, The Salvation Army cannot do everything. Primary health care is the priority and therefore patients requiring 'one off' clinical interventions such as high-tech surgery, specialist diagnostic services, most secondary and all tertiary level care will need to be referred to other health providers.

Secondly, the quality of Salvation Army health services will be enhanced through partnerships with other organisations. For example, the eye work at the MacRobert Hospital in Dhariwal, India, is an excellent example of a good partnership between The Salvation Army and Christian Blind Mission (CBM). CBM provide technical support, equipment and training for staff – The Salvation Army staff carry out more than 3,500 cataract operations a year restoring the sight of thousands of people. This type of quality partnership is definitely the way forward in the 21st century.

Conclusion

The ministry of healing is important for the health of Salvationists, for the future of The Salvation Army and for the health of the world. The ministry of healing is not an optional activity for Christians – we all need to be involved!

How can people get involved in healing? The first important and exciting insight that struck us repeatedly on our travels is that the best examples of the ministry of healing do not depend on doctors, nurses and other health professionals. Many people incorrectly think everyone must be super-qualified to get involved in the ministry of healing – it is not true. We have seen time and again the impact of 'small acts of kindness' – as Rhidian Brook memorably described The Salvation Army's healing ministry in his excellent book, *More Than Eyes Can See*.[300]

Since we began this appointment as International Health Services Coordinators for The Salvation Army we have a greater appreciation and understanding that the Church is an important part of the solution. The worldwide Church has the greatest penetration of any organisation into communities. Christians can get closer to people and individuals than any government or NGO programme because Christians live in those communities – we *are* the community! If every Christian was fully equipped and involved in the ministry of healing the health of the world would be transformed.

However, unless The Salvation Army continually engages in the ministry of healing – in its broadest sense – we will lose all relevance in the world. We are not saying that every corps needs a clinic staffed with doctors and nurses (although that works well in some places) but rather we all need to get involved in the Lord's work of healing our broken world.

However, one word of warning – we live in a very broken, unhealthy world. Engaging in the ministry of healing will expose us to suffering, pain and disappointment. It may carry a personal cost. We were deeply moved recently walking around the grounds of one large Army hospital in India which – like many others – is now struggling to survive. We tried to imagine what it had been like 50 years ago when it was a thriving and beautiful centre of healing. Now the buildings are falling down, the trees and bushes are overgrown and hope is fading fast. It reminded us that the ministry of healing is a fragile gift from God that needs careful tending. It can easily become crumpled by pressures from a changing world.

However as we have suggested in this chapter, Salvation Army ministry of healing is not dependent on hospital buildings – it is most effective as close to the family as possible. With a renewed emphasis on primary health care, Salvation Army hospitals, clinics and corps will be able to offer many opportunities for Christians, community volunteers and employees to engage in the ministry of healing.

[293] Majors (Dr) Eirwen and Dean Pallant have a joint appointment as International Health Services Coordinators for The Salvation Army based at International Headquarters in London. Eirwen, born in India, is a medical doctor with post-graduate qualifications in tropical medicine and general practice; Dean, born in Zimbabwe, has post-graduate qualifications in theology and management. They have been Salvation Army officers for more than 15 years serving in corps and health ministry in the UK and in Zambia. Dean served for three years as Editor of the UK weekly publication, *Salvationist*. They have two teenage children.

[294] The World Health Report 2008 can be downloaded from http://www.who.int/whr/2008/en/index.html

[295] Building From Common Foundations – The World Health Organisation and Faith-Based Organisations in Primary Healthcare, WHO, Geneva, 2008

[296] The Healing Church – Practical Programs for Health Ministries; Abigail Rian Evans, United Church Press, 1999

[297] Bill Hybels, *Courageous Leadership*, Zondervan, 2002

[298] Carl E Taylor and Daniel Taylor-Ide, *Just And Lasting Change – When Communities Own Their Futures*, Johns Hopkins University Press, Baltimore, 2002

[299] *Salvation Army Year Book 2009*

[300] Brook, R. *More Than Eyes Can See* Marion Boyars Publishers, London 2007

Bibliography

Ah Kow, A. *Mary Layton* SP&S, London 1957

Atkinson, J.E. *Dr Beer Returns* SP&S, London 1957

Baird, C. *Little Doctor VC* SP&S, London 1944

Baird, C. *William Stevens (Yesu Ratnam): Jeweller and Missionary* SP&S, London 1944

Barnes, C. *The Salvation Army in Ghana* 1978 International Heritage Centre, London

Bolton, B. *Booth's Drum – The Salvation Army in Australia 1880 – 1980*, Hodder & Stoughton, Sydney 1980

Booth Tucker, F. *The Life of Catherine Booth Vol II* SP&S, London 1893

Booth, S. *To Be or Not to Be* p. 11

Booth, W. *In Darkest England and The Way Out* International Headquarters, London 1890

Bradwell, C. *Fight the Good Fight – The Story of The Salvation Army in New Zealand* A. H. & A. W. Reed, Wellington 1982

Bramwell-Booth, C. *Bramwell Booth* Rich & Cowan, London 1933

Bready, J. W. *England Before and After Wesley* Hodder & Stoughton, London 1939

Brekke, Bo *Sally Ann – Poverty to Hope* The Salvation Army UK Territory, London 2005

Brengle, S. L. *Helps to Holiness*, The Salvation Army, London 1896, facsimile edition by Salvation Army Supplies Department, Atlanta 1992

Bridson, T. *Lightening the Lepers' Load* SP&S, London 1946

Brouwer, M. *History of The Salvation Army in Indonesia* The Salvation Army, Australia 1996

Brown, A. *The Gate and the Light* Bookwright Publications, Toronto 1984

Browne, S. G. *Heralds of Health – The Saga of Christian Medical Initiatives* Christian Medical Fellowship, London 1985

Campbell, I. *Voices of Our Global Family* The Salvation Army IHQ, London 2001

Cathcart, G. *The Medical Charities in the English Metropolis* Garland Publishing, New York 1984

Cook, C. *Mad, Bad or Sad* Christian Medical Fellowship 2006

Cook, H. *White Gujaratis* (Bramwell and Dorothy Cook) Christchurch, New Zealand 2007

Copping, A. *Serving the King's Men* Hodder & Stoughton, London 1918

Coutts, F. *The Better Fight – The History of The Salvation Army Vol VI (1914-1946)* Hodder & Stoughton, London 1973 du Plessis, P. *'Some Traditional Tonga Eye Remedies'* Zambia Medical Journal 1978

Dunster R. *'Drought and Hunger in Matabeleland'. The War Cry*, Australia 14 January 1984

Facts for Life – A Communication Challenge UNICEF1989

Fairbank, J. *Booth's Boots – Social Service Beginnings in the Salvation Army* International Headquarters, London 1983

Fairbank, J. *For Such a Time – The Story of the Young Florence Booth*, International Headquarters, London 2007

Gariepy, H. *Mobilized for God The History of The Salvation Army Vol VIII (1977-1994)* The Salvation Army, Atlanta, GA 2000

Gilks, W. *'Our District Nurses from a Field Officer's Point of View', The Deliverer* January 1896

Hansen. L. *The Double Yoke* Citadel Press, New York 1968

Johnson, D. *Mufwa Cibuka (The Story of Ibbwe Munyama)* 1989

Kirby, L. *Led and Protected by the Omnipotent God – Autobiography of Isabel and Leonard Kirby*

Larsson, J. *Saying Yes to Life – An Autobiography* International Headquarters, London 2007

Lowther, J. *The Story of a Hospital: The Salvation Army Emery Hospital, Anand, Western India. Centennial Celebrations 1903 – 2003* Published privately

Luttrell, W. *A Submission by The Salvation Army in Canada to The Commission on The Future Of Health Care In Canada* The Salvation Army, Canada 2002

Mack, L. *History of Health Services in Papua New Guinea 2005*

McCarty, C. *The Salvation Army USA Central Territory Health Services 1970 – 2005*

McInnes, B. *Flag Across the Zambesi* The Salvation Army, Zambia 1997

McKinley, E H. *Marching to Glory (Second Edition) – The History of The Salvation Army in the United States, 1880-1992* William B. Eerdemans Publishing Company, Grand Rapids, Michigan 1995 pp. 68-69

McKinley, E. *Somebody's Brother: A History of The Salvation Army Men's Social Service Department Lewiston, NY*, The Edwin Mellen Press 1986

Merritt, John G. (Ed) *Historical Dictionary of The Salvation Army* Scarecrow Press, Lanham, Maryland 2006

Morris, J. *The Spectacle of Empire* Faber and Faber, London 1982

Mortimer, K. *'The Sick African' All the World* 1946 p. 167

Moyles, R. *The Blood and Fire in Canada* AGM Publications, Edmonton 2004

Murdoch, N. Paper to USA Social Services Commission

Neeve, E. *Nurse by Royal Command* SP&S, London 1958

Parkhill, G. and Cook, G. *Hadleigh Salvation Army Farm: A Vision Reborn* The Salvation Army UK Territory, London 2008

Porter, Roy *The greatest benefit to mankind*, Collins London 1997

Potgieter, S. *'Family Health Programmes in Rural South Africa' in Rays of Hope*, Knowles, G. (Ed) The Salvation Army Australia Eastern Territory 1998 p. 103

Richards, M. *It Began with Andrews*, SP&S London 1971

Robinson, B. *Bodily Compassion* Ph D Thesis, Ottawa University

Robinson, B. *'The Revival of Parish Nursing' Horizons* The Salvation Army, Canada May-June 1997

Robinson, I. *'Singapore's Peacehaven Home' New Frontier*, June 3 2004 The Salvation Army USA Western

Sandall, R. *The History of The Salvation Army Vol II* Nelson, London 1950

Sandall, R. *The History of The Salvation Army Vol III* Nelson, London 1955

Sandall, R. *The History of The Salvation Army, Vol I* Nelson, London 1947

Schwartz, G. *Searching for a Meaningful Way to Help the Poor* Paper prepared for The Salvation Army's International Summit on Poverty 2001

Smith, S. *By Love Compelled* SP&S, London 1981

Smith, Trevor A. *The Falling Leaf* The Salvation Army, UK 2004

Stead, W. T. *The Star*, 2 January 1891

The Deliverer SP&S, London, 1889 onwards

The Salvation Army Year Book 1941

The Salvation Army Year Book 1952

The Salvation Army Year Book 1971

The Salvation Army Year Book 1975

The Salvation Army Year Book 1980

The Salvation Army Year Book 1983

The Salvation Army Year Book 2002

The Salvation Army Year Book 2005

Troutt, M. *The General was a Lady* J. Holman Co, Nashville 1980 p. 190

Turner, P. *The CBH for One and Twenty Years* Printed locally

Unsworth, M. *Great was the Company* SP&S, London 1963

Unsworth, M. *The Flower Called Faith in the Night* SP&S, London 1946 p. 7

Wackernagel, G. *'Glimpses of Medical Work in Africa' Officers' Review* 1937 p. 113ff

Watt, J. *Howard Beginnings* 1998 Unpublished

Watt, J. Vaenzi Vauya – *The Strangers Have Come* 1988 Unpublished

Wiggins, Arch R. *The History of The Salvation Army Vol IV* Nelson, London 1964

Wiggins, Arch R. *The History of The Salvation Army Vol V (1904-1914)* Nelson, London 1968

Wille, J. *Lys og Morke* Copenhagen 1950

Williams, H. B*ooth-Tucker, William Booth's First Gentleman* Hodder & Stoughton, London 1980

Williamson, V. *The Inside Story* New Zealand

Winston, D. *Red Hot and Righteous – The Urban Religion of The Salvation Army* Harvard University Press, Cambridge, Massachusetts 1999

Wood, H. *They Blazed the Trail* The Salvation Army, Canada p. 64

Yesudasen, U. B*rokenness as a Way of Blessing* ICSA Books, Chennai, India 2008

Index

Arawhata, 153
Argentina, 69, 72
Assurance Magazine, ix
Assurance Society, Salvation Army, 18
Auckland Rotary Club award, 152
Australia, xix, 14, 19, 40, 57, 69, 77f.
   99f. 154ff. 161, 166, 200
Australian Volunteers Abroad, 106

B

Bacon, Charles Sumner, 18
Baggs, R. E., 147
Baker, Keith, 76
Bandung, 30ff. 138
Bangladesh, 80f. 191, 197
Bapatla, 36, 115, 132, 140
Barefoot Doctors, xix, 38, 78,
Barnett, Alfred, 39f. 63
Barnett, Ted, xviii, 40, 52f. 64
Barrett, Frank, 34
Batala, 25f. 115
Battersby, Agatha, 43
Baugh, William, xvi,
Beatrix of the Netherlands, Princess,
   31f.
Bedwell, Cedric, 154
Beer, Stanley, 41, 60, 160
Begoro, 83, 130
Beit Trust, 73
Bell Shelter, Los Angeles, 185
Berge, Malene, 31
Bethany Colony Leprosy Association,
   133
Bethany hospitals, 18
Bethany Leprosy Society (UK), 133
Bethany leprosy village, 140
Bethesda Hospitals, 99f.
Bethesda House, Soweto, 171
Beveridge, Sir William, xviii
Bhore Report, xviii

Biafra, 130
Billups, Mary C., 5
Bingham, Gordon, 176
Blind school/institute/home, 80, 82,
   143, 161f. 217
Blowers, Arthur, xviii, 2, 39
Bofu, Benjamin, 125
Bolivia, 29, 104, 110f.
Boot, Marjorie (Neeve), 65
Booth Institute, Australia, 155
Booth Memorial Hospitals, 41, 43, 61,
   69, 89ff.
Booth Memorial Medical Centre,
   Queens, 91ff.
Booth, Ballington, 11,
Booth, Bramwell, 3, 7, 9, 23f. 44, 196
Booth, Catherine, xiv, xv, 3, 4
Booth, Emma (later Booth-Tucker), 6,
   8, 12, 23f. 37
Booth, Evangeline, 52f. 66, 88, 95, 132,
   134, 141
Booth, Florence, 7, 9, 10, 47
Booth, Herbert, 13
Booth, Maud, 11
Booth, William, xivff. 2, 3ff. 23, 95, 145
Booth-Tucker, Emma, 35
Booth-Tucker, Frederick (Fakir Singh),
   12, 25, 35, 63, 88, 137
Booth-Tucker, Louisa Mary, 137
Booth-Tucker, Minnie, 63
Boozers' parades, 146f.
Bosscha, K., 138
Bovill, Margaret, 88f.
Bown, Emma J., 12
Braden, Margaret, 86
Bradley, Fred, 118
Branch hospitals, 26, 36, 38, 40, 49, 60,
   64, 104, 141f.
Brand, Paul, 60, 134, 141
Braun, Heidi, 128
Brazil, 69, 71f.
Brengle, Samuel, 12

Bridge Programme, Australia, **154f.**

Bridge Programme, New Zealand, **152ff**

Bridson, Captain, 138

Brieseman, Melvin, 59

Brightmoor, Detroit, 186

Brinkman, Miss, 6

Brinsdon, David, 152

British Columbia, 183

British Journal of Ophthalmology, 30

Brown, Arnold, xx, 116, 162, 178, 198

Brown, Chester, 148

Buffet, Warren, 202

Bugangan, 27

Burfoot, Samuel, 39, 64

Burrows, David and Jean, 117

Burrows, Eva, 50, 74, 166, 197

C

Cage, Agnes, 67

Calgary Conference, 1995 182

Calgary Grace, 181

Callaghan, James, xxi, 198

Calvert, Graham, 121, 177

Cambodia, 159

Campbell, Ian, 57, 74, 122f. 157, **166ff.**
    176f. 196

Canada, xx, 14, 40, 43, 53, 69, 94ff.
    153, **177-184**

Canadian Hospital Association, 179

Capacity Development Programme, 134

Cape Town, 42, 155

Capsey, Mary, 113, 128

Captain William Jackman Memorial
    Hospital, 96, 180

CARES Programme, Omaha, 188

CARF (Commission on Accreditation of
    Rehabilittion Facilities), 187

Caribbean, 143

Carleton, John A., 18

Carmichael, Andrew, 157

Carpenter, George, 76

Carpenter, Minnie, 61

Carr, Hannah, 10, 40

Cass, Edward, 118

Caste, 55, 139, 217

Castle, Miriam, 10

Catherine Booth Hospital, Montreal,
    177, 181

Catherine Booth Hospital, Nagercoil,
    See also Nagercoil, xiv, 23-27, 36,
    38f., 49f. 58, 68, 70, 103, 137, 141

Catherine Booth Hospital, Zululand, 43

Catholic health services, 82, 89, 96, 99,
    129, 180

Cellar, Garret and Gutter Brigades, 6,
    9f.

Cepe, Mirriam, 80

Chaplaincy services, 97, 133, 149, 176,
    180

Cheela, Elijah, 121

Chicago (Andrews training), 25

Chikankata, xix, 44, 57, 61, 69f. 73ff.
    103, 118f. 135, 137, 166f.

Child survival initiative, 82, 197

China, 19, 41f. 67

Chini, 39f. 63

Cholera, 4, 35, 82, 129, 137

Chosen to be a Soldier, 145

Christian Medical Association of India
    (CMAI), 60, 103, 116, 160

Christian Mission Magazine, 5

Christian Mission, The, 2

Christian, Isudas, 58

Christmas Day, 5

Christmas Kettle Appeal, USA, 88

Churchill Fellowship, 152

Clarke, Rupert, 70

Cochabamba, 104, 110f.

Collins, Rosemary, 60, 160

Community development, 80, 168, 175,
    181, 197

Mobile clinic(s), xx, 110, 121f.

Mole, Bev, 77

Money, Dorothy (Cook), 65

Monk, Joshua, 153

Moone, Betty, 43, 126

Moorfields Eye Hospital, 35

Moradabad, 25, 37f. 53, 64f. 70

Morris, Jan, 1

Morrison, John Reid, 2

Mortimer, Kingsley, 59, 71ff.

Mortimer, Mavis (McKenzie), 73

Mothers' Hospital: Durban, 43

Mothers' Hospital: London, UK, 47,
86ff.

Mountain View Hospital, 43, 116

Mountbatten, Earl, xxi, 198

Mukarji, Daleep, 176

Mulder's Vlei, 156

Mungate, Rebecca, 126

Munn, Evelyn, 76, 126

Murdoch, Professor Norman, vii

Music library, Harbor Light, 148

Music therapy, 148

Mwiinga, John, 120

N

Nagasaki, Taro, 68, 190

Nagercoil, x, 13, 48-50, 59, 140f. 160f.
165

Nahari, Mrs Brigadier, 124f.

Napier, 158

Narraway, Dorothy, 68

Nash, Mrs Frazer, 7

Natal, 43

National Health Service (NHS), 87, 178

Ndona, Citizen, 128f.

Needham, Phil, viii, 176

Neeve, Eileen (Williams), 65

Neeve, Reg, 65f.

Netherlands, 43, 78, 200

New York, 11f. 61, 68f. 88-94

New Zealand, 13, 18, 39, 58, 69, 99,
150ff. 157f. 189, 200

New Zealand *War Cry*, 195

Newfoundland, xix, 40, 98

Nidubrolu, Andhra Pradesh, 53, 59, 66,
68f. 140

Nigeria, 75, 83, 130ff. 161f. 167, 197

Nightingale, Florence, 33, 35, 47,

Nku, David Imbie, 82, 130

Noble, Etna, 37

Noble, William, 37f. 58f. 61, 68, 140f.

NORAD, 163

Norman, Philip, 158

Nuffield Scholarship, 152

Nurse education, 5, 15f. 38, 40, 42, 50,
55, 67, 79, 87, 105, 124

Nurses Fellowship, SA, 61

Nutrition programme, 80f. 110, 129f.
196

Nutrition village, 124

Nxumalo, 122

O

Obstetric(s) see also maternity services,
xvii, 67, 85ff. 135, 181, 187, 188

Odura, Christiana, 83

Officer, The, 123, 126, 166

Oji River, 130ff. 161

Okello, Jane, 121

Okello, Julius, 121

Onamuga, 76ff. 107ff.

Ontario, 99, 180, 183

Operation Wesley, 108

Ophthalmology, 27-30, 42, 48, 61, 71,
181, 187

Order of Oranje-Nassau, Netherlands,
29

Order of the Blue Ribbon, Japan, 34

Order of the Dannebrog, Denmark, 29

Trinidad, 170
Trinity College, Cambridge, 35
Tshelanyemba, 75f. 126f.
Tsunami (2004, 1997), 57, 109, 159
Tuberculosis, xix, 27, 32, 42, 51, 74, 80, **137f**. 185
Tubingen, 70
Turen Hospital, Java, 31, 70
Turner, Minnie (Mayger), 48
Turner, Percy, xvii, 2, 19, 23f. 35ff. **48-50,** 53, 56, 63, 88, 103f. 137, 143
Tutton, Ken, 60, 160
Twins, 107
Typhus, 28

Williams, Harry, ix, 51f. 56, 60, 65f, 77, 100, 111, 121, 141f.
Williams, Henry W., 16 ff. 56
Williamson, Vera, 39
Winchell, Wallace, 146
Wind of change, 116
Winnipeg, 14f. 89, 95f. 98, 177
Wong Too, Rex, 122
Woodward, Leonard, 79
Woolcott, Ruth, 60, 160
World Council of Churches, 125
World Health Organisation (WHO), 105, 197, 203f. 211
World Humanity Award, xxi, 198
World Mission Associates, 191
World War One, 25, 39, 44, 86, 88, 143, 146, 196
World War Two, xviii, xix, 30, 32, 77, 97, 190

Wright, Doris, 76
Wylie, Keith, 60, 160

Y

Yale School for Study of Alcoholism, 148, 153
Yamamuro, Gunpei OF, 32f.
Year Book (Salvation Army), 113, 163

Z

Zaïre, 82, 116, 167
Zambezi, 72f., 118, 122
Zambia, xix, 43f. 66, 72ff. 103, 166, 197
Zimbabwe, 44, 68f, 72f. 76, 112f. 119, 124ff. 137, 203
Zululand, 43